Iranian Refugees in Transit

Iranian Refugees in Transit

Exile and the Politics of Survival in Turkey after the 1979 Revolution

Maral Jefroudi

I.B. TAURIS
LONDON • NEW YORK • OXFORD • NEW DELHI • SYDNEY

I.B. TAURIS

Bloomsbury Publishing Plc, 50 Bedford Square, London, WC1B 3DP, UK
Bloomsbury Publishing Inc, 1359 Broadway, 12th Floor, New York, NY 10018, USA
Bloomsbury Publishing Ireland, 29 Earlsfort Terrace, Dublin 2, D02 AY28, Ireland

BLOOMSBURY, I.B. TAURIS and the I.B. Tauris logo are trademarks of
Bloomsbury Publishing Plc

First published in Great Britain 2024
This paperback edition published 2026

Copyright © Maral Jefroudi, 2024

Maral Jefroudi has asserted her rights under the Copyright, Designs and Patents Act, 1988, to be identified as Author of this work.

For legal purposes the Acknowledgments on pp. viii–ix constitute an extension of this copyright page.

Cover design: Adriana Brioso
Cover image © Reza Allamezadeh

All rights reserved. No part of this publication may be: i) reproduced or transmitted in any form, electronic or mechanical, including photocopying, recording or by means of any information storage or retrieval system without prior permission in writing from the publishers; or ii) used or reproduced in any way for the training, development or operation of artificial intelligence (AI) technologies, including generative AI technologies. The rights holders expressly reserve this publication from the text and data mining exception as per Article 4(3) of the Digital Single Market Directive (EU) 2019/790.

Bloomsbury Publishing Plc does not have any control over, or responsibility for, any third-party websites referred to or in this book. All internet addresses given in this book were correct at the time of going to press. The author and publisher regret any inconvenience caused if addresses have changed or sites have ceased to exist, but can accept no responsibility for any such changes.

A catalogue record for this book is available from the British Library.

Library of Congress Cataloging-in-Publication Data
Names: Jefroudi, Maral, author.
Title: Iranian refugees in transit : exile and the politics of survival in Turkey after the 1979 revolution / Maral Jefroudi. Description: London, UK ; New York, NY, USA : I.B. Tauris, 2024. | Includes bibliographical references and index. | Summary: "This book examines the dynamics of Iranian political refugees settling in and migrating through Turkey after the 1980 coup and how they were able to influence its asylum policies. Maral Jefroudi presents a comprehensive picture of one of the biggest migration waves in contemporary history. Bringing together interviews with refugees from the period, analysing the cultural products by and on them, and tracing their footsteps in newspapers, archives, and scholarly literature, this book presents a thorough ethnography of Iranians in transit in Turkey after the 1979 Revolution"– Provided by publisher.
Identifiers: LCCN 2024006287 (print) | LCCN 2024006288 (ebook) | ISBN 9780755648092 (hardback) | ISBN 9780755648139 (paperback) | ISBN 9780755648115 (epub) | ISBN 9780755648108 (ebook)
Subjects: LCSH: Refugees–Iran. | Refugees–Turkey. | Iranians–Turkey.
Classification: LCC HV640.5.I73 J447 2024 (print) | LCC HV640.5.I73 (ebook) | DDC 305.9/0691409561–dc23/eng/20240419
LC record available at https://lccn.loc.gov/2024006287
LC ebook record available at https://lccn.loc.gov/2024006288

ISBN: HB: 978-0-7556-4809-2
PB: 978-0-7556-4813-9
ePDF: 978-0-7556-4810-8
eBook: 978-0-7556-4811-5

Typeset by Newgen KnowledgeWorks Pvt. Ltd., Chennai, India

For product safety related questions contact productsafety@bloomsbury.com

To find out more about our authors and books visit www.bloomsbury.com and sign up for our newsletters.

To those who could not flee

Contents

Acknowledgments		viii
Introduction: Our Shared Pain		1
1	Flexible or Precarious? "One and a Half Million Iranians" in Turkey	17
2	When Does Exile Begin?	39
3	"Their Categories and Ours": Politics of Differentiation	61
4	"Not One of Those Women": Negotiating Womanhood in Transit	85
5	The Collective Memory of Being in Transit in Turkey	103
Concluding Remarks		119
Epilogue: Turkey as a Transit Hub Today		131
Notes		149
Bibliography		179
Index		193

Acknowledgments

This book has been written across diverse time periods and locations. Consequently, acknowledging all the individuals who have made contributions would be challenging. Therefore, I maintain a concise list and express my gratitude to those whose impact was direct.

The origins of this book can be traced to the Atatürk Institute for Modern Turkish History (ATA) at Boğaziçi University. Offering a critical, interdisciplinary perspective, the institute's lively intellectual community played a pivotal role in shaping my project. My fellow graduate students, especially those in Tez-Koop, nurtured a strong sense of camaraderie that remains unmatched to this day. Çiğdem Oğuz encouraged me to contact I.B. Tauris and supported me all the way. I am grateful to Prof. Cengiz Kırlı, who supervised the initial version of this study. His supportive yet critical approach was admirable. Similar to many other progressive institutions in contemporary Turkey, my alma mater Boğaziçi University and ATA are currently facing repression. In 2022 Prof. Kırlı was removed from his role as the director of the institute and in 2023 he had to leave ATA where he had dedicated twenty years. I stand in solidarity with him and other resilient Boğaziçi University professors, students, and staff.

I am indebted to all the people who sincerely shared their stories with me. My uncles Rouzbeh Djalaei and Maziar Jafroodi not only shared their personal experiences but also welcomed me into their homes, introduced me to their friends, and provided valuable connections in Sweden and Germany. I am truly thankful for their warm hospitality. I express my gratitude to Massoud Maffan and Reza Allamezadeh for their invaluable support. Reza Allamezadeh generously shared a behind-the-scenes photo from his film *The Guests of Hotel Astoria*, which we featured on the book's cover. All personal aspects of this book have been lived alongside my mother, Afsaneh, thus making her an integral part of its essence.

Acknowledgments

I wrote this book while working full time as codirector at IIRE, the International Institute for Research and Education in Amsterdam. I am thankful to Alex de Jong for codirecting with me and also being a long-standing member of my close community. He has not only been a supportive colleague and friend, but also opened up his personal library and provided insightful comments on various parts of this book.

The editorial team at Bloomsbury were wonderful to collaborate with, and their supportive approach was exceptional. The anonymous referees who reviewed the entire manuscript contributed with engaged consideration and constructive criticism. I am thankful to them. Many other people will contribute to the production of this book after I write these lines. I appreciate their work.

Sometimes, solidarity and kindness manifest in unique and unforeseen ways. During a challenging period in my life, Paula Ribas graciously welcomed me into her beautiful apartment in Intendente, Lisbon, where I wrote the proposal for this book and submitted it to the publisher. Without her generosity and kindness, this book might have taken longer to reach its readers.

Introduction: Our Shared Pain

There was a hostel at the Rahmanlar seashore in Istanbul—Sezil Camping—a huge ping-pong table stood in the foyer, beaded curtains divided the foyer from the lobby, and a TV set was placed at the corner of the room. I remember a few things: a shared kitchen, the heart-shaped burn on my hand caused by the splashed oil of the fried sausages, and turnip soup cooked by a curly haired man with stubble, wearing a white sweater. And Bereket, the owner's chubby cat. It was 1986. I was four years old and had just migrated to Turkey from Iran with my 24-year-old mother without any concrete plans on the following step of our journey. We had first landed in As Hotel in Taksim and later on moved to this homelier hostel. We lived with other Iranians waiting in Turkey to resume their journey to "the West" for several months. This book has its origins in those days spent with Iranian transit refugees in Sezil Camping. In times spent with people coming from various backgrounds, strangled in deals with human traffickers, supporting each other, and leaving each other without a formal goodbye. We stayed, others left.

Many Iranians who left Iran in the aftermath of the Islamic regime's consolidation initially arrived in Turkey. Their passage to Western countries took a couple of weeks for some, while many had to stay in Turkey for much longer. Although due to lack of a visa regulation between the two countries, the route to Europe through Turkey was one of the most frequently used ones, the Iranian transit migrants of the 1980s attracted the attention of journalists of the time,[1] but not that of researchers.[2] When referenced in the scholarly literature, their stories were appropriated for constructing the genealogy of Turkey's experience with migration and did not go beyond forming a background for other stories. These narratives often focused on the number of the Iranians in transit, their assumed class background, and a causation inferred from that on the relative ease of their passage to the West compared to the current transit migrants in Turkey.

It is correct that time eases the pain suffered. It also makes it less visible. Also, the political climate of a bipolar world made some border crossings easier than others. The fall of concrete walls brought an end to the capitalist block's performative hospitality. As I will discuss in the following chapters, there have been significant changes in the way the Western European countries were receiving refugees in the 20th century and today. However, none of these facts can lead us to assume homogeneity in the experiences of Iranian refugees crossing Turkey after the 1979 revolution. An abstract picture of Iranian transit migrants as a background lacks historical quality. A perspective without historical quality not only distorts the past but also hinders our understanding of the present situation and taints our vision to find solutions necessary to cater for specific needs.

Having lived with the reality of seeing many Iranians living in transit in Turkey throughout the 1980s and early 1990s and observing the absence of this experience in the migration studies in Turkey in early 2000s urged me to write this missing chapter of Turkey's history on transit migration as a part of my graduate work at the Ataturk Institute for Modern Turkish History in Boğaziçi University, Turkey, in 2008. I wanted to register the footsteps of those Iranians who fled from the very revolution they fought for and arrived in Turkey with the intention of making their way to "the West." I wanted to record the footsteps of the people I met in my childhood, with whom I shared bread and moments of joy and precarity.

Later on, I worked as a volunteer interpreter for refugee advocacy groups in Turkey assisting Iranian and Afghan asylum seekers in their application processes. Most of the interpretation was done over the phone. Over the phone I connected asylum seekers living in various satellite cities with refugee legal aid advisors in NGO offices in Istanbul. I interpreted traumatic experiences of war, gender-based violence, and discrimination over and over again. I heard people speaking about war breaking in their neighborhood, them being separated from their loved ones living on the other side of the barricades, their kids being kidnapped by warlords and being sold, and finding an escape no matter what. Many life stories that felt as foreign as belonging to other times or parallel universes.

I moved to the Netherlands in 2010. The popular uprisings in Syria that started in 2011 were brutally repressed and turned into an international war in 2015 displacing millions of Syrians in search of a safe place. The ineptness of the international organizations and rulers of the advanced capitalist countries turned this situation into a "refugee crisis," where thousands of people lost their lives on their way to safety. Meanwhile, the intensified authoritarianism in Turkey particularly after the suppression of Gezi Movement in 2013, end of Peace Process with the Kurdish PKK, and then the failed coup attempt of 2016 pushed many people from Turkey to exile. More than three decades after living in Sezil camp, I was once again with refugees and undocumented people in Amsterdam. This time it was the sea and not the mountains that they had to cross to flee persecution and war—the same sea that drowned many others on their way to Europe.

Turkey is both a country of origin for many refugees and the country with the highest number of refugees in the world now.[3] The former is not new. People from ethno-religious minorities, such as Greek, Armenian, and Jewish people, who survived massacres and persecutions in late 19th and 20th centuries, were among the first emigrants from Turkey. Later on, groups effected by the military coups of 1960 and particularly 1980 joined those millions of people originally from Turkey living abroad. When Iranians arrived in Turkey, starting from early 1980s, many people from Turkey were in exile in Europe fleeing a postcoup authoritarian state. Between September 1980 and February 1983, when Turkey transitioned to a somewhat civilian regime, sixty thousand people had been arrested due to their political activities in Turkey.[4] Following the coup, half a million people from Turkey filed asylum applications in the 1980s, amounting to more than one million applications in the following two decades.[5] Based on a 2002 UNHCR report, Danış recounts that among countries in the process of integration to the EU, Turkey had the highest number of citizens asking asylum (23,389) in a EU country between 1997 and 2002. The next in that list was Romania with 557 people.[6] Even before the last wave of emigration from Turkey following the suppression of Gezi movement, the end of Peace Process, and the rising authoritarian rule after the failed coup attempt in 2016, the number of people originally from Turkey living abroad was estimated to be more than six million.[7] While numbers and identity of the refugees and migrants from

Turkey can differ from era to era, emigration is a constant phenomenon for Turkey.

However, Turkey being the country with the highest number of refugees is a new phenomenon. Turkey has not lifted its geographical limitation to the 1951 Geneva Convention on the status of refugees, yet. Thus, as I will elaborate in the following chapters, the Turkish State does not recognize anyone fleeing persecution and asking for asylum as refugees unless they are coming from Europe.[8] Nevertheless, the war at its borders and the said ineptness of the international asylum system made it impossible for Turkey to deny residency and basic rights to millions of Syrians fleeing war and destruction. More than 3.5 million Syrians are under special protection in Turkey. Turkey continues to be a country of transit migration too. More than a hundred thousand Afghan undocumented people were arrested in 2022 and tens of thousands of Afghans, Iraqis, and Iranians are in asylum procedure in Turkey to be resettled in a third country. Many Syrian refugees I met in Amsterdam have been in transit in Turkey long enough to be able to speak the language and talk about the precarious life conditions and discrimination they faced there.

Similar to what occurred with post-1979 Iranians and post-Halabja massacre Kurds, the concrete historical realities, which will be explored in the epilogue, generated dynamics that brought the necessity of regulation in one way or another. The new situations had to be defined; names and categories were created to regulate. Thus, while there are continuities in some of the experiences of documented and undocumented foreigners living in Turkey since the 1980s, such as de facto obstacles in using one's rather limited rights, corruption and interpersonal violence in relations with authorities, precarity, and the constant state of uncertainty due to being in transit without concrete plans for future, many things have also changed. Introduction and enforcement of satellite cities where asylum seekers are supposed to settle, official collaboration of state institutions and NGOs, introduction of a specific temporary protection category for Syrians living in Turkey, and Turkey's evolution to being the principal guard of European borders are among the most impactful changes in refugees' lives in the 21st century.

Iranians in transit were coming from various backgrounds in terms of their age, gender, ethnicity, and political experience among others. Without an intersectional approach that takes into account the multiple forms of oppression shaping their experiences before and after their flight, we cannot grasp the plurality of experiences of living in transit in Turkey. This does not mean that there were no common denominators. However, it means that similar conditions can affect people in different ways. To understand this plurality, in this book, I delve into the conflicts, struggles, and tactics of the people in transit, thus their *politics of survival*. Refugees' relations with the Turkish and international authorities in charge of dealing with transit migration, their own history of struggle and exile before they come to Turkey, and the relations among the community of Iranians in transit are the main sites these conflicts, struggles, and tactics are traced in this book.

While the chapters on the Iranian refugees crossing Turkey after the 1979 revolution sheds light on a forgotten and understudied part of the history of Turkey's now very established position as a transit hub for refugees on their way to "the West," this book does more than filling a—rather significant—historical gap. The case of post-1979 Iranian refugees crossing Turkey provides a productive field to discuss many issues and concepts that are central to the lives of refugees and migrants and to the study of migration. A non-exhaustive list of these includes the taxonomy applied to migrants and refugees and its consequences, the conditions under which those categories evolve or stay intact, how autonomy is seen to be an existential contradiction to being a refugee, how norms about roots and belonging are social constructions, how people make and remake their identities through their everyday life activities, and how gender oppression and its norms enable and hinder its subjects at the same time. Revising and expanding the 2008 study made it possible to discuss these issues further and also to contemplate the continuities and changes in Turkey's asylum regime over the last four decades. Completed in the latter months of 2023, the book is embedded in the theoretical discussions of its time.

The main material of this research involves interviews conducted in 2007 with twenty-one refugees (six women and fifteen men) living in Sweden (Stockholm, Malmö, and Lund) and Germany (Cologne), whose first stop after leaving Iran was Turkey.[9] They had mostly fled Iran in the mid-1980s, the earliest being in 1982 and the latest in 1990. Their stay in Turkey ranged from two weeks to two years. We spoke in cafes in the neighborhoods selected by them, in their homes or in their workplaces. All the interviews were conducted in Persian and tape-recorded. During the interviews I assured the interviewees that their identities would not be revealed, and thus pseudonyms are used.

Interviews were not the only form of narrative that is used in this book. Mehri Yalfani's novel *Afsaneh's Moon*, Abbas Kazerooni's autobiographic novel *The Little Man*, and most importantly Reza Allamezadeh's movie *The Guests of Hotel Astoria*, among others, are referenced both as narratives of Iranian refugees and as products in circulation that kept the memory of being a transit migrant in Turkey alive. In 2022, I also interviewed the director Reza Allamezadeh in the Netherlands.

In Sweden, I had the opportunity to have the project announced on a Swedish radio channel broadcasting in Persian before my visit there and I had one respondent who had left her telephone number after the radio broadcast. The interviewees in Germany (one-third of the total interviews) knew each other and were from the same organization, the People's Fadaiyan. In Sweden, people interviewed were from more varied backgrounds. All in all, the interviewed refugees were mostly political refugees, and the most salient political affiliation was with the People's Fadaiyan. Most of them were still engaged in politics, not in terms of political affiliation with a party or organization but in terms of engaging in discussions by writing articles published in online journals or blogs. Among the interviewees there were mother-tongue (Persian) teachers, photocopy shop workers and shareholders, maids in nursery schools, journalists, and people from various occupational groups such as a restaurant owner, a taxi driver, a publisher, a psychologist, a librarian, and a pharmacologist. Most of the interviewed refugees were in their forties, with the exception of four refugees in their late fifties and early sixties.

Iranian Refugees in Transit does not claim to narrate some "authentic experiences" of Iranian transit migrants while challenging the de-humanized narration based on mere numbers. Kobena Mercer's discussion on the "burden of representation" in the cultural politics of Black British cinema is helpful in understanding the unfruitfulness of this claim to authenticity.[10] Mercer demonstrated how in order to challenge stereotypical representations of Black people in mainstream cinema in Britain, where they were seen either as the source of the problem or as passive bearers of social problems and thus victimized, Black cinema makers resorted to a documentary realist approach to "tell it like it is."[11] This political responsibility has endowed Black cinema makers with a burden of representation, which invisibilizes Black experiences that do not fit in this collective representation or does not challenge those stereotypes. When limited access to resources such as funding and production is taken into account, this burden of representation gets heavier.[12] To present what burden of representation means further, Mercer quotes a character in *Passion of Remembrance* (1986) by Sankofa: "Every time a black face appears on screen we think it has to represent the whole race," to which comes the reply, "But there is so little space-we have to get it right."[13]

This is a problem many historians of marginalized communities face. Although the community in question may experience marginalization and oppression through their collective identity, this does not imply the absence of power dynamics within it. Being marginalized does not exempt the community from internal politics or prevent them from oppressing others. Taking into account the limited "stage" time these communities can acquire in public, choices often are made to present a homogenized picture or to prioritize the "bigger problem," where marginalization of a segment of people can be invisibilized until the liberation of the collective identity takes place. While this is a frequent issue with historians of oppressed nations, we can also see it in narratives on refugees, undocumented people, LGBTQI people, and other marginalized groups. Moreover, the representation of nonnormative practices in those communities would face serious backlash from the community. Burden of representation renders every narration on a marginalized community a political one.

The primary question during the writing process was the validity of taking the narrated experiences of transit migrants as the representation of "what happened." Taking experience as an unmediated source of knowledge would disguise the social and material mechanisms underlying the construction of these experiences. As goes the famous quote, people do make their own histories, but they make them under already existing circumstances.[14] Shedding light on those circumstances, which often have a collective impact, and contextualizing narratives in that framework of already existing circumstances is crucial to understanding the dynamics of not only the era under study but also current experiences of migration through Turkey.

Moreover, oral sources are no less reliable than the written ones categorically. Alessandro Portelli underlines that factual credibility cannot be seen as a monopoly of written documents as those written documents have not always been written either. Written documents are very often "only the uncontrolled transmission of unidentified oral sources," Portelli writes.[15] Thus the objectivity those written sources claim disguises the production processes of those written sources. National and company archives are full with letters and reports written by informers who claim things without any tangible proof. In this respect, oral sources are not categorically different from written sources with respect to objectivity or credibility.

However, in particular cases, oral sources can tell us more than the written documents. As Portelli argues, oral history gives us information not only about illiterate people or social groups but about people, whose written history is either missing or distorted.[16] It tells us more than "what people did, but what they wanted to do, what they believed they were doing, and what they now think they did."[17] Thus, resorting to oral history gives us not only "more history," but also a lead to the meaning of that history.[18] Studying oral sources has been a key methodology for researchers engaged with the histories of marginalized people, as their histories have seldom been found important enough to be reported on and registered in institutional archives. Working on Iranian oil workers for my PhD in various archives involving national archives of the United States, Iran, and the UK, and the company archives of British Petroleum, I can attest to this observation. Information on precarious workers who have not been on regular payroll, on women living in company towns, on ethnic minorities, or on other marginalized populations have been hard to find in those archives. We know they existed, but we would not have enough information on their experiences or gather data to be able to reconstruct their history by working solely at institutional archives.

In this book, oral sources are not juxtaposed with the written ones, but the written sources' construction of a homogenized group of people in transit is refuted by the tools oral sources render possible. Thus, the narrated experiences are taken into account with the histories of the narrators and the dynamics of the social space in which those experiences took place. Therefore experience is taken as a process in making and a key to understanding the social reality of the studied era.[19] The selection of the sources for the study was not secondary to the formation of its cause either. This study started as a response to the lack of histories of the Iranian transit migrants of the 1980s in a literature that initiates Turkey's experience of transit migration with the very arrival of those postrevolutionary Iranians in Turkey. As will be seen in the subsequent pages, it was the extraction of their stories in the written, academic accounts that urged me to search for Iranian transit migrants' footsteps elsewhere. Thus I began to search for the traces of transit life in Turkey through memoirs, novels, movies, and most importantly the oral narratives of Iranians who had been in transit in Turkey in the 1980s. And those narratives revealed that there is more to the written history of being a transit migrant in Turkey.

Discussion on sources goes beyond the quality of sources themselves. The conditions of their accessibility and the dynamics of working with them are impactful in the study as well. When I first decided to work on the history of Iranian refugees passing from Turkey after the Iranian Revolution, my thesis supervisor Professor Cengiz Kırlı had encouraged me to study the experiences of the present-day Iranian refugees in Turkey instead. I did not choose to do so due to two main issues related to methodology and reflexivity. Attending a few conferences on refugees in Turkey, it was hard for me to see the foreigners' branch of the General Directorate of Police being given a platform, let alone be exposed to their technocratic propaganda. Having firsthand experience of psychological violence, material neglect, and discrimination imposed by the same agents, it was not possible for me to take them as credible peers for information exchange. Moreover, due to lack of transparency in the state's tracking and storing qualitative and quantitative data on foreigners and refugees in Turkey, it did not take me long to understand that I had to work with the police who had the monopoly on not only data but also the permits I would have needed at different stages to conduct the research. This was one aspect of my identity converging with the research topic. The other involved my relationship as a researcher with the interviewees. Researching the experiences of the present-day refugees would mean witnessing their plight without being able to make a change and constantly trying to keep a critical distance. My experience as an interpreter for refugees had already shown me the limitations of this effort of a critical distance and the power dynamics that exists between people who share a similar language and culture but not similar lives. I did not want to be a bystander to their current plight, but a narrator of harder days that have already became history for them. None of these concerns can be taken as given for all researchers working on current-day refugees in Turkey.

That's why we need an intersectional approach not only in our analysis of the people we interview, but also in dealing with the reflexivity of the researcher. My identity, which proved challenging in my interactions with institutions and present-day Iranian refugees, played a facilitating role in my dialogues with refugees passing through Turkey after the 1979 revolution. First of all, the power dynamic was somewhat reversed at least in one aspect: they were the ones who had been able to make it to "the West," while my family and me were the ones who had not made it. Also, I was also one of them; they were my parents' generation. Each of our families had to leave Iran around the same year, had similar experiences in Turkey, and was living in an involuntary distance from our country of origin.

While oral and written sources are complementary to each other, the different nature of working with oral sources must be acknowledged. Oral sources are living sources; therefore, it is not possible to conduct a study based on oral sources without the subjects' participation in the process. Thus, unlike written sources, oral sources respond and react to the way they are being studied. However, this is more an opportunity than a challenge. It provides a more open interaction between the agenda of the interviewee, the source, and the agenda of the researcher.[20] Starting with a set of questions and finishing the interview only with the responses given to those questions would block the possibility of such an interaction. The practice of oral history necessitates and requires dialogue.

I engaged in a *thick dialogue* with the interviewees, which allows for more space to answers than questions and enables a dynamic process between questions and answers.[21] Portelli makes a distinction between a questionnaire and thick dialogue according to how much space the answers would have in the interview and how those answers would have an impact on the following questions. While a questionnaire gives the researcher more comparable data, the thick, open-ended dialogue can tell us more about the experience.[22] The concept of *thick dialogue* is derived from the concept of *thick description*, a concept popularized by anthropologist Clifford Geertz in his 1973 article "Thick Description: Toward an Interpretive Theory of Culture." Discussing Gilbert Ryle's notion of *thick description*, Geertz underlined the importance of semiotics in studying culture. At every level of observation, the ethnographer interprets what they see. Following Ryle's famous example, contracting eyelids and winking are two different things even if they, on the surface, seem to be same. You need to contextualize to understand the difference. A thick description of events goes beyond the surface, contextualizes, and interprets. A thick dialogue goes beyond the answers, and it helps interpret why certain topics are prioritized to be narrated and what function some stories carry.

Thick dialogue made it possible to obtain information on the grounds that did not seem to be important for the study before engaging in dialogue with the refugees (i.e., intergroup distinctions). Asking open-ended questions with more emphasis on "how" and "why" rather than "what" rendered it possible to have responses not particularly to the questions that I thought were important, but to the ones that were important for them, which later turned to be important for the study too. Even though my agenda was key in the formation of this study, in terms of asking the primary questions, selecting themes, and organizing the study, its content and focus would be quite different if it were not for the responses of the refugees.

Asking people to share the most significant and often most painful days of their lives required a more relevant excuse than mere academic engagement. I explained my purpose and the reasons for undertaking such a topic for research before starting the interview. At times, I shared my story with them, as I did not want to be in a position of *extracting* their story for my individual, academic purposes without reciprocating. Most of the time, our dialogues continued off the record and we exchanged telephone numbers and emails.

Revealing things about myself was helpful in having a dialogue.[23] This became apparent after the first interviews. In the first interviews, even though I had some prior information, I planned not to ask the interviewees about their organizational background to make them feel safer. However, each time our dialogue brought us to a moment that organizational backgrounds were revealed. And after that moment my personal history was important to build rapport with the interviewees. I was the same age as their children, if they had any; had family members who had been members of those organizations; and had lost dearest ones in similar ways they did. I did not share my story to learn more, but particularly to be able to continue to speak especially in times of rupture, such as an elder brother's account of his brother being killed under cross fire or a mother's account of shouting at her son attempting to take a piece of bread that was being saved for the next day. Ahmad Shamlu, the distinguished poet of 20th-century Iran, whose verses were undoubtedly also read by my interviewees, wrote: "I am not a tale you can tell / not a song you can sing / not a sound you can hear / or something you can see / or you can know / I am the shared pain, cry me out!"[24] Our shared pain was the enabler of our dialogue.

One of the limitations of working on transit migrants is the lack of resources to project a detailed composition of people in transit. As I will demonstrate in the following pages, the lack of regulations and other particularities of the time and place when Iranians were passing from Turkey renders this estimation even harder. The reasons to flee a postrevolution country in the midst of a war are more complex than what asylum forms expect you to fill in. I have engaged in the debate regarding the number of Iranian transit migrants in the 1980s in Chapter 1, "Flexible or Precarious? 'One and a Half Million Iranians' in Turkey." There are various attempts at describing that population. It is widely agreed that the migration flow from Iran in the 1980s was more politically oriented than the post-1990 flow.[25]

According to the unofficial UNHCR sources of 1987, referenced in Janet Bauer's study, the biggest group of recognized Iranian refugees in Turkey was composed of anti-regime activists (57 percent) and draft evaders (25 percent). With respect to the refugees' political affiliations, 36 percent of the refugees claimed to be affiliated with the People's Mojahedin, 35 percent with leftist organizations (such as Fadaiyan, Komala, and Tudeh), 12 percent with monarchists, 4.5 percent with Muslim religious opposition groups, and 0.5 percent with nationalist opposition groups.[26]

This book presents the narratives of the refugees who claim to be political. However, some of the stories did not include "political reasons" for flight in terms of affiliation with a certain anti-regime group. The question of "what is political" is beyond the scope of the present study. However, despite my usage of "political" particularly with reference to leftist political activists in this study, I do not deny the political quality of non-leftist Iranians' reasons of flight. In other words, I am not suggesting that the reasons driving women and LGBTQI individuals to flee, which stem from gender oppression and violence, are any less political than those of leftist political activists seeking refuge. Instead of ascribing identities to people, I take their self-identification as the main reference. This is also linked with the discussion on the centrality of semiotics and interpretation in ethnography. Political or in Persian, *siyasi* refers to a certain identity, the meaning of which is shared by the people involved in this study and it refers to leftist, revolutionary activists against the Shah regime and the Islamic Republic. This has been employed as the operational definition of the term throughout this book.

The thematic chapters of *Iranian Refugees in Transit* explore different dimensions of transit life in Turkey, each offering its own reading experience. Together, they provide the reader with a comprehensive picture of the post-1979 Iranian refugee life in Turkey connected with critical literature on the global depiction of refugees, the systemic inadequacies of the international asylum system, and the broader discourses of racism and sexism.

Chapter 1, "Flexible or Precarious? 'One and a Half Million Iranians' in Turkey" provides a historical and political setting for the Iranian refugees' temporary stay in Turkey. Iranians in the 1980s arrived in a country that was ruled by a postcoup authoritarian regime, which had its own internal political and ethnic conflicts, intersecting with the conflicts that had pushed them to leave Iran. Turkey's newly shaping asylum regime was formed by this political dynamic and prioritizing security concerns over protection of refugees. Refugees deserted and resisted this arbitrarily regulated asylum system. Precarity is introduced as a key concept to understand the transit refugee lives in Turkey particularly before its first asylum regulation in 1994.

For a great number of Iranian refugees, exile had started long before they left Iran. Chapter 2, "When Does Exile Begin?," portrays the flight of refugees from Iran to Turkey and elaborates on the impact of their political affiliations on their routes and ways of flight. Fear of persecution did not manifest itself at the same time for all refugees. I introduce two portraits, those of Said and Mahnaz, to highlight the diversity of these experiences and to delve into the intricacies of crossing the Iran-Turkey border. The concept of internal exile is presented as both an endangering and an empowering experience for political refugees' lives in transit.

Chapter 3, "'Their Categories and Ours': Politics of Differentiation," studies the institutional efforts to categorize and pick the "genuine refugee." These institutional classifications are contrasted with an alternative form of categorization based on self-identification: the ongoing endeavors of political refugees to distinguish themselves from fellow travelers in transit. Interviews with refugees reveal that the system's litmus test to check the degree of choice and compulsion in people's motives of flight fails to assess their situation thoroughly and punishes those who demonstrate agency. I argue that the technicalization of discussions about categories obscures the history and politics of the asylum system.

Chapter 4, "Not One of Those Women: Negotiating Womanhood in Transit," expands the politics of differentiation in the third chapter to refugee women's discourse on decency and "being the right kind of woman." Similar to the approach taken in the previous chapter, the concerns of refugee women are analyzed in conjunction with the intellectual and political influences that have shaped these concerns as well as the narratives stemming from various symptoms of gender-based oppression. This chapter explores gendered dimensions of displacement and its wide array of effects on women of diverse backgrounds.

The book's last thematic chapter, "The Collective Memory of Being in Transit in Turkey," seeks to look at Turkey and Istanbul through the eyes of the Iranian transit refugees. What does Turkey, as a first stop, represent in the narratives of migrants from Iran on their way to the West? How is this representation circulated and how does it impact the Iranian refugees' perceptions of having been in Turkey? In this chapter, in addition to interviews, I use novels, memoirs, and a particular movie, *The Guests of Hotel Astoria* by Reza Allamezadeh, to discuss representations of Turkey in cultural artifacts on/by Iranian refugees and the impact they have on the collective memory of being in transit in Turkey.

"Concluding Remarks" explores the shift in the interpretation of the concept of autonomy when applied to refugees, the tendency to isolate refugees as a categorically distinct group, and transit migration as a challenging category to the existing asylum system. Demonstrating the interconnectedness of these phenomena, this concluding chapter aims to shed light on the limitations of the prevailing approach on addressing refugees' needs and offers alternative perspectives.

Finally, to provide readers with insights into the current state of transit migration in Turkey, where the largest population of refugees in the world resides today, the Epilogue examines the situation of Syrians and Afghans in contemporary Turkey. This exploration delves into the continuities and changes in Turkey's approach to transit migration. The particularities of Turkish politics are considered in conjunction with its engagement with the global reinforcement of Western borders following the events of 9/11.

Iranian Refugees in Transit reintroduces political context into the abstract depiction of Iranian transit migrants in the 1980s. It predominantly highlights the experiences of leftist refugees, recognizing that their experiences may not fully represent all Iranians passing through Turkey during that period. The leftists I interviewed came from diverse ethnic backgrounds; however, the central focus of this study is on their identity as political refugees rather than their ethnic affiliations. Numerous untold stories remain, each with its unique focus. These include the lives of Iranians belonging to a wide array of ethno-religious minority backgrounds as well as those having nonnormative gender identities and sexual orientations. Exploring the constant psychological state of being in transit, even after what might be considered a "successful" migration to the destination country, is another valuable theme to investigate further.

1

Flexible or Precarious? "One and a Half Million Iranians" in Turkey

The Iranians who had to escape in the aftermath of the revolution they fought for landed in a country with its own history of political and ethnic conflicts. When they arrived in Turkey, it was under martial law following the notorious 1980 coup. The country had neither experienced a large wave of transit migration before, nor did it have any legal structure to regulate it. The main scholarly narrative on Turkey's history of irregular migration refers to a policy of pragmatism and flexibility, granting some protection to de facto refugees before 1994 despite the lack of any codified regulation.[1] Yet, as I will demonstrate in the following pages, this "pragmatic and flexible policy" facilitated corruption in the asylum system, intensified inequalities among the refugees, and rendered them precarious.

The concept of precarity has been used widely in explaining the human condition under neoliberal capitalist rule. From flexibilization of labor relations to the making of disposable populations, the concept of precarity helps us unpack a common condition shared by many dispossessed people without dismissing the heterogeneity of their experiences. When it comes to the Iranian transit refugees passing from Turkey after the 1979 revolution, precarity emerges as a core concept defining the experiences of those people in transit. Refugees present an archetypal "ideal case" of precarious subjects. It is when the noncitizens' condition of lack of autonomy and secure attachment to one's surroundings are extended to larger segments of the population and when the scope of a disposable population is stretched out, then the concept of precarity became popularized both in the academia and beyond.

In this chapter, I map the cornerstones of the making of Turkey's first asylum regulation, which exposes the moments triggering the Turkish State's national security-centered response to the refugee question and discuss what these flexible and pragmatic policies entailed for refugees. Discussing these experiences through the perspective of precarity debate, I demonstrate that what was flexible for the Turkish State was precarious for the Iranians in transit.

The Making of an Asylum Regulation

The 1951 Convention Relating to the Status of Refugees, which was a product of post–Second World War conditions, defines a refugee as someone who:

> As a result of events occurring before 1 January 1951 and owing to well-founded fear of being persecuted for reasons of race, religion, nationality, membership of a particular social group or political opinion, is outside the country of his nationality and is unable or, owing to such fear, is unwilling to avail himself of the protection of that country; or who, not having a nationality and being outside the country of his former habitual residence as a result of such events, is unable or, owing to such fear, is unwilling to return to it. (Article I/A/2)

Article 2 of the Convention states that "events occurring before 1 January 1951" should be understood to mean either "events occurring in Europe before 1 January 1951" or "events occurring in Europe or elsewhere before 1 January 1951" and that any contracting state adopting the former alternative may extend its obligations at any time by adopting the latter alternative.[2]

Turkey chose the former alternative, thus introducing a geographical reservation to the Convention—undertaking to grant asylum only to persons fleeing persecution in Europe as a result of events prior to 1951. The 1967 *Additional Protocol Relating to the Status of Refugees* lifted the geographic and time restrictions of the Convention. However, Turkey dropped the time limitation but kept the geographical reservation.[3] From 1960 when the UNHCR opened its first office in Turkey until 1980s, Turkey worked together with the UNHCR to process refugees from Soviet Union and Eastern Europe to settle them in a third country.[4] The rise of authoritarian regimes in the Middle East and their human rights violations rendered Turkey's geographical reservation obsolete in time. Millions of people from Iran and Iraq arrived in Turkish territories on their way out. Thus, by the 1980s, Turkey had been transformed into a transit country of de facto, non-Convention refugees.[5]

Iranians fleeing the Islamic Republic founded after the 1979 revolution constituted the first populous wave of transit migration to Turkey. Ahmet İçduygu defines three distinct periods of irregular migration to Turkey in the 20th century: 1979 to 1987, 1988 to 1993, and 1994 to 2001. 1979 points to the Iranian Revolution; 1988 to the massive arrival of asylum seekers from Iraq, Bulgaria, and former Soviet Republics; 1994 to Turkey's first asylum regulation; and 2001 to the beginning of a period of "degeneration" of irregular migration to Turkey, where smuggling and trafficking became more organized.[6]

This periodization needs further elaboration when it comes to the Iranians in transit. The years between 1979 and 1987 involved two distinct migration waves. The first two years were characterized by the migration of monarchists and those associated with the Pahlavi regime. Halleh Ghorashi names this period as "the spring of freedom," which ended with the consolidation of the Islamic Regime. As she also argues, this spring of freedom was a period of horror for those associated with the Pahlavi regime.[7] Ervand Abrahamian writes that revolutionary courts in Iran executed 497 people in the twenty-eight months between February 1979 and June 1981. These involved a former prime minister, ministers, generals, colonels, intelligence agents, and Baha'i businessmen accused of spying for Israel.[8] Fereshteh Ahmadi Lewin's classification is more exhaustive as it starts from the pre-revolution days. People affiliated with the Pahlavi regime, some of the industrialists, investors, financiers, and high-ranked officials fled from Iran starting from the summer of 1978 till the winter of 1979. This pre-revolution migration was followed by the flight of ethnic and religious minorities and the remaining Pahlavi-related people after the Islamic clergy's victory in February 1979.[9]

The first revolution-related migration wave to the United States, *starting before the revolution*, is argued to include "high-status migrants" who had high levels of education and income. For example, writing in the late 1980s, Bozorgmehr and Sabagh stated that Iranian nonstudent migrants had a much higher average individual income compared to those born in the United States and other foreign-born residents in 1979.[10] These "high-status migrants" do not characterize the postrevolutionary Iranian migration wave. However, there is a general perception that the first postrevolutionary Iranian migrants had a higher economic status than the subsequent ones.[11]

Lewin notes the removal of the first elected president Bani Sadr in 1981 and the subsequent clashes between the regime forces and the opposition movement as the launch pad of another migration wave composed of people with strong political affiliations.[12] The trajectory of Islamic Republic's consolidation involved the persecution of revolutionary opposition after the anti-revolutionaries. Between 1981 and 1985, revolutionary courts in Iran executed more than 8,000 people. As Abrahamian underlines, the revolutionary state killed more revolutionaries than anti-revolutionaries.[13] With the evolution of the target population of the new regime, more people sought ways of fleeing Iran. The escalation of Iran-Iraq War (1980–8) added draft evaders to this wave. This book studies this second, post-1981 wave.

The subsequent migration wave to Turkey before the establishment of 1994 Asylum Regulation was from Iraq and Bulgaria. The Kurdish refugees from Iraq and Turkish refugees from Bulgaria did not receive the same treatment by the Turkish State that has a history of discrimination and oppression of its own Kurdish minority, who form Turkey's biggest internally displaced population (IDP).

The Bulgarian State's forced assimilation of its Muslim minorities between 1984 and 1989 pushed many Turks from Bulgaria to seek refuge in Turkey. This Bulgarian "revival process" that involved bans on Turkish language and cultural and religious rituals was the push factor behind the mass migration wave in 1989, when more than 300,000 Turks, also pushed by the Bulgarian State, arrived in Turkey.[14] The 1989 refugees were welcomed by the Turkish State and were granted social rights and citizenship not as refugees but according to the settlement laws that defined a migrant as an individual of "Turkish race/lineage and who has ties to Turkish culture."[15]

Kurds sought refuge in Turkey with the intensification of the systemic persecution of Kurdish population in Iraq with the dynamics of Iraq-Iran war. Following the Halabja massacre of 1988, 50,000 Kurds sought temporary shelter in Turkey. Half a million Kurds from Iraq joined them in 1991 when the post–Iran-Iraq war uprisings in northern Iraq were crushed violently by the Saddam Hussain–led Iraqi State.[16] Sixty-thousand Asian workers and their families fleeing Iraq during the 1990 Gulf War comprised another temporary migration wave from Iraq to Turkey.[17] These refugees from Iraq were sheltered in Turkey close to Iraq border on humanitarian basis and were later on repatriated, both voluntarily and with force,[18] or moved to third, Western countries. Kirişçi relates that these Kurdish refugees were referred to neither as refugees nor as Kurds at the time. They were called by the Kurdish name *peshmerga* or "temporary guests"[19]—names employed to acknowledge neither their ethnic identity nor their right to asylum. The usage of the term "guests" for refugees who are not legally recognized is a practice that continues until today.

While Turks from Bulgaria, at least initially, received a warm welcome, Kurds from Iraq found themselves in turmoil. Kirişçi points to the contrasting treatment these two groups of refugees received. In the case of refugees from Bulgaria, legal provisions were made to convert their Bulgarian currency to the local currency, to import their cars, and to accelerate their citizenship process. Housing projects and employment assistance were organized to integrate them into the society.[20] Nevertheless, Kurds, also being an oppressed minority in Turkey, were sheltered at border towns and were supported with bare minimums. The main concern while receiving the Kurdish refugees was their accelerated repatriation, which after intense negotiations with European states ended up in creating a "safe heaven" in northern Iraq for them to move to.[21] While Kurds from Iraq, who also had family ties in Turkey, were from the very first moment unwelcome, 50,000 Turkmen refugees from Kirkuk and Mosul were given a preferential treatment.[22] As Kirişçi argues, being of "Turkish descent and culture," defined not in terms of language but ethnicity and religion has been the core of Turkey's immigration and asylum policy from early days of the Turkish Republic.[23] As he strikingly shows through examples, citizenship through immigration and asylum was reserved not even for all Muslims but for those following the Sunni line.[24] However, later on, Muslims from Kosovo and Bosnia did not benefit from the same welcoming policies as the refugees coming from Bulgaria did. Refugees from Bosnia and Kosovo were settled with their relatives and repatriated as soon as possible.[25]

Kirişçi defines the 1994 Asylum Regulation, Turkey's first asylum regulation, as a reflection of "the ascendance of national security concerns over refugee rights."[26] Until the mass arrival of Kurdish refugees, the Turkish authorities managed to do with the aforementioned "pragmatic and flexible" lawlessness.

However, the influx of half a million Kurdish refugees invoked national security concerns for the Turkish authorities, who at times only became aware of them at the time of their departure and did not let them leave.[27] The early 1990s mark a tug of war between the UNHCR dealing with the mostly Kurdish Iraqi, non-Europeans' asylum procedures, and the Turkish authorities, who took the Kurdish refugees' presence as a security threat given the activities of the PKK in those years. The State's assumption of PKK militants' presence among those Kurdish asylum seekers who had entered from the Iraqi border and it disrespecting the principle of *non-refoulement* for non-Convention refugees stiffened the disputes further.[28]

Thus, the 1994 *Regulation on the Procedures and Principles Concerning the Mass Influx of Foreigners in Turkey Requesting Residence Permits with the Intention of Seeking Asylum from a Third Country*[29] did not stem from the concern of legalizing non-European transit migrants and regulating their already undefined and nebulous situation, but from the state-centric logic of defeating the "security threats" generated by the recent flow of Kurdish refugees.[30] With the 1994 Regulation, the Turkish State took control of determining the status of the non-Convention refugees and regulating their asylum procedures by making it obligatory for refugees to register with the police upon their arrival. Its practices following the 1994 Regulation aggravated the situation.[31] A time limit of five days for asylum applications to be filled was imposed. This made it possible for officials to reject late applications without taking into account the actual substance of the applications.[32]

The Turkish State was not impartial to many conflicts in Iran that rendered the refugees' lives vulnerable both in Iran and in Turkey. Both countries have been going through similar—albeit to different extent—ethnic and political conflicts. This made the Iranian Kurdish refugees' lives even harder than the other Iranians. In an open letter written by the Iranian Refugees' Alliance's vice president Mona Afary to the then minister of interior Meral Akşener, on April 7, 1997, it was claimed that in the previous 1.5 years, eighty-five Kurdish Iranian refugees were refused to be registered at the police in Şırnak and were deported to Zakho in northern Iraq. The refugees argued that their papers were confiscated and they were pushed to bribe the authorities.[33] Iranian Kurds were reported to be regularly interrogated about PKK and were accused of cooperation with them. Perhaps the most striking claim is that Turkish paramilitary village guards, *köy korucuları*, had raided Iranians' dwellings in Şırnak to use them as temporary operation bases against PKK guerillas.[34]

The 1994 Regulation did not stay unchallenged. International refugee advocacy groups, the UNHCR, and the struggle of the asylum seekers themselves had a collective impact, and the Turkish State developed closer relations with the UNHCR in the three years following the Regulation.[35] Kirişçi points to the role of courts in this process. He states that although there was precedence and a general legal opinion that foreigners could "challenge an administrative decision preventing the entry or requiring expulsion in court," asylum seekers and refugees did not try that option until 1997 due to a lack of confidence in the Turkish police and appeal system as well as the fear of aggravating their situation by challenging the authorities.[36] However, two UNHCR-recognized Iranian refugees in resettlement process went to court and won the case against the Ministry of Interior's decisions calling for their deportation for violating the time limit in their asylum application in 1997.[37] These two trials set forward other refugees taking their cases to court, which was encouraged by the UNHCR. These actions rendered the Ministry of Interior's decisions open to judicial review and appeal, created precedence for future cases, and drew attention to the technical misinterpretation of the time clause disregarding the substance of the asylum applications.[38]

The resistance of the refugees to the arbitrary deportations involved not only individual attempts of taking their cases to the court, but also organizing collective actions such as a major sit-in act that lasted ten months in the Ankara office of the United Socialist Party (USP). The protestors involved refugees whose cases had been rejected by the UNHCR and were under the risk of deportation. They demanded the UNHCR to reopen their cases and take action against deportations. Starting in the early days of August 1995, the sit-in came to an end in June 1996 with the intervention of Ankara police. In a Turkish leftist weekly, *Söz*, it was reported that the Iranians at the USP office in Ankara were from various organizations including the Worker Communist Party of Iran, People's Mojahedin, the Kurdistan Democrat Party, and Shah supporters.[39]

The Iranian Refugees' Alliance, which was formed in New York for supporting the asylum seekers in Turkey in 1993, was their main supporter. The alliance defined its activities as providing financial support and legal help for Iranian refugees as well as disseminating news about their situation and linking them to human rights organizations.[40] Its reports state that the sit-in started with the participation of nearly 160 refugees (representing 70 families/files) in the USP's Ankara office and ended with 80 participants in the newly formed Freedom and Solidarity Party's (ÖDP) Ankara office. At the time of the police intervention, 10 refugees were on the twenty-fifth day of a protest hunger strike at the office of the Human Rights Association.[41]

In an article written at the time of the protest, Kirişçi stated that refugees had deferred deportation by means of the publicity surrounding their case.[42] Moreover, refugees added a new demand to their list during the protests: "even if their cases were rightly rejected in the first place, they should now be considered refugees *sur place*."[43] The protesting refugees demonstrated in front of the Iranian Embassy in Ankara and were highly exposed as their pictures were taken and published. This meant that a new condition was created in Turkey (thus *sur place*) that by itself created a basis for having "well-founded fear of persecution" in case of return. However, this was seen as abusing the conditions of protection and the UNHCR did not reopen their cases. Nevertheless, as they were highly exposed and their deportation would mean that their lives would be at risk, the UNHCR convinced the Turkish State to extend their residence permits by means of which the threat of deportation was evaded.[44]

Fewer deportations and more cooperation between the UNHCR and the Ministry of Interior constituted the 1999 revision of the Regulation that increased the time limit of application from five to ten days.[45] The cooperation between the UNHCR and the Turkish government required the asylum seekers' applications to both authorities. From then on asylum seekers were guided to apply to the UNHCR for refugee status and to the Turkish government for "temporary asylum," being reminded that the UNHCR would not conduct an interview with them or their families and would not decide their case unless they had first registered with the police in their "assigned city."[46] Thus, a two-tier system was introduced.

The 1994 Asylum Regulation affirmed the legal status of the non-Convention refugees' stay in Turkey, which can be seen as a constructive contribution to non-Convention refugees' lives. However, it was an outcome of the internal security concerns of the Turkish State with respect to the increasing numbers of Kurdish refugees and its implementation was tainted with this perspective. Moreover, the 1994 Regulation coded this new category of non-Convention refugees as *sığınmacı*, which is just another word for refugee, this time not in Arabic (as in *mülteci*) but in Turkish.[47] This term has been used simultaneously as indicating a status prior to being a refugee as in "asylum seeker" and as non-Convention refugee. However, at an increasing rate, it has also been used as a category of its own to define people for whom nothing more than a temporary protection is envisaged. Even though *mülteci* and *sığınmacı* are synonyms, the former's Arabic roots has rendered the word a technical term referring to refugees, while the latter, coming from a verb used in daily life meaning seeking protection, has underlined the vulnerability of the people under question without giving them a special status.

The pre-1994 so-called flexible and pragmatic policies and the post-1994 regulated policies do not belong to two distinct and opposing life worlds. Criticizing such an assumption of linear evolution of the state of law, Nadir Özbek notes that such ideal and abstract concepts of two states, one based on premodern arbitrariness and coercion and the other based on law, are not sufficient to explain concrete historical situations.[48] He argues that there is no such "ideal state of law" or "state based on coercion," but formations based on different strategies suitable for different concrete historical situations. The genealogy of the 1994 Regulation is a good example of these changing strategies of the government with respect to transit migration. Moreover, it sheds light on the presence of actors other than the state in the process. The pre-1994 and post-1994 policies were products of a conflictual social space and formed new arenas of struggle.

In this light, the resistance to the 1994 Asylum Regulation can be seen as a product of the Regulation itself. The pre-1994 "pragmatic and flexible" policies did not define the non-Convention refugees legally, which rendered them vulnerable to the arbitrary power of the police. The two interviewees, who chose to be registered with the police as they even did not have fake passports, stressed the maltreatment of the police in charge of interrogating them and "deciding" to grant them temporary residence permits the first time they went to the police station. The temporary residence permit was given not on a legal basis, but as an arbitrary favor and thus intermediaries had been formed. For example, there were lawyers known for "arranging residence."[49] "Arranging" meant charging money and acting as intermediaries to bribe the police in charge of granting temporary residence permit.

In Search of Figures

The 1990s were also marked by an increasing concern of human rights violations in Turkey. Most of the NGOs now actively supporting refugees in Turkey and documenting these violations were founded in the 1990s. The Organization for Human Rights and Solidarity for Oppressed People, Mazlumder, was founded in 1991; Helsinki Citizens' Assembly that gave birth to the Refugee Advocacy and Support program in 2004 was founded in 1993; Amnesty International Turkey Branch was founded in 1995; and the Association for Solidarity with Asylum-Seekers and Migrants was founded in 1995.[50] The only exception is the Human Rights Association of Turkey (IHD), which was founded in 1986. Yet, its activities pertaining to refugees do not date back to the 1980s. IHD supported the Iranian asylum seekers' protest actively in 1995.[51] Nevertheless, Turkey's experience with transit migration and violation of refugees' human rights predates 1990s. Starting from the 1980s, Iranians have been among the biggest migrant groups in transit in Turkey. Even in the period subsequent to the 1994 Asylum Regulation, until May 2004, 21,601 of 35,162 asylum applications in Turkey were filed by Iranians.[52]

Despite the increasing number of studies on transit migration and non-Convention refugee groups living in Turkey, it is hard to pursue the traces Iranians have left in the 1980s. Their presence in Turkey is generally accounted as background information for the assessment of the period studied. Most of the studies refer to the quantity of the Iranians passing through Turkey. However, the estimates of the Iranian population passing through Turkey in the 1980s vary to a great extent. Although it is mostly estimated to be "up to one and a half million," the number varies from half a million[53] to three million.[54]

Referring to those fluctuations between estimates, Stéphane De Tapia introduced the case of Iranian nationals in Turkey "as a perfect illustration of the difficulty of determining the statistical reality of irregular transit migration and the fantasies surrounding it."[55] Even though not published regularly, various statistics on Iranians of the time provided by a number of Turkish ministries are available. For example, numbers exist for "foreigners arriving by country of residence/nationality," "foreigners leaving by country of residence," "foreigners who live in Turkey by their nationality and reason for presence: (resident/education/work/other)."[56] Yet, they are far from giving a comprehensive account of the Iranians in transit. According to the border crossing statistics (foreigners arriving by country of residence/nationality) derived from the Ministry of Tourism, there were 3,689,514 Iranian entries in the years 1984–99.[57] Nevertheless this by no means conveys their actual "reason for presence" as Turkey evolved into a center of attraction for Iranian tourists after the 1979 revolution because of its geographical proximity and lack of visa requirement.

The UNHCR figures do not help to solve this ambiguity of numbers either. According to the UNHCR figures, only eight Iranians registered with the UNHCR Ankara, and only one person was recognized as refugee up to 1985 (see Table 1.1). According to Ahmet Güder, former UNHCR Ankara, National Resettlement Officer, the reliability of these records is questionable as the UNHCR was using a manual cards system in keeping the archive of registrations up until 1985 and it is assumed that there might have been mistakes in data processing.[58] In our interview Ahmet Güder stated that it was pointless for Iranian refugees to apply to the UNHCR before 1985–6, as no systematic resettlement was employed then. Thus, knowing that the Turkish State did not accept refugees from non-European countries, refugees did not apply to the UNHCR. As arrivals increased by 1984–5, the UNHCR came to an agreement with the Turkish State not to deport the new comers until they had evaluated their cases and resettled the recognized refugees in a third country. This shows that the UNHCR's resettlement policies emerged from the necessity produced by the Iranian refugees of the mid-1980s. Furthermore, a special status was created for the draft evaders composing a significant part of the Iranians applying the UNHCR as they did not fit the UNHCR's general framework of asylum. They were recognized as refugees on humanitarian bases, as it became the case for a great number of Somalis later on.[59]

Lack of an official non-Convention refugee status before the 1994 Regulation in Turkey added up to the ambiguity of numbers. The pre-1994 de facto protection involved a temporary residence permit for the asylum

Table 1.1 Iranians under the UNHCR Mandate (1980–90)

	Iranian registrations		Iranian recognitions	
	Cases	Persons	Cases	Persons
1980	–	–	–	–
1981	1	2	–	–
1982	–	–	–	–
1983	–	–	–	–
1984	6	6	1	1
1985	76	78	17	17
1986	1,420	1,568	464	487
1987	3,382	3,867	1,169	1,269
1988	2,968	3,584	1,745	2,042
1989	1,049	1,198	407	479
1990	907	1,192	446	576
Total	9,809	11,495	4,249	4,871

Note: The asylum procedure might take more than a year, so numbers do not indicate the recognized cases that were registered in the same year.

Source: Compiled by the author from the data provided by Ahmet Güder, UNHCR National Resettlement Officer, Ankara, Turkey, April 21, 2008. Previously published in M. Jefroudi, "Migration across the Turkish-Iranian Border," in *Migration, Asylum, and Refugees in Turkey: Studies in the Control of Population at the Southeastern Borders of the EU*, edited by Nurcan Ozgur Baklacioglu and Yesim Ozer (Lewiston, NY: Edwin Edgar Melen Press, 2014), 324.

seekers registered to the police. However, registration was not a prerequisite for the UNHCR application and refugees, especially those who suffered from fear of persecution in their country of origin did not choose to register with the police. By rejecting the "pragmatic and flexible" protection of the Turkish authorities, political refugees avoided the threat of being victims of those "pragmatic and flexible" policies, which could have involved being part of a cartel or deportation without having access to asylum procedures. Celia Mannaert noted the presence of such "security arrangements" between Turkey and countries such as Tunisia and Iran. These cartels involved the immediate repatriation of opposition activists.[60] Although most of the time it is hard to have access to the details of such "security arrangements," what is known in the case of such agreements between the Islamic Republic of Iran and Turkey is enough to understand the aversion of the political refugees to police registration.

In its May 31, 1987, issue, the widely circulated weekly *Nokta* cited a Ministry of Interior officer stating that Turkey found the opportunity to maintain "critical stability" by signing bilateral agreements with its neighbors.[61] The

Agreement on Repatriating Criminals was reported to be an example of such bilateral security agreements between Turkey and the Islamic Republic of Iran, which approved the repatriation of the asylum seekers that had been found guilty in their country of origin. Such agreements actually led to the reciprocal repatriation of opposition activists. While the subjects of these bilateral security agreements were mostly people from leftist guerrilla movements in the mid-1980s, it became mainly militants of Kurdish opposition movement in the late 1980s and 1990s. This not only reflects the Turkish State's evolving perception of threat, but also gives clues for the composition of the Iranian migrants in the subsequent periods. Interviews with former transit migrants in Turkey reveal the awareness of such agreements.

Farhad is one of such refugees living in Cologne. He lived in Turkey for two different periods. As a Kurdish Party professional from Sanandaj, he first fled to northern Iraq, then to the USSR, went back to Iraq, and entered Turkey in 1988. He applied for asylum through the UNHCR, which he later abandoned. However, he fled to Germany and came back to Ankara as an exchange student with a German passport in 1993 to pursue political activities, which he termed "class activities," focusing on logistics—organizing safe accommodation for the militants from his organization in transit. He claims that the Turkish police kept a list of Iranian opposition activists according to their degree of importance in order to exchange them with Turkey's opponents that sought refuge in Iran.[62]

According to a 1988 Amnesty International Report on Turkey, Sirali Huseyin Zadeh, an UNHCR Ankara interpreter who was detained for three weeks in Ankara to be deported to Iran, disclosed that he was accused of being in touch with Amnesty International, the Kurds, and the Communist party and he was tortured to give their names.[63] The threats to the lives of political refugees extended beyond detention and deportation. The most well-known cases of political assassinations in Turkey involved the murder of Ali Akbar Ghorbani (1992), a member of People's Mojahedin; Zahra Rajabi (1996), a member of the National Council of Resistance of Iran (NCRI); and Abdolali Moradi (1996), a NCRI supporter.[64] According to the 1993 Human Rights Watch World Report on Iran, Hojatoleslam Ali Fallahian, the head of the Iranian intelligence service at that time, acknowledged the involvement of Iranian agents in the assassination of opposition members abroad.[65]

Iranian State was not alone in jeopardizing political refugees' lives in Turkey. A 2010 newspaper article in Sabah, Turkey, published the confessions of a former member of JITEM, the Gendarmerie Intelligence and Anti-terror Unit, titled as "Former Specialist Turned into a Covert Informant: We Killed and Buried 40 Refugees." The informant, previously working at Hakkari, Yüksekova, stated that he participated in the murder of forty refugees in 1997 and that he could point the mass graves. According to his claim, refugees were mostly from Iran, Pakistan, and Afghanistan and they were shot handcuffed. Killed in the border town Van, Başkale, the massacre was officially registered as shooting PKK militants infiltrating Turkey.[66]

The awareness of such interstate agreements and extralegal violence can also be traced in representational works on and by Iranian transit refugees. The movie I will discuss in more detail in Chapter 5, *The Guests of Hotel Astoria* by Reza Allamezadeh, acknowledges these interstate agreements as well.[67] The film tells the story of a group of Iranians who stay in Hotel Astoria in Istanbul while trying to find a way to continue their journey to "the West" in the 1980s. The prominent political activist in the film, the engineer Mr. Mohseni, is identified in a regular police raid at the hotel and taken into custody and beaten by the police, who did not even give him time to get dressed. Toward the end of the film we learn that he is deported and handed over to the Iranian government with four other Iranian political activists and is subsequently executed. We learn from his interrogator at the Turkish police that he had been working with Armenian and Kurdish political organizations in Turkey. Throughout the film there are few clues about his identity despite some references to the collective memory of Iranian exiles. The only thing mentioned about him is that he is an engineer and his final destination is France, the popular destination for Iranian revolutionary leftists.

We can read the presence of post-Iranian revolution refugees in the literature on transit migration in Turkey through Roland Barthes's explanation of myth as "depoliticized speech." Depoliticized speech "organizes a world which is without contradictions because it is without depth ... it establishes blissful clarity: things appear to mean something by themselves."[68] Used as background information for the history of Turkey's experience with irregular migration, Iranian refugees of early 1980s are represented as a homogenous group of middle or upper middle class, which then "naturally" means that they have transited smoothly through Turkey. Barthes stated that "myth is constituted by the loss of the historical quality of things"[69] and it does distort the reality rather than hiding it. The most important distortion is carried out by assuming the homogeneity of the one million or so Iranians in Turkey in the 1980s and the identity of their experiences. The facts presented might not be "false" such as the UNHCR's and the Western European countries' comparative receptiveness of Iranian refugees in 1980s or the high percentage of middle-class or upper middle-class Iranians' presence among the ones in transit. Yet, these facts do not speak for themselves and other facts might be selected and juxtaposed to them.

Janet Bauer's study on Iranian women refugees in Turkey and West Germany, based on her research in 1987–8, is a rare work conducted on those "more than one million Iranians in Turkey." About choosing Turkey and West Germany as her field, she argued that "the class background of the exiles in these locations are more varied than those of exiles in the United States."[70] In her fieldwork, she was able to contact some of the individuals that she had known from the working-class areas in Iran before the revolution. Among her fifty interviewees there were leftists from Tudeh, Peykar, and Fadaiyan, members of the Mojahedin, monarchists, and "unaffiliated teens wanting a better chance," all of whom sought political asylum.[71] Her findings are contradicting the myth of the Iranians in the 1980s' Turkey. Bauer states that all of her interviewees in Germany had paid someone for their journey to Germany while those remaining in Turkey, from three weeks to four years, had neither the money nor the family connections to continue their journey. They were either waiting for the UNHCR recognition or resettlement in a third country. She argued that the majority of those in transit in Turkey were from working-class areas of Tehran or from the provinces.[72] Two cases she cited underline the diversity of transit migrants' experiences:

> Nahid, a member of a Marxist organization, was a teacher in Iran before fleeing. She was injured in street fighting in Tehran and spent time in prison before being married in a proletarian ceremony to a comrade. After fleeing first to other parts of Iran, she came over the western mountains with a small, sickly infant to Turkey, where she stayed several months before a smuggler arranged her passage to Germany when the border with East Berlin was still open. "It was very difficult, especially in Turkey," she said. By

contrast, Parveen and her sister, with no political affiliations, said "We had a great time for two weeks in Istanbul while waiting for a smuggler to take us to Germany."[73]

These are not exceptional stories. Transit migrants' experiences differ with respect to their class, gender, age, ethnicity, and political affiliation as well as the duration of their stay and their motivation. Therefore, constructing a narrative of a smooth transition of well-off Iranians in the 1980s excludes, abstracts, generalizes, and omits the experiences of those living in Turkey as transit migrants in 1980s. Before further delving into the variety of those experiences, I would like to elaborate on the relevance of the concept of precarity when it comes to understanding the transit refugee lives, particularly under "flexible and pragmatic" regimes.

Flexible Is Precarious

I use the concept of precarity to describe the experiences of Iranian transit refugees throughout this book. Precarity is not only one aspect of being in transit but has been a central attribute of the transit refugee experience. From the first moment of feeling the need to flee, throughout different stages of their journey, and temporary stay on their way to the "final" destination, institutional and societal factors render refugees' lives precarious. Even though the concept is often used as an adjective to describe the insecurities refugees face in their asylum process, it is seldom studied as a core attribute of refugee lives in transit.

Sabine Hess is one of the few researchers using the concept to explain the phenomenon of transit migration. In "De-naturalising Transit Migration," Hess argues that while transit migrant experiences are varied, living in "precarious transit zones" or "precarious settlements" is a common denominator. Hess demonstrates that European border regimes do not stop mobility but create these precarious settlements where people are "stuck in mobility," changing their plans and trajectories to be able to survive.[74] Being stuck has been a continuous trope in describing transit refugee lives in Turkey, as is done also in this book through the narratives of refugees describing the neighborhood of Aksaray in Istanbul as a swamp, themselves stuck in limbo or in a waiting room.[75]

However, the fact that this situation did not necessarily mean immobility but a different kind of mobility is a novel argument. Hess underlines the dynamism, the mobility in waiting. This mobility might not be linear or productive at most times and constitute a significant factor of precarity, of not being able to have any secure attachment to one's surrounding.

The concept of precarity has been discussed primarily with respect to labor conditions. However, as the milestones in its conceptualization and its contexts of appearance in academic and popular discourse demonstrate, from one's relationship to the state, to living in uncertainty, to lack of access to political representation, autonomy, or independence, labor condition is life condition under racial capitalism. In the following pages I am presenting those milestones in precarity debate to unpack this interconnectedness.

Following the trend of de-regularization of the labor market with the rise of neoliberal policies and austerity measures, the concept of precarity has been used to describe the condition of people in flexible labor relations. Guy Standing, who popularized the term in his 2011 book *The Precariat*, initially described it to mean basically all working people who do not have a standard employment relationship characterized by working full time, having a permanent contract, being employed directly, and working at the employer's designated place, among others.[76] Standing later on defined the precariat as people whose labor is insecure, unstable, associated with casualization, and informalization.[77] The precariat is "exposed to chronic uncertainty, facing a life of 'unknown unknowns,'" Standing writes.[78] Moreover, he extends the phenomenon from labor relations to one's relationship with state. He claims that the precariat has fewer rights than others.[79] "More and more people, *not just migrants*, are being converted into denizens, with a more limited range and depth of civil, cultural, social, political and economic rights," Standing writes[80] (emphasis mine).

Standing's book *The Precariat* came out during a wave of anti-government protests, starting with the *Arab Spring* of 2010–12, which popularized the term and the more specific Latin language context which I will describe later. Protests against poor living conditions, unemployment, and economic stagnation were set off with self-immolation of Mohamed Bouazizi, a street vendor selling fruits and vegetables in his hometown Sidi Bouzid in Tunisia. Working without a permit and tired of giving bribes, the police confiscated his scale and he set himself on fire in front of the governor's office after not finding any authority that would listen to his complaint.[81] Protests for better life conditions and freedom spread to Libya, Egypt, Yemen, Bahrain, and Syria. Each country had its own root causes and different processes, while sharing some attributes, which could be summarized as having capitalist regimes focused on speculation, extraction, and overdeveloped service sector, ruled by corrupt, patrimonial states.[82]

These structural particularities aside, the Arab Spring riots also had shared attributes with following riots at the west side of world. These were mainly a crisis of political representation and unequal impact of neoliberal austerity measures on the population. It was first in Spain and then in Greece where large waves of protests against austerity measures took place. Initiated by occupying Puerto del Sol in Madrid, *indignad@s* in Spain, the indignants, protested against high unemployment rates, corruption, and austerity measures that made the working people pay, unequally, for the financial crisis of 2008.

In Latin language contexts, at which *precarius* means mainly uncertain or pertaining to entreaty,[83] in Spain, Italy, and Portugal, movements reclaimed the word precarious even before the 2008 crisis. As Marcel van der Linden demonstrated, the movement even got its patron saint, San Precario, in Italy in 2004.[84] *Precarios en movimiento* in Spain and *precários inflexíveis* in Portugal reclaimed the word representing insecurity and helplessness, to represent a rebellious, collective identity. As Catarina Principe argues, in Portugal, the anti-austerity movement articulated precarity to go beyond a labor condition to encompass "questions of independence, self-determination and life planning, as well as discrimination and racism."[85]

Meanwhile the narrow description of precariat referring to people who are not in a standard employment relationship was criticized widely in the academia as well. The main argument against this narrow definition was that it was a Eurocentric argument focusing on countries where standard employment relationship was widespread at some specific, post–Second World War, period. Not only labor was precarious at all times, but also millions of people used to work and continue to do so at odd jobs and without contract, informally before and after the worldwide neoliberal age. While precarization can be a useful concept to describe further flexibilization of some sectors or relations of production in certain context, we cannot reserve the term for that only.

Looking at the origins of the popularization of the concept in academia and its widespread employment in Latin language contexts, we can take the concept of precarity referring not only to a lack of standard employment relationship, but to a "life condition" that evolves around uncertainty, insecurity, and lack of autonomy. This does not exclude the increased rate of precarization of labor in neoliberal times, but includes people whose relationship with uncertainties, insecurities, and lack of autonomy goes beyond their labor condition.

Moreover, it is clear that the labor condition and life condition are connected and cannot be separated under racial capitalism. The denizens of the world, irregular migrants, refugees, and undocumented people, compose the largest segment of informal labor force as well. According to International Labor Organization (ILO), noncitizens are mostly employed in sectors such as domestic labor and agriculture, which are less regulated,[86] or in industries such as construction and tourism, which are immediately affected by economic downturns, which make them more vulnerable to job losses than others.[87] Moreover, the prevalence rate of being in a forced labor relationship is three times higher for adult migrant workers than that of adult nonmigrant workers.[88] Women's position in the formal-informal labor spectrum is not favorable either. ILO's Women at Work Trends report reveals that women are not only more likely to be unemployed than men, but when they work, they are overrepresented in informal labor relations, which end up them having less access to employment-related social protection and old-age benefits.[89] This latter point highlights that particularly when the welfare state is shrinking all around the world and noncitizens are structurally kept away from the allocation of those already shrinking resources, work relations are never only work relations.

Highlighting the intersectional distribution of precarity corresponds to another thread of thought on the concept that focuses not on the lack of resources but on their differential allocation, either structurally or temporally. Ayse Parla's work on migrants from Bulgaria in Turkey, *Precarious Hope*, takes precarity as a condition that is marked by the sense of losing a privilege. Parla is concerned that the ever-expanding deployment of the term "precarity" in the current scholarship makes the term lose its analytic edge.[90] Going back to its theoretical roots in English language critical theory, mainly credited to Judith Butler's 2004 *Precarious Life*, and building up on her fieldwork with migrants from Bulgaria, Parla focuses on the "differential distribution" of uncertainty, unpredictability, and insecurity in studying precarity.[91] She highlights that it is the relationship to structures of privilege that defines where someone is situated in the spectrum of precarity.

Similar to its Latin roots of "obtained by entreaty or prayer," Parla uses it with reference to dependence on the "words, acts, and whims of structurally more powerful others, whether they be border police, officials at police stations, police on the street, employers, or migrant association representatives."[92] Elaborated in a rather thorough manner, Parla's argument of existential "dependency on the acts of others," at its core, is not different from Guy Standing's more simplified account of one's position in labor relations and their relation with state. The former involves dependency on the will of employers, and the latter involves dependency on state's laws and regulations However, in Parla's account, the concept of dependency is expanded to the community as well. What is stimulating in her argument is that it is the loss in privileges that one had or thought to have in the past that makes someone feel precarious in present.[93] Her argument is based on the experiences of migrants coming from Bulgaria, whose past is shaped with memories of communism and the favorable reception the first generation received in Turkey.

While it is logical that one can probably feel the lack of something deeper if they once had access to it, it is doubtful that having access to secure life conditions, health, housing, education, and the right to work, among others, renders someone privileged. Also, even if we take precarity not as an objective situation but a subjective assessment of the conditions one lives in, there are limits to normalization of poverty and insecurity. Unless we are isolated from society totally and do not have physical and sensory experiences of insecurity, cold, hunger, and so on, the ones who never had access to secure living conditions will still feel insecure. That is where the circle closes: going back to Butler, all lives are precarious as all human beings need food and shelter and are dependent on social and labor relations.[94] It is not the universal condition of life's precariousness, but the differential distribution of the condition of precarity that matters. Thus as Butler argues, while precariousness is an ontological concept, precarity is a political one as it is a product of political orders rendering the lives of one segment of population valuable and the others disposable.[95]

The neoliberal, flexible labor relations lead to lack of employment, job, income, work, or representation security for the dispossessed curtailing their autonomy. Similarly, flexible asylum regimes, which defined Turkey's asylum policies in the 1980s and early 1990s, limit refugees' access to basic human and social rights curtailing their autonomy. Lack of regulation and flexible employment of those existing regulations made transit refugee Iranians more prone to arbitrary state violence at and beyond borders, fraud and corruption, and interpersonal violence. Yet, depending on their personal history and identities, they experienced the condition of precarity in differing ways, which I demonstrate in the following pages.

2

When Does Exile Begin?

"They were getting closer," said Sohrab, narrating his flight from Iran. He had left Iran with a forged passport that had a crooked photo of him and with a serious stomachache that would accompany him until Germany. Flight was not his first choice, but "*they* were getting closer"; so he had to leave.

The reason for their flight is the main question refugees face in their asylum interviews. International asylum regulations give "the validity of the fear of persecution" the leading role in the assessment of the applicant's eligibility to be a recognized refugee. However, for the newcomer or the noncitizen, being inquired for their reasons of arrival is not exclusive to the official spaces. Encountering an Iranian, an Afghan, or a Somali in their neighborhoods, the locals feel that it is their right to know the reasons for the foreigner's being in "their" territory. Foreigners' mere presence is a situation to be explained.[1]

The conditions of flight and the refugee's preflight life in their country of origin are influential in the way they perceive transit migration or exile. People carry an intangible baggage with them everywhere they go. A baggage of memories, struggles, pains, and hopes. Most of the time this baggage stays intact, never opened. The memories of their preflight lives and the conditions of flight itself form the basis of the dispositions that shape the refugee's interaction with the new environment they find themselves in. The history of being a refugee does not begin in the country of reception where one is recognized as a refugee, it starts the very moment one goes into hiding and looks for ways to escape.

This chapter elaborates on the Iranian refugees' routes and ways of flight, as well as their preflight lives, focusing on the relation between the degree of political affiliation and the beginning of exile. Two different stories of flight are presented with flashbacks to their preexile lives, followed with a general portrait of flight and two characteristics of the flight of political refugees being internal exile and the dominant sense of unpredictability.

Said's Story

March 9, 1985, Tabriz: Said had an appointment in front of the Tabriz Communication Center (*Mokhabarat*). He was waiting for the five other passengers traveling with him and the "guide" that would lead them to the Turkish border. Iraqi warplanes were in sortie, and he did not dare wait in front of the *Mokhabarat* building in case of having been reported. Wandering around the building, he saw the "guide" he had met in Tehran a week ago. In those days, when demand was high for them, it was hard to find a trustworthy smuggler. He had heard stories of people who had been left on the road, literally on the mountains, even before passing the Turkish border. It was not rare for guides to disappear after taking the first part of their money. However, he thought he had no other choice than to trust this guide, who had "helped" his friend Nasser to Turkey before. Nasser, now residing in Istanbul, had given him the guide's phone number.

Among the other five passengers there was only one that he knew, a comrade. Passengers included a young Baha'i couple with their baby girl, a man in his late thirties, and a boy in his mid-teens. He would travel with them for five days, yet his knowledge on their "origins" would remain based on assumptions. They would not speak of anything about their lives in Iran. The only conversations they had were based on their daily routines on the road, frequently stemming from necessity. This condition of limited conversation, not in terms of frequency or length but in scope, would become the norm when they arrived in Istanbul. It was not the "foreigners," be it citizens of Turkey, Sweden, or Germany, but the "natives" with whom the Iranians on the road would abstain from coming into contact. Given the fact that the people fleeing the newly established regime did not compose a homogenous group and that in a great number of cases fellow travelers involved sympathizers or members of various organizations, not always friendly to each other, explains the dominance of mistrust in the exilic relations. Furthermore, it was well known that agents of the Islamic regime did stroll in the Iranian populated neighborhoods in Turkey and even queued in front of the UN building in Ankara to gather information. This is not unique to the Iranians in Turkey in the 1980s. Political disagreements do not disappear once people leave their country of origin. However, the institutions that regulate asylum are blind to these intercommunity conflicts. Even today asylum seekers have to share camps and be roommates with people who they have been in severe political conflict in their country of origin. Thus people sharing a language often feel safer not being in contact with each other.

Said's travel mates included a Marxist guerilla, a Baha'i couple, and a "un-identifed" middle-aged man. Said was a member of the Marxist guerilla organization, People's Fadaiyan—the Minority (*Aqalliyat*). His first choice had been not to leave Iran, but as more and more of his comrades were arrested, or "hospitalized" as it was coded, the more he felt that the ring was closing on him. Feeling the threat of being arrested each day, leading a secret life was getting harder. During the previous few months before he left Iran, he had left Tehran and sought refuge in a provincial town of Gilan district in the north of Iran. Leaving Tehran did not mean putting an end to the political struggle. On the contrary, leading a secret life was a prerequisite to resuming his political activities in the "years of suppression," which are mostly taken as starting from 1981 when the mass executions began.[2] Halleh Ghorashi, herself a leftist militant in the revolutionary era, would cite a young woman militant's perception of her political activities in those years as such:

> It was during those years of suppression that our political activities became really serious. ... On the news you heard daily about 100 names of executed persons. ... It was then after 1981 that the organization started its underground activities. For me it was the beginning of the serious political work. ... The period of suppression was a period of becoming tempered for me.[3]

However, the period of suppression did not have the same starting point for everyone. The organization that Said was a member of (Fadaiyan) was split in June 1980 into two branches, the Minority (*Aqalliyat*) and the Majority (*Aksariyat*), on the basis of different analyses of the postrevolution Iran. The terms "Majority" and "Minority" did not refer to the quantity of the supporters of the factions, but pointed to factions' representations in the central committee of the organization.⁴ The Majority branch supported the Islamic Republic of Iran on the basis of its presumed anti-American character. In the bipolar world of the Cold War era, being anti-American was seen as proof of the government's revolutionary character as well as proof of its anti-imperialist nature, which is similar to today's campist analyses of the international world order. For the Minority, Iran was still a dependent capitalist state and the revolution had not been completed yet. Moreover, the Minority emphasized the antidemocratic stance of the Islamic Republic vis-à-vis the question of women and ethnic minorities.⁵

Organizations' stances toward the Islamic Republic of Iran determined the extent of their activities as well as the extent of the suppression they faced. The People's Mojahedin and the Minority branch of Fadaiyan occupied the first ranks on the government's black list. However, Iran's oldest leftist party, Tudeh, and Fadaiyan the Majority did not endorse armed struggle against the government and were able to pursue their political activities until 1983. Nikki R. Keddie states that Tudeh "was allowed to publish and spread its influence" until 1983, and it was in May 1983 that both Fadaiyan and Tudeh were declared illegal.⁶ The spring of 1983 became the witness of Tudeh and Fadaiyan the Majority leaders' arrest and their televised "confessions" that marked a cornerstone in the elimination of the revolutionary left.⁷

Therefore, being a member of the Minority, Said's experience during the suppression years had a far longer history than most of the other dissident militants. He had succeeded at leading a secret life in Tehran for a couple of years and then had moved to Gilan, in north Iran. Later he would say that those years of secret life or his "internal exile"⁸ had provided him with the necessary tools to survive in Istanbul. While in "internal exile" he had pursued underground political activities. He wanted to remain close to Iran and resume those activities even when he had to leave to be able to survive both physically and politically. However, his organization's strong presence in France rendered the country an inviting destination. He was thinking of reaching Turkey successfully, then getting in touch with the organization's Paris headquarters, and continue his journey to France with their help. Yet, he did not know anything about the route and it became harder to get help from the organization by 1985.

Following the advice of his friend Nasser, he had found the smuggler who had told him to wait in Tabriz and follow the guides. He did so. Gathering in front of the *Mokhabarat* building, all passengers got into one car. Four men sitting at the back seat and the Baha'i couple with their baby in front arrived at Salmas, the border town near Van, Turkey. Although there were police on the road, no one stopped them; it looked as if everything was arranged. In the car, the guide told the young woman to give pills to her baby to make sure that she would keep silent on the road. After half an hour, the driver who was their guide left them outside Salmas. Someone was waiting for them there. It was getting dark and the real "flight" was then beginning.

They were told to hide behind rocks until they reach an orchard on the other side of the road. Then they were to run through the orchard as fast as they could until they were told to stop. Someone was going to be waiting for them in the orchard. However, it was not only the new guide, but also the "guardians of the revolution" waiting at a checkpoint at the other side of the orchard. So, they had to keep silent and find the guide waiting for them in the orchard. He was their key to passing the checkpoint. The sense of unpredictability of the conditions stemming from lack of information that Said was struck with in front of the orchard would accompany him all through his journey. He thought passing through the orchard meant reaching Van. He ran as fast as he could. He heard someone among the bushes telling them to bow their head, stop, or run. He did not know when the orchard would end. He stopped when he was told and continued to run when someone through the bushes said so. He was told not to look behind. He should have just run without knowing when the orchard would end. Finally he came to the end of the orchard. Yet, he was not in Van.

The man waiting for them told him to wait for the other passengers. The boy in his late teens had preceded him. His face was pale. They were all out of breath. It wasn't just because of running, but of the fear that followed them through the orchard. It was the lights of the checkpoint and the whispering shouts of the "guides" telling them to stop or run. The baby girl in her father's lap was wrapped in a blanket. She was still and soundless. She was fed cough syrup to keep silent.

They walked a few kilometers led by their guide and stopped when they saw two men with horses, some already loaded. They continued their journey on horses. One of the smugglers took the baby and each of the refugees was given a horse. The boy shared a horse with the other smuggler, as he did not know how to ride. Besides, the other horses were loaded with goods that were being smuggled alongside them. However, it was harder to sit on the back of a horse because its bones pricked and were sharp. So the boy wanted to sit on the saddle of a horse and one of the loaded horses was spared for him. Loads were reorganized and he got a horse of his own.

Later, Said would tell that his inner thighs became sore and bleed, as he didn't know how to ride a horse. "You shouldn't stick to the horse when it moves, you should move along with it." "Otherwise it would be like sticking to a chair that doesn't stand still and hits your thighs continuously." He didn't know, so he stuck to the horse. They rode all the night. They reached a village at sunrise. They were brought to a house, welcomed by armed men. The house belonged to a family affiliated with the Kurdish armed struggle. The local people's familiarity with routes through the mountains and their knowledge of bypassing the checkpoints rendered them tailor-made for the business. Sometimes it was goods or drugs that were smuggled, sometimes people, sometimes both. That time Said and his travel mates were to be smuggled alongside goods; they had no idea what the goods were.

They had to wait until late afternoon to continue their journey as they could easily be identified walking on the snowy slopes. The light of the shimmering sun reflected as it shined upon the snow-covered hills. Even when the light was not so bright, they had to hide in the snow when they were told to do so by their local guides. The duration of moments hiding in the snow was not calculable either. They were told not to ask questions, but Said said they would not have asked even if they had not been told not to ask. Following the orders seemed to be the most practical way to get out of that unpredictable mess. At times nights ceased to be secure either. When the sun gave its place to moonlight, they would be vulnerable to be espied by inquisitive eyes. In *The Guests of the Hotel Astoria*, the movie directed by Reza Allamezadeh, himself taking the same route, a former nursery schoolteacher Pouri sitting in the lobby of the hotel narrates their march through mountains as such:

> You come through the mountains yourself, you know. You can't expect anything from anyone there, everyone is on their own. The march, sleeplessness, the worst is the fear … it would pull even the most professional smugglers down. I don't even mention people like us. And think of Kurdistan's ice-cold weather. It was almost chapping our skin. Damn the

winter moonlight! You can even see a rabbit from far away; I don't even mention fifteen to twenty people with horses and mules.⁹

It was not only the weather that intensified their feeling of insecurity. They were guided by armed men and even hosted by them. No one would dare object them. Said recalls the smugglers' handling of the forged passports they had been promised before. They had not given the teenage boy a passport, telling him they had not been able to arrange one. He had objected at first, but understanding the insanity of objecting to an armed man in the mountains, he had kept quiet. The boy, sent by his family to avoid conscription in the Iran-Iraq war, had cried all through the mountain route.

After riding for more than ten hours, they took a break at a village near the border. They were still in Iranian territory. They washed their faces and ate the food given by the host family. After resting for four or five hours, they started to ride again. They had to walk and ride for an additional day to pass the border. On their third day of walking and riding, at midnight, they approached the border. They stopped in several houses on the way. Every time Said dismounted, it took a while for him to feel his legs again and walk properly. His legs would tremble and resist to band together. After passing the border, their guides informed them about soldiers on the road from time to time and they dismounted and hid in the snow. On their third and fourth days they did not wait until late afternoon to resume the journey. They walked until they reached Başkale, Van.

Said had given more than a hundred thousand tomans (approximately 1,200 dollars at the time) to the smuggler. He had an additional 500 dollars sewed into the lining of his coat and 16,000–17,000 tomans (approximately 20 dollars) in his pocket. When they arrived at Başkale, he had already lost or spent the money in his pockets. Although they were not supposed to pay on the road, extras dragged on. He had given all the money he had in his pockets to the people hosting them along the way. He was not verbally obliged to pay them, yet in those conditions, he did not dare object. They spent a few hours in Başkale before they left for Istanbul. Their guide dropped them by the Van road and told them to wait for a bus to pick them up.

Five men, a woman, and a baby in ragged clothes, weary of walking, waited in panic. It was obvious from their looks that they were not "ordinary passengers," and in fact, their appearance was the main reason for their panic. However, as they had been told, a regular bus stopped and picked them up after two hours of waiting. They were not asked any questions until the bus approached checkpoints, when the driver's assistant came and asked them for money to pay the soldiers on the way. Said did not have any money left; the young couple gave all they had. Soldiers who were conducting regular checks stopped the bus and the driver dropped off the bus before the soldiers got on. They did not see any money exchange, but assumed that it had taken place as they were skipped over at the ID check.

After four days of walking and riding in the snowy mountains, traveling in a bus was the greatest comfort to them. Yet they could not sleep immediately. Said recalls what he was feeling when they passed the border. It was not only relief. At the moment he left Iran, he was thinking of the day he would return. He had to assure himself that he was not leaving Iran for his own well-being but in order to be able to continue the struggle. On the road he thought about writing to the French base of the organization informing them of his presence in Istanbul and wait for their advice to make his next plans. Initially, he wanted to get in touch with his comrades who lived in Istanbul and then leave for Paris. For the time being, the forged passport given to him by their guide in the mountains was his sole source of anxiety. It was so badly forged that he did not know whether he would even be able to use it. On their fifth day, they arrived in Istanbul. Not knowing where to go, Said followed his travel mates and found himself in Baran Hotel in Aksaray.

Mahnaz's Story

Tehran, 1989: Two policemen were knocking at the door. They were not wearing uniforms, but introduced themselves by showing their identification cards to Mahnaz. They asked for Hossein, her husband. He had been absent from his regular signing in at Evin prison for a long time. She told them she did not know where he was. He had left home nearly four months earlier and she had not heard any news of him since. She said she was worried about him and that she did not know where to report him missing. The men told her to visit Evin the following morning at 8:00 a.m.

After Hossein's flight, Mahnaz was frequently "visited" by the police. A militant of the Fadaiyan (later of the Majority branch), Hossein had been a prisoner both before and after the revolution. After being released in 1986, he was continuously harassed by the police and finally sought peace in seeking asylum in Sweden. Mahnaz was twenty-eight when Hossein left and Hossein was thirty-eight.

They had discussed how to find a way to get released from daily police surveillance for a couple of months. Hossein had to visit Evin each week, so they could not leave Tehran legally. They did not even think of moving to a provincial city, as it would not stop the police control over them. Hossein had to sign in and inform the authorities about his whereabouts every week in another prison or office wherever they moved. Moreover, their moving to a provincial city would make them look more suspicious. There was no legal way out, so they decided that Hossein should flee first and seek asylum in Sweden. Mahnaz and the children would join him later. Due to his former connections, Hossein had learned about Sweden's asylum procedures. Most of his friends had fled to Sweden and written letters to him from the camps they had been placed in. His case seemed to be a strong one: he could easily prove his membership in the Fadaiyan, he was jailed both before and after the revolution, and the surveillance of the police did not cease after his release. He lived under constant threat, as he had to inform the police of his every act each week. At the time when Hossein and Mahnaz decided on Hossein's flight to Sweden, they believed that after Hossein's admission to the refugee camp, they would not have to wait long for his family's acceptance to the camp.

Hossein did not have a passport. With the help of his friends, he got in touch with a smuggler who provided him with a forged passport to leave Iran. He did not need to get a visa to travel to Turkey, so he bought a ticket and flew to Turkey with his forged passport. After staying in Istanbul, Aksaray, for two days, he left for Bulgaria and from there continued his journey with the "guide" that had been waiting for him in Bulgaria. The guide was taking thirty people with him to Sweden with a ship leaving from Poland. Hossein fled to Sweden in 1989, yet despite his assumptions, he had to wait in the camp for three years until his asylum process was finalized and he was given a residence permit as a political refugee.

Before his flight, they had sold their house and Mahnaz had moved to her parents' house with their children. Hossein had taken 5,000–6,000 dollars from the sale and the rest was with Mahnaz to support her in Hossein's absence. They had some debts to be paid as well. Thus, when the police knocked on the door, Mahnaz was in her parents' house and was thoroughly informed of her husband's flight. For the children's and her own sake, she had to behave as if her husband had abandoned her.

Before Hossein's flight, they had even thought that it might be a good idea to blame the police for Hossein's absence, but she did not do anything except imply that. The only thing Mahnaz worried about was her parents' involvement in the case. They were conservative people who did not have anything to do with political dissent. They were always afraid of Mahnaz's suffering with her children because of Hossein's case. So she decided not to tell them about her "invitation" to the notorious Evin prison. She would leave in the morning and tell them afterward.

On a cold and gray Tehran morning she went to Evin, where she was blindfolded and taken to an interrogation room. Evin was so big that she was put in a car and given a lift to go to the building in which she would be interrogated. Blindfolded, she was told to sit and questions started. Mahnaz objected to be blindfolded as she "was not political," but "the wife of a political." She was asked whether Hossein had written letters to her and she said he had not. They asked whether she was also planning to leave Iran as she had applied for a passport and she said she had not. They told her that she had to inform them if she was to leave Iran and she said she would do so. When she returned home, her family was having lunch. She told them of her morning visit to Evin prison. She did not tell them she was blindfolded.

Taking over Hossein's role of being questioned by the police, Mahnaz waited for his call to leave Iran. After learning Mahnaz was requested to visit Evin, Hossein told her to take the remaining money and leave for Turkey and wait there until he got his residence permit. It had been nearly one year since he had been placed in the refugee camp so he thought it would take less than a month for his papers to be arranged. In addition, he had met an Iranian in the camp who had offered to forge a Polish visa for Mahnaz, and one of his camp mates had offered him to arrange for her to stay with his relatives, two young women attending to university, living in Ankara while waiting for the arrangement of her travel by the UN. Mahnaz and Hossein had a nine-year-old son and four-year-old twins, a boy and a girl. Thinking that her "passage" would not last more than fifteen to twenty days, she decided to travel to Ankara and apply to the UN to join her husband in Sweden.

Recalling the police's warning that she should inform if she was to leave Iran, she was worried about not being able to pass the border securely. Yet, she had to try. Not informing anyone, even her parents, she took a bus from Azadi Square to Ankara. She had an address in Ankara. It seemed straightforward. She was truly motivated to join her husband. She had bought two tickets for the children and herself. The twins were on her lap and her son was sitting next to her. When they approached Khoy, an Iranian city close to Turkish border, the bus stopped. Revolutionary Guards (*Pasdaran*) got on the bus and took a few men off the bus. One of the taken men did not get back in. Mahnaz was not afraid of being taken by the Guards as there were no legal charges against her. She was only afraid of not being able to leave Iran in case the police at Evin had informed the border police. She could not do anything but waiting. For the time being, she was trying to keep her children silent not to attract attention.

They arrived at Bazargan border (the Iranian side of the Iran-Turkey border), yet it was plain that they would have to wait long until they could really "arrive at" the border. Esmail Fassih, in his novel *Sorraya in a Coma*, which was published in 1985, describes the Bazargan border of 1980 as such:

> The Bazargan Transit Building is a big, old single-story edifice, with only one narrow Dutch door now open, but controlled by Islamic Revolutionary guards. Hundreds of travelers are crowded in front of it. There is no sign of regular police force. Only a few boyish *hezbollahi* youths, quiet and polite, with G-3s and Uzi machine guns dangling from their shoulders, are assisting the passengers and attending to what has to be done. It is clear that one must wait for hours, perhaps even days, before getting through the rigamarole here. … A bearded, middle-aged man shouts out through the narrow doorway: If anyone has extra currency, or gold, or any other valuable objects with them, they must be handed to the customs authorities and get a receipt. Otherwise, if anything is discovered, it will be confiscated, and the passengers turned back.[10]

In the early 1990s' Bazargan, the boyish *hezbollahi* youth were present whereas their Uzis were out of sight. However, the military uniforms of the Revolutionary Guards implied that Uzis were not far away. Mahnaz and the other passengers were led by their driver, who was trying to open a path for his passengers to get into the checkpoint as quickly as possible. It was not hard for him as he was acquainted with most of the employees there. It was harder for individual passengers to reach to the checkpoint.

Mahnaz had been informed that she could not take the money remaining from the house sale with her legally, so she had hidden the money inside the lining of one of the suitcases. It was a known, yet still successful tactic. In those days, even children's dolls would be disemboweled in search of money, gold, or drugs. However, a professionally sewed back lining was still the most secure way of "smuggling" a small amount of money. She had to keep calm until they had passed through the checkpoint. Nevertheless, the possibility of being rejected by the guards terrified her. Nothing happened and she got on the bus successfully. After waiting for a couple of hours, the passengers of their bus gathered together. Some had to hand over the jewelry that they had tried to take with them, but no one had been returned. After passing the border, Mahnaz could not stop crying. She thought she would never be able to return to Iran. She had not even said goodbye to her family. However, the thought of joining Hossein gave her strength. The police checks resumed after passing the border. Every half an hour they saw soldiers on the road. Most of the time they were not stopped by them, but every one or two hours, soldiers would get on the bus and check their identity cards or passports.

Finally, they arrived in Ankara. Mahnaz had the address of the house Hossein's friend had arranged, so she took a taxi and found the apartment easily. Two young Iranian women were living in that apartment. Mahnaz and the children were welcomed by them. One of the women wanted to learn how long she would have to stay in Ankara before her travel arrangements were made. She recounted what she had thought: ten to twenty days. After a couple of days, she was advised to stay in a nearby hotel where Iranians stayed, the Hotel Tandoğan. Trying to manage three children in an apartment of strangers, going to a hotel instead seemed to be a good idea. After all, she was thinking that her stay was not going to be long so there was no harm in spending some of the money she had "smuggled" to Turkey. That's how her two-year-long stay at the Hotel Tandoğan, waiting for Hossein's residence permit in Sweden, begun.

Transit Routes

Turkey has been among few countries that do not require visa for Iranians, which is one of the reasons why it has been a favorite country of transit for a great number of Iranians fleeing from Iran in the 1980s and later on. Pakistan, India, and Dubai were also used as transit routes to the West in the 1980s. However, the geographic condition of the borderland between Iran and Turkey and the presence of predominantly Kurdish extended families living on both sides of the border experienced in smuggling rendered Turkey a favorite route, particularly for the people who could not leave Iran legally. Between 1987 and 2003, mostly due to the political conflict and military violence between the Turkish State and the PKK, the region was ruled under martial law, with security forces having heavy military presence at the borders,[11] which did not, yet, succeed in stopping undocumented border crossings but changed the conditions severely.

For the Iranians leaving Iran in 1980s, getting out of Iran was, in most cases, harder than reaching the country of destination. Political militants under surveillance did not dare apply for passports. Most of them were young and had not left Iran before. Also, young men and boys who had not served in the military, even if they were in their early teens, were not allowed to leave the country. Therefore, despite the fact that some sought other ways such as leaving "legally" with a forged passport, mountains seemed to be the only possible route for the rest of them.

The stories of Said and Mahnaz picture two different forms of flight. While their stories might not represent all, they are far from being exceptional. I interviewed twenty-one refugees who had left Iran in the years 1982–90. Six of them were living in Cologne, four in Malmö, one in Lund, and ten in Stockholm. There were six women and fifteen men. Among the twenty-one refugees, seven had fled by way of the mountains, nine had traveled by bus (via the Bazargan border), and five by plane. The routes employed were very much related to their degree of political affiliation as well as other official barriers of exit (i.e., military service). The route through the mountains was not the first choice. Nevertheless, the lack of a genuine or finely forged passport made it one of the most popular ways.

All of the travelers on foot were leftist militants from various organizations (three of them were from People's Fadaiyan—the Majority). There was only one party professional among on foot travelers. Fleeing in the first half of the 1980s, two of the party professionals had left Iran by plane and one by bus. Four of the interviewees were party professionals and all of them were male. These party cadres should be taken as a separate group as their experience varied to a great extent from those of the other travelers. Their journey was mostly guided by the party and they were introduced to contact persons to meet in Istanbul. All the four interviewees said they carried telephone numbers of contact persons who would ease their "passage" through Turkey.[12] Furthermore, two of them had been on duty when they were in Turkey. They had come to Turkey to serve as "logistic managers" for the incoming refugees. Having passports, genuine or finely forged, two of those cadres, Farhad and Hooman had traveled before. Farhad had been in Iraq and the USSR before he came to Turkey and Hooman had been in Dubai.

Farhad defined his work not as a political activity, but as a "class activity" (*fa'aliyat-e senfi*). Nevertheless, it was only the militants of his organization and their families that he was responsible for helping, which at the time of the interview he criticized bitterly.[13] "Logistic management" involved meeting the newcomers at Aksaray hotels and settling them into the houses they had rented in "quieter" neighborhoods where fewer Iranians lived. Farhad had rented a house in Tarabya and Hooman in Bahçelievler.[14] Keeping away from Iranians was their main security precaution. They were transit migrants themselves, yet their duty shaped their experience immensely.

The degree of political affiliation mattered for the quality of flight plans too. Most of the political militants, not party professionals, had made all the arrangements for their travel themselves. Those arrangements mainly involved finding and coming to an agreement with a smuggler, usually a tried and advised one, and then finding and bargaining for a cheap hotel after arriving in Turkey. Sympathizers shared the same destiny.

Most of Iranians recognized as refugees in the 1980s and the early 1990s were given asylum for political reasons, which made them officially "political refugees." In addition to that, although some recounted "reasons for flight" were not related to political activities, most of the refugees called themselves as political (*siyasi*). However, their stories reveal that a further differentiation among the political(s) is necessary to understand the non-homogeneity of their experiences. Therefore, we can categorize the people interviewed as party professionals, political militants, and sympathizers of dissident groups. There was also one refugee, Mahnaz, who did not call herself political but "the wife of a political."

In this book, "political" refers to the people who engaged in the revolutionary movement that gave birth to the 1979 revolution and participated in the anti-regime struggle after the foundation of the Islamic Republic of Iran. This definition is compatible both with the conventional usage of *siyasi* in the Iranian context and with the terminology relevant with the asylum procedures.[15] However, using such a "thin description" of the political does not mean that frequently recounted causes of flight such as rejecting to comply with the suppressive laws against women, refusing to participate in war, and being subject to discrimination on the basis of one's religion or gender are not political. When we take into account the structural barriers against the flight of the people participating in the anti-regime struggle after the foundation of the Islamic Republic of Iran and the internal exile to which most of them were exposed before leaving Iran; expanding the definition to encompass everything political would obscure the diversity of the refugee experiences. This would have led to the generalization and abstraction of the refugee experience.

The assessment of the quality of refugees' political affiliation is mainly based on their own self-identification. Taking into account the plurality of motivations in the case of the Iranian refugees of the 1980s, it is not easy to draw clear borders between refugees' degrees of political affiliation. Moreover, the organizational form of the dissident groups renders it hard to differentiate between cadres and militants. Before and after the revolution, there were no classical leftist political parties except Tudeh, which had a clearer structure. Despite the lack of an official structure, the refugees' narratives enable such a categorization, which matches the narratives of former Fadaiyan guerillas as well. In her piece in the compiled volume *Fada'i Guerilla Praxis in Iran 1970–1979*, Nahid Qajar argued that "there was a more or less clear ranking amongst members and sympathizers, such as clandestine members, semi-clandestine members, overt members and the outside sympathizers."[16]

Among the twenty-one refugees I interviewed, four claimed to be professionals (*herfei*). Two of them (Farhad and Hooman) had been in

Turkey to facilitate their comrades' flight and carry out organizational work as mentioned before, and the other two had left Iran after fulfilling their two-year obligatory clandestine work. They were from the same organization. They had left illegally and were living in Cologne at the time of the interview. Three of them had used forged passports while one had traveled through the mountains. They all had contact numbers to call when they arrived at Istanbul.

The axis of legal-illegal exit involves the routes traveled as well as the documents used. We have mentioned that seven refugees had used the mountain route. However, twelve refugees had employed illegal means in their flight. That points to the frequent use of forged passports. Employing illegal means of exit also suggests the existence of structural barriers imposed on dissidents. The figures indicate that the objective conditions of flights (legal-illegal) are compatible with the subjective self-assessments of the refugees. While all the party professionals and most of the militants had to leave Iran illegally, sympathizers and nonpoliticals fled Iran via legal means.

However, the categorization of political affiliations needs further elaboration. While it is easier to recognize cadres and nonpoliticals, it is harder to assess the difference among sympathizers/nonpoliticals or sympathizers/militants. Except for one refugee who was granted asylum to accompany her husband who got the refugee status beforehand, all refugees claimed to be political (*siyasi*) themselves. Nevertheless, their narratives demonstrated that some had actively engaged in political activities while others had not. I chose to name everyone who called themselves *siyasi* as political without asking further questions. Nevertheless, the people who did not mention any political cause for their flight are taken as sympathizers.

There were four "sympathizers": they had left Iran in the first half of the 1980s and had mixed motivations, such as pursuing better opportunities for education, fleeing the suppression imposed on women by the Islamic government, and joining family members who had left before. The people named as political militants, eight people, had mainly used illegal ways as they were actively engaged in the political struggle against the Islamic Republic of Iran, while the rest, three people, had left the country before the threat had become serious. Political militants shared sympathizers' sense of unpredictability stemming from lack of knowledge that marked their travel plans as well as the cadres' experience of internal exile and dealing with insecurity. The sense of unpredictability mainly stemming from lack of knowledge is not specific to the beginning of the journey but can be tracked all through the transit period of the refugee life. Thus, before elaborating on the further stages of their transit migration, these two shared attributes, namely refugees' internal exile before they fled their countries of origin and the sense of unpredictability marking the travel will be reviewed.

Internal Exile

In *Ways to Survive, Battles to Win*, Halleh Ghorashi quotes Minoo saying: "Our refuge began actually back there [Iran]; it just became clearer here [Netherlands]."[17] Most of the people defined as political militants in this study stressed that their lives had undergone a serious change even before leaving Iran. The postrevolution years of suppression had not started at the same time for members of all organizations. Some had had to live secretly for several years before leaving, some had changed their houses or their cities, and some had to double-check the streets they used everyday to avoid being followed. Sitting in a cafe in Cologne in 2007, Sohrab, who had left Iran in 1986 in his mid-twenties, would recall those days as such:

> By the year 65 [1986] things turned to be really bad. They were arresting, executing, a lot of my friends had been arrested, they had arrested a number of them, they had executed a great number of them, they were getting closer ... When we were walking in Iran, on the street, we had to check our back all the time. Returning home after work we had to be sure that no one was following ... When we wanted to go to the bakery, we had to be sure that no one was following us to learn where we lived. Everywhere, everywhere we went, we checked our back. We would double-check. The stomachache that I had in Iran was because of all this. Fear, terror, when I saw a *pastar*, a *basij* [revolutionary guards], I was always thinking that someone was following me. In fact, they were getting closer, most of my friends had been arrested. I wasn't afraid that much in Turkey. We knew those kinds of things. [laughs] That's why we could make our way easier, because we knew those things. We knew where we should knit ourselves to, where we should refrain from. Politicals did make their way faster. ... They were able to organize themselves faster.[18]

Sohrab related his stomachache, which had followed him all through the journey to the feeling of insecurity that haunted him. The stomachache had disappeared on his first day in Germany. He had been hiding his identity both in Iran and in Turkey, where the many smugglers at Aksaray hotels, where he stayed, fueled his sense of insecurity. Nevertheless, his experience of dealing with insecurity had helped him to keep calm and continue with his plans. He claimed that the suppression that they, the *politicals*, had faced in Iran had empowered them to live in exile. In other words, they had acquired the know-how of living in exile already in their homeland.

In conformity with Sohrab's narrative, Hammed Shahidian argues that Iranian secular, leftist activists' exilic life had started before they left Iran.[19] Taking the term from Abu-Lughod, Shahidian defines this experience as "internal exile."[20] However, he introduces this term especially to stress the social estrangement that he claims had rendered Iranian leftists "social strangers" in their own society. He states that it was the ideology and the praxis of the Iranian left that shaped their exile at home. This ideology and praxis involved activism in the name of people, among whom those "new intellectual activists" lived "vicariously."[21] Therefore, Shahidian claims that the political activists had become strangers in their home, especially because of their ideology.

Nevertheless, Shahidian's "lonely intellectual" is not the only explanation for feeling like a stranger in the home country. There are narratives parallel to Sohrab's, stressing the role of the state's suppression in the estrangement of the political militants. For example, Halleh Ghorashi cites another woman exile's, Taraneh's, account of "the lost home inside home":[22]

> The worst thing for me was that I became a stranger in my own country during that terrible period of suppression. This is a very bad pain, and when you think of it you really suffer. ... The most terrible thing was that you had to lie constantly to protect yourself and the people whom you loved. We had to do everything in secret; we did not live there anymore. *It was actually then that we became refugees: it was as if we were not there anymore.* It was really painful, you saw a high and thick wall between you and other people and you told lies to protect yourself. You made up stories. You were obliged to do it. You had to do things that you did not believe in. *All those things you had to do because of the pressures from outside.* (Emphasis mine)

Taraneh's account conveys how being a stranger in one's own home is not necessarily a subjective assessment—a feeling of "otherness" among the people who do not share your ideology. Keeping one's identity secret was seen as a prerequisite for survival for many political activists after the revolution. Three decades later, another political refugee in Turkey, Syrian writer Yassin Al-Haj Saleh would also argue that it was in their own land where Syrians were "exiled" without political and legal rights or cultural and social life.[23]

The living conditions of political activists under the suppression of Islamic regime are intrinsic to the definition of internal exile. The refugees interviewed for this study were from different parts of Iran (Kurdistan, Azerbaijan, Gilan, Tehran, and Fars) and from families of various social classes. It was not the feeling of "otherness" among the masses that had forced them to live precarious lives under surveillance, but the suppression by the government they were fighting against. The fact that they hid their identities did not stem from their being challenged by conservatives or Islamists for being Westernized, as Shahidian claims, but from the increasing suppression of the dissidents by the government, which included arrests and executions. Nevertheless, his account of the practical conditions of "living in exile" that refugees had experienced while living in Iran and its influence on their adaptation to their exile in the West renders his introduction of "internal exile" helpful for our analysis. Shahidian states:

> Political activism under two dictatorial regimes has meant improvisation, quick adaptation to a changing and harmful environment. After the Islamic Regime's widespread attack on the opposition in the summer of 1981, many activists had to migrate to new areas inside Iran where they could live incognito. They often had to familiarize themselves with new ways of life or even learn a new language—an experience not too different from living in exile.[24]

The forced internal exile of the political militants empowered them to deal with the harsh conditions of flight from Iran and living in exile. Agreeing with Shahidian's analysis of political activism's quality under Iran's two regimes, I argue that this experience of internal exile, which was not necessarily a direct outcome of strong party connections, had a serious impact on the formation of the "political refugee" subjectivity, which I will discuss further in the following chapter.

Living with Unpredictability

None of the political militants interviewed had prior knowledge of the mountain route's length. Some of them did not even know the conditions of the climate or geography of fleeing via mountains. Some said they would not have dared to use the route if they had had prior knowledge of it. The inability to assess the duration of the journey was mostly relevant to the users of the mountain route as the others had traveled with plane or buses, which had a somewhat standard route and timing. However, even for those who had used plane or bus, the checkpoints along the way were sites of anxiety and vagueness. For political refugees, precarity had its most robust manifestation in unpredictability. I will first elaborate on the sense of unpredictability intrinsic to the mountain route and second on the anxiety of passing the checkpoints.

All the mountain travelers had started their actual flight in Salmas, the border town between Iran and Turkey (Van). Brought to Salmas by car, they were told to run through the orchards outside the town. However, most of the interviewees stated that they did not know what was waiting for them on the other side of the orchard. Furthermore, two interviewees out of seven, Said and Khosrow, said that they thought they would arrive at Van when the orchards ended.[25] They were given no information about the road and did whatever their guides/smugglers told them to do. They did not know how far they had to run to find the other guide that was waiting for them in the orchards, how long they had to ride to reach a village nearby, or even how long they had to hide in the snow until it was safe to stand up.

Azadeh's narrative exemplifies the extent and impact of this unpredictability. Fleeing Iran in 1983 with her husband and two-year-old daughter by the mountain route, Azadeh said that her daughter had not been able to drink water or pee for more than ten hours as their guide had lost the way because of the snow-covered roads. In addition, she had not thought that their journey would last long and had only taken one small bottle of water and their clothes were not appropriate for cold weather. She had told her daughter not to pee her pants to keep her away from freezing. She stressed that the worst thing was the inability to assess the next step of the journey. It was the feeling of being totally dependent on the smugglers who did not seem to be reliable, which troubled her seriously.[26]

It is true that the conditions producing the sense of unpredictability in the mountain route were much more severe as they were consequential to the travelers' immediate life chances. Nevertheless, the people who even had a slight possibility of not being able to leave the borders legally were stuck in constant anxiety while passing through the checkpoints in a similar way. It was only at the moment that the Iranian border control was passed that most of the passengers relaxed. As cited earlier, Mahnaz was afraid of losing the money left from their house during the border control and of not being able to leave the country as she had been told to inform the police of her absence. The fear was more intense for people who had actively been engaged in political opposition. One of the four party professionals I interviewed, Mahmoud, described his passage from the border control as such:

> They were distributing the passports. … At the last moment he read my name and gave my passport. I, even then, didn't understand what was happening. I had my bag in my hand, I was thinking of running away. The doors of the bus were open. I would get down, and one way or another would reach Khoy. Bazargan was not far from Khoy. … We were in the middle of two sets of fences. One side was Iran and the other side Turkey. … I had a different feeling when I was between the fences. … I thought no one could take me to the other side. *Later, I learned that you cannot trust Turks.*[27] (Emphasis mine)

Both in his entrance and in his exit from Turkey to Germany, he was threatened by officers who refused to let him in or out without taking money. The first time, he was able to pass with the help of his fellow travel mates. However, he had to insert 100 marks into his passport to be able to pass the border in his exit from Turkey. This practice of inserting money in passports was cited frequently by the interviewed refugees.

The unpredictability of the conditions, not being able to evaluate the very next step in their journey, and the inability to stick to plans were not only a matter of their flight or a factor contributing to the harsh living conditions of exiles, but were constitutive to the precarious medium shaping "the political refugee subjectivity."

Every story has a beginning. Most of the time, the starting point is chosen by the storyteller according to its relevance to the chain of events to be narrated, the causality that is prescribed to the events, or simply to gather the attention of the reader/listener at the first instance. Our stories of transit migration started with the flight. In fact, most of the time, the interviewees themselves asked the first questions. My responses given to the questions of "What do you want to learn?" or "What is interesting for you?" determined the selection of the beginning point. I asked them to tell me about their flight "from the beginning." So, it was again their turn. "The beginning" had various meanings. Most of the time I contented myself with the answers and did not want to disturb them by asking questions, especially on their organizations or the details untold, unless I felt it was possible to ask for more.

Refugees' premigration experiences were indispensable to understanding their lives in transit in Turkey. Although most of the Iranian transit migrants stayed in the same hotels and strived to find the same smugglers or the same routes to resume their journey, the conditions of their flight from Iran and the extent of the pressure to which they were subjected in their "home" were influential in the way they experienced transit migration and, all in all, the way they experienced being a refugee.

In this respect, the precarious life conditions in Iran, which were reified in the internal exile that most of the interviewees had experienced one way or another, according to their degree of political affiliation, were significant in their stories. The experience of going through internal exile was empowering as it rendered them familiar with exile conditions. It was also inhibiting as the conditions that pushed them to internal exile meant that deportation would have devastating effects for them. Most of the time, it was not the harsh physical conditions of flight, but the unpredictability of those conditions that was more detrimental for refugees.

The stories of flight and internal exile experienced in Iran are necessary to convey that the one and a half million Iranians cited in the statistics did not constitute an undifferentiated mass, and while some transited easier than others, many had walked for days through mountains; had feared to lose their frozen, blackened toes; had drugged and cautioned their babies to shush in order not to be killed; and had left their friends behind arrested or executed. Flight and their preflight life in Iran constituted the beginning of a story to be developed through their lives in Turkey, to be continued in the "final" destination.

3

"Their Categories and Ours": Politics of Differentiation

At a conference on international migration to Turkey taking place in Istanbul in 2007, the director of the Asylum, Migration, and Citizenship branch of the General Directorate of Security Affairs of Turkey intervened in the discussion to object to a researcher's usage of the word *integration* for the Iraqi transit migrants in Turkey. He argued that *integration* is not a term to be employed for illegal migrants.[1] One year later, Helsinki Citizens' Assembly Refugee Legal Aid and Advocacy Program published a report, the first of its kind, titled "Unwelcome Guests: The Detention of Refugees in Turkey's 'Foreigners' Guesthouses'" based on interviews with forty refugees from seventeen countries examining refugees' access to procedural rights and conditions in detention centers in Turkey. Before the report's official release, they sent a copy to Turkey's Ministry of Interior. In return, after three months, they got an informal email response centered on the argument that the report was not based on information gathered from refugees but illegal migrants, and thus the findings were inaccurate.

The illegal versus legal divide imposed by national security forces is not the only categorization refugees are exposed to. The UNHCR documents stress the level of freedom of choice as the main difference between migrants and refugees. It is stated that "migrants, especially economic migrants, *choose* to move in order to improve the future prospects of themselves and their families" (emphasis in original), while "refugees *have to* move if they are to save their lives or preserve their freedom"[2] (emphasis in original).

Such definitions are far from being explanatory, as real people with real motivations of flight hardly constitute such ideal types. As I will demonstrate in this chapter, refugees are exposed to many classifications by decision-giving authorities, whose main motivation is to limit the number of asylum statuses given and they respond by creating their own classifications, which tell more about their experience than the official categories do.

The lack of fair assessment of the individual motivations of flight, ignoring the plurality of those motives, and the assumption that these categories are fixed and immune to change over time invoke the need for questioning the formal categories. The institutional assessment criteria are not exclusive as political, sociological, and economic reasons cannot be easily separated and analyzed. As the famous words of Audre Lorde pioneering an intersectional approach in 1982 goes, "There is no such thing as a single-issue struggle because we do not live single-issue lives."[3] Refugees do not live single-issue lives either. In a world shaped by a long history of structural inequalities, the motivations of leaving will often be multifarious. The case of the Iranians in the 1980s showcases plurality of migrants' motives for leaving their countries as well as of the shift in their categorical status over time.

Taking into account asylum seekers' flight conditions, falling into illegality at some point in their journey due to fear of persecution is more the norm than the exception. Most of the time this highlights the inadequacy of laws and regulations that should provide a safe passage and asylum process for refugees rather than refugees' criminality. Most of the interviewed refugees in this book were or became illegal in Turkey at some point and became recognized refugees in Europe. As we have seen in the previous chapter, illegality covers a wide spectrum including but not limited to unauthorized border crossings, forged passports and documents, or overstaying visas, all of which are parts of many refugees' lives.

Using degree of choice in their flight to differentiate refugees and migrants is misleading as well. Even if limited, we all have a degree of choice in shaping our future, and as the narratives of post-1979 Iranian refugees expose, they also had certain preferences particularly on their final destination. Moreover, authoritarian regimes rule by creating ambiguous gray zones, where you live on a knife-edge. Thus it would be very hard to assess whether one had to leave or chose to leave.

More often, it is not the will of the people on the move but the will of status-ascribing authorities that determine who is a refugee and who is a migrant. Taking categories as fixed and explanatory in itself, these "technical" debates also miss that categories are products of their own historical making. The international asylum regime that emerged in the context of the Second World War for the protection and the resettlement of the refugees produced by the war has evolved into a restrictive system characterized by reluctance to admit asylum seekers and grant asylum.[4] Khalid Koser takes the 1973 oil crisis and the end of the Cold War as the cornerstones of that restrictive approach.[5] While the former paved the way for the restriction of economic migration with the decline in the demand of foreign workers, the latter ceased the ideological or strategic motivations to resettle people "escaping from communism."

9/11 with the consequent rise of Islamophobia and its political implementation in anti-terrorism laws is another cornerstone in this restrictive approach. On the one hand, the United States' response to 9/11 in attacking Afghanistan and Iraq killed hundreds of thousands and displaced fifteen million Afghans and Iraqis.[6] On the other hand, many European countries joined the Islamophobic trend to limit the rights of immigrants with a Muslim background and fortifying their walls against new migrants. Denmark, France, and Germany were among the first countries in post-9/11 world to limit family reunifications of immigrants, impose selective measures for labor migration, and heavier surveillance over immigrants coming from predominantly Muslim countries.[7] As Jeremy Harding puts it, it did not matter whether you were Caribbean, Asian, Turkish, or North African in Europe anymore, the defining term was "Muslim."[8] What is even more ironic is that a significant number of refugees, women, and LGBTQI people in particular, escaping religious authoritarianism in predominantly Muslim countries, are subjects of the same Islamophobic migration policies that hit all the people perceived as Muslims in the Western world.

However, when legal doors are closed, illegal ones are opened. "The end of West's sympathy," in Behzad Yaghmaian's terms, has resulted in a wandering population in search of smugglers.[9] This restrictive approach resulted not only in increasing the numbers of asylum seekers, but also in the convergence of economic migrants and political refugees under the name of asylum seeker, which generated a "crisis" for the system that attempted to sort out the "genuine" refugees in need of protection and block the "bogus." Koser calls this the migration-asylum nexus.[10] Pointing to the significant numbers of refugees that were settled in Europe in 1970s and 1980s and their role in filling labor market needs, Koser links diminishing annual quotas of European countries to accept refugees in a systematic way and the decrease in their demand for foreign labor in creating this migration-asylum nexus. When the only way to come to Europe is through an individualized process of applying for asylum and having to prove your individual reasons for seeking asylum, it is not surprising that this route will be employed by people who feel the need to migrate. Also as Koser underlines, even though the primary reason for a refugee to leave their country can be political, where they want to resettle can involve economic motivations too. It is logical that refugees would like to apply for asylum in a country where they have an existing network and possibilities to work.[11]

In their study on Iranian exiles and immigrants in Los Angeles published in a volume titled *Iranian Refugees and Exiles since Khomeini* in 1991, Mehdi Bozorgmehr and Georges Sabagh discuss the US government's assessment of refugees. Until the 1980 Refugee Act, imposed to bring the US policy in line with the UN definitions, the US refugee policy favored persons coming from communist countries and the Middle East. Thereafter, individual motivations for leaving a country and a well-founded fear of persecution became the decisive criteria for granting refugee status. However, Bozorgmehr and Sabagh argue that it was the US government's view of friendly and unfriendly nations that defined who a refugee was. While migrants coming from countries with "friendly governments" such as El Salvador and Haiti were seen as being economic rather than political, migrants from "unfriendly nations" such as Cuba or Vietnam were easily defined as refugees.[12]

Bozorgmehr and Sabagh conducted interviews with 671 Iranians (including Muslims, Armenians, Jews, and Baha'is), each representing a household, to classify exiles and immigrants in Los Angeles. Asking an open-ended question on "the most important reason for leaving Iran," they found that "only 35.1 percent of exiles, and as many as 15.8 percent of immigrants, were admitted as legal refugees or, after arrival obtained legal refugee and asylee status," which reveals the unreliability of the legal categories.[13] They stress that the immigrants mostly gave educational reasons for their presence in the United States. Citing educational reasons for their presence in the United States was not specific to the immigrants in Los Angeles. However, in LA, this can be explained by the high presence of Iranian students living there before the revolution, who did not return to Iran after 1979.

The dominance of educational reasons among the responses demonstrates more than the former students' choice to stay. The Iranian Revolution of 1979 proceeded with the 1980 Cultural Revolution that brought forth the closure of universities until 1983, when they were reopened with purging interviews and even identifications of the leftist, revolutionary students by their pro-regime former classmates.[14] The militants were purged, as well as the sympathizers of leftist organizations, the people related to them, and women who had not lived according to the Islamic rules of conduct in the pre-1979 era. Thus, it is not hard to recognize the great number of people who lost their chances of education during the Cultural Revolution. The revolutionary political refugees[15] of the postrevolution era were mainly young people in their twenties and even in their late teens, which explains the frequent mentioning of educational reasons for flight. The majority of the revolutionary political refugees of the 1980s I interviewed responded to the question on the reason for not wanting to stay in Turkey as the existence of better educational opportunities in the Western European countries. Fleeing conscription for the Iran-Iraq War (1980–8) was also among the leading motives for refugees who were in their late teens or for the "immigrants" who had teenage sons when the conscription age was reduced to the early teens. Thus, fleeing conscription and pursuing educational opportunities may also be taken as adjoining motivations for leaving Iran for young refugees.

In an endnote to her article "Desiring Place: Iranian 'Refugee' Women and the Cultural Politics of Self and Community," Bauer participates in the discussion on the futility of assigning people to distinct categories. Referring to the experience of being in both categories at different times, she writes:

> Some tried to become students first, applying for asylum later; some applied for asylum but after entering my sample were denied refugee status. Should I throw them out? Layla, for example, was a political refugee (ex-Tudeh) in Europe, who became a citizen of her host country, only to immigrate to North America because of racism. ... Mehran who was a student in Germany, working with a political organization, returned to Iran after the revolution, lost student status, returned and reapplied for refugee status, was not accepted in Germany but then became a refugee in Norway, from where he then applied for student status in Germany.[16]

As Bauer demonstrates, shifting to different categories may stem from the regular, procedural evolution of asylum seeker into refugee and refugee into citizen as well as intended by people as a survival strategy. Religious conversion points to such an intentional change in categories that can also be taken as a recent migration strategy used by some asylum seekers in Turkey. Şebnem Köşer Akçapar argued that "the length of stay in the transit country, often much longer than anticipated, leads migrants to find different ways of maintaining themselves, resulting in specific strategies and skills that are certainly crucial."[17] Conversion is at times an outcome of such prolonged transit migration. She claimed that conversion is used for increasing their chance in asylum procedures by Iranian asylum seekers who have been rejected by the UNHCR in the first place. Conversion not only provides them the chance of readmission to the UNHCR asylum process, but also provides access to social networks both in the country of transit and in the country of resettlement.[18] This is by no means a claim about all conversion cases.

Another current example of resisting the limitation imposed by the asylum system to choose one's destination is presented by the Dublin Brothers based in Amsterdam. According to the 2003 Dublin Regulation, asylum seekers have to apply for asylum in the first European country they arrive to avoid multiple applications for asylum in several Dublin member states. This means that refugees concentrate in the border countries of Europe, such as Greece and Italy, and have not been able to travel to their preferred country of destination.[19] The disproportional concentration of refugees in these border countries, combined with the inefficiencies of local resources and the increase in right wing hostility against refugees, renders these first countries of arrival unpopular destinations for refugees. Their attempt to continue their journey to safer spaces is responded with detention and deportation. Dublin Brothers, a group of fifty young Eritrean refugees with Dublin claim in Italy and living in the Netherlands, has rejected forced settlement in Italy where they had detrimental experiences by avoiding detention for the period they have to fill in (eighteen months) in temporary shelters with the support of solidarity networks. After spending eighteen months in the Netherlands, these refugees have been able to apply to asylum in the Netherlands.[20]

There is more to challenging these categories. The logic of depicting the refugee as the passive victim of the migration process, who had no other choice than flight, needs to be unpacked as well. Mina Agha criticizes the perception of exile as a "process suffered" due to external pressures.[21] The harshness of the circumstances does not sweep away the choice factor in flight. Agha narrates the personal history of Robab, an Iranian refugee in Germany, to illustrate the decision of flight's being a multidimensional process. Robab explained her reasons of flight:

> I didn't want to live underground or die a martyr in prison .... I was also very worried about my children. I had to save them, because they had no future and might even die in the war. This is what made me decide to flee .... I also thought that I could be more effective in my political activities abroad than in Iran, because the regime had destroyed all of the opposition groups there.[22]

Agha states that it was the threat of political persecution that directed Robab's decision. However, her decision was a result of her rational assessment of the alternatives with which she could not identify. She argues that flight should be seen as a "meaningful course of action taken with the aim of saving oneself and at the same time creating new social freedom for oneself."[23] Robab's exhausting process of recognition as a refugee demonstrates the logic of asylum law on "passive" refugees. Robab states:

> It was stupid that I wrote in my application for asylum that, besides being persecuted on political grounds, I also wanted to save my children from the Iran-Iraq war. This led to the authorities not believing my political reasons for fleeing, so that I had to fight for my recognition for six years.

Hence, Robab was punished for her recognition of her flight as a "motivated action" and not solely as a forced action.[24] Moreover, her experience as a political refugee with mixed motivations of flight shed light on the voidance of the assumption of "ideal types" of migrants in a context in which multiple factors determine one's life conditions. Robab stressed the lack of opportunity for pursuing political activities in Iran in her reasons for flight. She believed she could be more effective in her political activities abroad. Apart from physical survival, exile provides the political self to resume their political activities, thus becoming a tool for "deterritorialization of politics."[25]

The narratives of the revolutionary political refugees I talked to exemplify this empowering aspect of exile further. Without exception, all the leftist political refugees of the mid-1980s wanted to stay close to Iran as they carried the hope of a regime change and worked for that cause. Thus, not the United

States or Canada, but Western European countries were preferred as destination countries. Although most of them had quitted professional political activity in terms of being a member of the opposition groups in exile at the time we met, they had resumed political activities in the countries they had settled for a number of years. For example, the former militants of People's Fadaiyan I met in Cologne had taken part in various positions in the Cologne branch of the organization immediately after their arrival.

Moreover, the choice of destination countries did depend on the aspiration of pursuing political activities in a great number of cases. Though settled elsewhere, most of the leftist militants did plan to go to France in the first place. "Paris is host to almost all of the leaders of the Iranian opposition," stated Vida Nassehy-Behnam in her account of "Iranian Immigrants in France" published in the previously cited 1991 volume.[26] This statement is far from exaggeration. Both the political opponents of the Islamic Republic and the founder of the regime that those people fled from sought refuge in Paris. The name of the commune in which Khomeini lived in Paris, Neauphle-le-Chateau, is later given to the street where the French Embassy is located in Tehran. The most famous and active leaders of Iranian opposition, the last prime minister of the Shah, Shapur Bakhtiar, leading the National Resistance Movement in France in the path of Mosaddeq's National Front; Ali Amini, the grandson of Qajar Shah Mozaffar ad-Din, former prime minister of the Shah and the leader of the monarchist group the Front for the Liberation of Iran (active until 1986); former president Bani-Sadr; and the leader of Mojahedin, Masud Rajavi, lived as exiles in France.[27] France was also host to the headquarters of the Marxist guerrilla organization People's Fadaiyan and the Kurdistan Democratic Party once led by Qasemlu. Therefore, going to France meant more than physical survival and promised interaction with anti-regime organizations, which was important for leftist militants who were unable to pursue political activities in Iran any longer. Moreover, the existence of such networks did ease their process of adaptation in the countries they settled in. At the same time, due to the same reasons, refugees who did not want to be part of the said organizations anymore chose not to go to France.

There are also literary and scholarly texts reflecting on asylum and exile leading to other classifications. For example, Edward Said differentiates between exiles, refugees, expatriates, and émigrés. He argues that the word refugee suggests "large herds of innocent and bewildered people requiring urgent international assistance," while exile indicates "solitude and spirituality."[28]

Yassin Al Haj Saleh, a prominent Syrian writer and political activist living in Turkey after leaving Syria, approaches exile similar to how Said defines and rejects to use the term to describe his life in Turkey. He argues that the term has elitist connotations in Syria and he is just one among many displaced Syrians. Also, with the violence continuing in Syria and his friends, family, and acquaintances missing, he feels connected and not distanced from the circumstances in Syria, which seems to be a prerequisite of being an exile.[29]

Writing on Iranian refugees, Hammed Shahidian used exile, refugee, and expatriate interchangeably[30] while Annabelle Sreberny and Ali Mohammadi differentiated exile and refugee. Sreberny and Mohammadi took the degree of choice in their flight, the motivations, and the "desire to go home" as three main criteria to differentiate refugees and exiles. According to their description, exiles have personal motivations and more choice over their flight. Refugees' motives, on the other hand, are state influenced or external, thus beyond their control. They add that exiles want to "go home" while refugees "seek a permanent home" outside their country of origin.[31] Nevertheless, the most popular axis of differentiation in the literature is yet the economic-political divide.

Iranian refugees in transit were not only classified by the institutions and states regulating the asylum system. There were also classifications refugees themselves employed. These classifications were formed through a continuous interaction between their past experiences and their chosen actions at particular situations. By this very fact of their formation through interaction and self-identification, these categories were not necessarily transitional in the same way the official, assigned ones were. As I will demonstrate in the following pages, refugees' everyday life struggle to survive was interlinked with their everyday life struggle to maintain the identity they related to by differentiating themselves from the rest of the Iranians in transit. The current asylum regime, starting from border policies to refugee camps, de-individualizes the people on the move and contributes to the imagery of a homogenized mass. In times of uncertainty and involuntary blurring of differences among people, refugees create their own boundaries by differentiating themselves from other refugees they do not want to be affiliated with. Existential survival involves both the material and the symbolic realm. I will start with the material survival.

Bread and Butter in Transit

As introduced in the previous chapters, the widespread scholarly and popular assumption about Iranian transit migrants in the aftermath of 1979 revolution is that they were from middle or upper middle class, which is thought to bring the automatic conclusion that they did not have to engage in daily struggle over means of subsistence. This correlation is hard to prove. The quality of life in transit depended very much on the duration of being in transit. The longer the passage took, the harder became the material conditions for transit migrants as they would be living on the money they had brought from Iran or money sent to them by relatives abroad. Thus, while some of the Iranians in transit had to spend cautiously from the beginning of their journey, when the periods of stay became longer than anticipated, most of them sought ways for decreasing their expenses further or finding alternative ways of making money.

Eating less was the primary way of spending less. At times, when no money was left, the diets were mostly composed of bread and soup or bread and yogurt. Going to markets at late hours to buy cheap goods or to collect the dispersed fruits or vegetables, though not frequently, were mentioned. Khosrow told that they used to wait till late afternoon to visit the Sarıyer fish market, where they could get cheap or free fish. Mahnaz remembered buying meatless chicken bones to make soup for her children. Besides eating less or having a lower-quality diet, cooking and eating collectively was a widely used way of decreasing expenses. Cooking and eating collectively was also preferred as it made it possible to eat more elaborate, time-consuming recipes of traditional Iranian food by pooling resources together. The other widely used way of spending less was walking instead of using any means of transportation. For the people who lived in shared apartments, illegal use of electricity and water was also referred to being one of the ways of saving money.

In addition to individual attempts such as selling pistachios brought from Iran or finding temporary jobs in construction, making money out of the state's obligation imposed on them was a common practice. Most of the Iranian transit migrants in Turkey, particularly the ones who had valid passports and avoided registration, stayed in Turkey with their three-month visa, which meant that they had to exit Turkish territory every three months to be able to renew their visas, a practice widely referred to as doing *giriş-çıkış* (literally enter-exit). It was obligatory for Iranians who did not want to risk deportation in case of police arrest. Bulgaria and Cyprus were among the most favorite *giriş-çıkış* routes. Buying tax-free alcohol and cigarettes, which were hard to find in Turkey in the 1980s, and selling them in the hotel lobbies was the most common way of earning money from *giriş-çıkış*. But it was not the only way. In addition to cigarettes and drinks, some sold jeans in Bulgaria and bought canned food that was much cheaper there for their consumption in Turkey. Such transactions compensated the expenses of the obligatory *giriş-çıkış* and served as an opportunity to make some money.

These ways of decreasing expenditure are not particular to transit migrants. Necmi Erdoğan and Aksu Bora demonstrated similar experiences in their studies on urban poverty in Turkey.[32] Buying old bread from bakery, buying bones to boil for food, using illegal electricity, and using public transport discount cards that they are not entitled to are listed among ways of urban poor living expense-reducing tactics.[33] Erdoğan takes these practices as forms of "the art of making do" (*idare etme sanatı*).[34] Following Certeau, he argues that these tactics involve appropriating the power-ruled spaces with deserting, making use of opportunities, and dissimulating, which helps the urban poor to get away without leaving the labyrinth constructed by the power of capital.[35] Erdoğan argues that these forms of "the art of making do" is composed of unsystematic, quiet, and individual attempts that do not target a systematic change but an improvement in the living conditions of individuals and their families, who resort to them.[36] In this sense, he states that these attempts cannot be seen as forms of everyday resistance in the way that is defined by James Scott, as they are not anti-systemic practices that target the state or power relations.[37]

James Scott, who had popularized the concept of "the weapons of the weak," had classified similar tactics as forms of everyday resistance.[38] In "Everyday Forms of Resistance," Scott argues that resistance has many different forms, and open political action is only one form that takes place in political conflicts.[39] While nonconfrontational tactics that aim to improve one's living conditions may look banal when taken in its singularity, they could have serious consequences when widely practiced.[40] Scott underlines that most of these singular to the plain sight activities do often rely on a form of cooperation among subordinate groups.[41] He gives examples of poaching in

England between 17th and 20th centuries, peasant tax resistance in Malaysia, desertion from Confederate Army in the United States, and agrarian resistance in China and Soviet Union to demonstrate that resistance against regimes of appropriation can have many faces that seem individual, nonpolitical, nonorganized but serve to a common purpose. Moreover, as his example of poaching demonstrates, some of these experiences, which have been mundane parts of everyday life subsistence, become everyday life resistance because legal regimes of power rendered them illegal.[42]

Dissimulation to fit in the recognized refugee category was also a part of refugees' politics of survival. The UNHCR seeks "well-founded" fear of persecution as a prerequisite for granting asylum and has sophisticated methods for assessing the authenticity of the applicants' claims. However, its authority does not stay unchallenged. Despite the warning of refugee advocacy groups and the UNHCR itself, refugees search for ways of strengthening their applications as their actual reasons are seldom recognized. For example, the presence of "story selling" people in the hotel lobbies of the 1980s or the contemporary satellite cities where asylum seekers live points to such an effort. There are other ways of "deceiving" the authorities that do not recognize the actual reasons of refugees' flight as well. These tactics add to the difficulties that block the researchers' means of access to the actual composition of the studied population. The widespread claim of political causes for flight among postrevolutionary Iranian refugees can be read with this insight as well. Being the most "legitimate" reason for flight, it was unlikely for the people who did not want to live in postrevolutionary Iran not to claim political reasons for their flight. Therefore, consistent with Scott's usage, dissimulation should be taken as an important tactic for the Iranian refugees of the 1980s.

Resorting to such tactics does not necessarily imply the insincerity of their claims of fear of persecution, but at times, to the inability of the decision-making authorities to assess those claims in a fair and accurate way. Gaim Kibreab recounts refugees' attempts at thwarting censuses in the refugee camps and resettlements for increasing their share of benefits and their splitting of their families into different camps for getting more compensation as examples of refugees' tricks against the "faceless" institutions such as the UNHCR and the NGOs aiding refugees.[43] He points to refugees' lack of participation in the allocation of resources as the reason underlying these tricks. In today's

Netherlands, where it is quite usual to see couples living apart, young refugee couples having separate cases are given no other option than living together. To be able to escape this discriminatory practice and secure their right to housing irrespective of their relationship status, those young people often chose to lie on their relationship status.

Following Scott's argument, we can conclude that the main difference between everyday forms of resistance of subordinate groups and pragmatic action of individuals to improve their life conditions is not necessarily whether they are collective, conscious, or classically "political," as most of the acts did demonstrate certain degrees of these mentioned attributes, but whether the widespread practice of these acts would challenge regimes of power and domination. In that sense, some of the tactics of survival by refugees can be seen as forms of everyday life resistance while some are not. Some of these survival tactics might even strengthen regimes of power and domination, as is the social negotiation on being the right kind of woman that I will elaborate on in next chapter.

Moreover, crossing borders illegally and living undocumented are the most widespread practices by refugees, which are examples of everyday life resistance to nation-state regimes that claim authority over borders and deny basic human rights to noncitizens. Asylum seekers' dissimulation on their reasons of flight, their evasion from registering with the police to avoid threat of deportation, and even the widespread collective act of refugees helping the ones who do not have money to pay to flee from hotels without paying can be taken as forms of everyday resistance as they involve denial of the UNHCR's claim of assessing their fear of persecution, the state's claim of registering and controlling the refugees, as well as advancing refugees' claims to the right of accommodation. In as much as each of them can be taken as singular attempts of improving one's life chances, they are practiced widely, involve social cooperation, and threaten the existence of the regimes of power and domination. While many of the abovementioned survival tactics were commonly practiced by refugees in transit irrespective of their background or particularities, some were employed particularly to mark boundaries, maintain their difference from other refugees in transit, and claim a specific subjectivity. Being political (*siyasi*) was a salient subjectivity refugees interviewed cared to identify with and actively engaged to maintain.

Political versus Normal

As seen in the previous chapters, most of the refugees I interviewed identified themselves as political—*siyasi*. Throughout this work, I have referred to them with their own words of identification.

"I did not apply for a Swedish passport when I got the right to have one. It took several years. I didn't want to take it. I had a political refugee passport. I considered being a political refugee was my identity (*hoviyat*),"[44] said Khosrow, in the south Stockholm home where he lived with his wife and daughter. A member of the revolutionary leftist organization the People's Fadaiyan, he had fled Iran in 1984 by means of a smuggler to avoid the draft for the Iran-Iraq war. At the time of the interview he was a Swedish journalist in his mid-forties. What Khosrow defined as "political refugee identity" is a prominent axis of self-differentiation among the Iranian transit refugees of the 1980s. It is also a good example of the impact of subjectivity in the assessment of categories related to refugees. That is, while the linear development suggests an evolution of asylum seeker to refugee and refugee to citizen of the receiving country, being a political refugee might resist this development. In the context of the postrevolutionary Iranian refugees, being a political refugee was not necessarily a transitional category.

According to the framework of the international asylum system led by the UNHCR, fear of persecution on the basis of one's political ideas is among the five recognized reasons of eligibility for being a refugee. Thus, the people who claim to be political refugees have to prove that the basis of their fear of persecution is due to their political ideas. They have to define their degree of political affiliation as well as the suffering they faced prior to their flight. Therefore, the reason for flight is taken as the primary basis to one's being a political refugee. There are, of course, exceptions to that, as we saw in the case of the *sur place* Iranian refugees protesting in the United Socialist Party in Chapter 1. One can be a political refugee after flight if they engage in political activity in the first country of asylum that puts them in danger of persecution in the case of their return. In both cases, it is assumed that political activities precede the status of "political."

This premise seems to be straightforward. However, those "objective conditions" of being a political refugee is not sufficient to understand the way it was experienced. While for most of the cases the abovementioned "objective conditions" might have been effective in the official ascription of the category, it was also the activities pursued *after* being an official refugee that rendered a refugee "political" for some. If we recall Serebeny and Mohammadi's argument, exile can be taken as "the fundamental political strategy of current times," which paves the way to resuming political activities.[45] Thus, being a political refugee also means being political *and* a refugee or being a refugee to be able to continue political activities. Therefore, it may even resist the abolition of the official refugee status and cease only with quitting political activity.

However, it is not a static category and is formed through the refugees' subjective assessment of their categories and their everyday life activities. Therefore, it is also the experience of living as a political refugee that brings forth the formation of the category itself. Or to put in more aphoristic terms, "the political refugee was present at their own making."[46] Interviews with Iranian refugees in Sweden and Germany indicate such formation of political refugee subjectivity through experience. In other words, refugee narratives reveal that their lives as political refugees had not started in their country of destination, which had recognized them as refugees, but had a much longer history, and their experience in Turkey was integral to the making of their political refugee subjectivity. For "making," we borrow E. P. Thompson's definition: "*Making*, because it is a study in an active process, which owes as much to agency as to conditioning" (emphasis in original).[47] In their discussion on gender performativity, Judith Butler also underlines how identity formation is a process and is negotiated daily. They argue that identity formation is performative not in the sense that it is made up and not genuine but that it is formed through "a repetition and a ritual, which achieves its effects through its naturalization."[48] It is the "expectation that ends up producing the very phenomenon it anticipates."[49] Butler's discussion on performativity and acts is illuminative as it also underlines how collective a "personal act" can be. "The act that one does, the act that one performs, is, in a sense, an act that has been going on before one arrived on the scene," they argue.[50] Refugees with the choices they made in their everyday life and behaving according to the expectations customarily laid before them took consistent and active part in maintaining and forming the identities they cared for.

Refugees' accounts of celebrating the International Workers' Day (May 1) and the International Women's Day (March 8) can be read as another form of their struggle in the symbolic realm. Staying in Turkey for one year, Mahin remembered celebrating May 1 in 1988 in a collective way, at a time when the International Workers' Day celebrations were prohibited in Turkey. She recounted her participation in such a celebration with other Iranian refugees from various leftist groups in a suburban park in Ankara. She recalled nearly 200 people having picnic in the park and singing revolutionary songs. They were present in the park from morning until late afternoon, celebrating the day in the guise of having picnic. Many years after these interviews, residing in Amsterdam as a migrant myself, I also observed that May 1 and March 8 were the two dates in a year when the spark of being a political refugee could be captured vividly. These were the two rallies, where leftist migrants and refugees particularly from Iran, Turkey, Kurdistan, and Latin American countries would be represented disproportionately. These were the dates when flags of political organizations that refugees had a historical and emotional connection with rather than ties of active participation caught some sunlight.

Iranian Fadai guerrillas' narratives of their life in safe houses before revolution point to celebrations of the International Women's Day as well. A former Fadai guerrilla, Nahid Qajar narrates one case when the women guerillas had forgotten about the date until they were presented with grilled carrots, a reasonable treat considering their low budget, by a male comrade to celebrate the International Women's Day. She remembers celebrating the day reciting poetry and talking about the difficulties of womens' lives in their full diversity including women workers, peasants, mothers, and young women under "double oppression."[51]

The discussion on the making and function of rituals, anthems, collectively shared images, and celebrated or commemorated anniversaries has been extensively done in relation to the formation of a communal identity in social anthropology and cultural studies. Benedict Anderson's discussion on "imagined communities" and Eric Hobsbawm's introduction of "invention of traditions" have advanced these discussions to the level of the formation of political identities.[52] In this light, the International Women's Day and the International Workers' Day should be taken as two prominent moments when an internationalist, leftist political identity, occupying a wide spectrum (from

Stalinists to social democrats), comes into being. This list could be extended to the singing of anthems and songs such as *The International* and *Ciao Bella*, among others.

Irrespective of, but not totally irrelevant to their reasons and ways of flight, most of the refugees I interviewed stated that other Iranian transit migrants they met, either on the way or in the hotel, were "normal" while describing themselves as political. By "normal," they referred to young draft evaders or people who sought better opportunities, both for education and for employment, in the Western countries. When the political refugees' narratives are taken into account, we encounter a clear pattern of behavior focused on self-differentiation strategies. This pattern is formed in dialogue with a set of norms that can be collected under the label of political morality or revolutionary rule of conduct. However controversial, political morality refers to the value system, in which political refugees have been socialized and not necessarily morality in the realm of political activity.

The political refugees' uneasiness in socializing with nonpoliticals is also mentioned in the previously cited Bauer's study on Iranian transit migrants in Turkey.[53] However, despite the reluctance of many refugees to socialize with other Iranian transit migrants in Turkey, especially due to security concerns, they often inhabited the same hotels. Moreover, the longer their stay became, some even rented shared apartments with those other transit migrants they called "normal." However, this cohabitation did not result in the borders' fading out. On the contrary, differentiation became the very tool of restating their political stance in life, or rather a restatement of their existence as a political refugee. Azadeh and Behram's narrative indicates such a need to differentiate:

There were only Iranians ... Everyone was just waiting, waiting for a call, making a call ... They were sleeping all through the day and staying awake till morning. Playing cards ... Children were running from this room to the other. It was disastrous![54]

When we arrived at the hotel, we ran into a family that we knew from Iran, coincidentally. After the very first or the second day, we confronted them. *"What kind of a life is yours?" we said.* They had a little child. You are awake till the middle of the night, sitting in, suffocated with smoke, backgammon and drinking ... Then you sleep till 13.00-14.00. The next day, it is the same. Our friend told us that if we stayed in the hotel for one or two weeks, we would start to act like them. *We stayed for two months and so but did not become like them.* ... We made plans not to spend our time in vain. We made plans for ourselves, we got up early ... And went to the market. It wasn't far away, we used to walk. We did our daily shopping and then returned to the hotel. We cooked—we had bought a hot plate. After meal, we used to leave the hotel and go for a walk.[55] (Emphasis mine)

We were trying not to be like them. So we had an organized life. We were waking up timely, going to walks.[56]

Azadeh and Behrouz's narratives both point to the determination of assessing their difference vis-à-vis the other Iranians at the hotel and to the determination of leading an organized life under unorganized conditions, or to restate their existence as political subjects.

Anthropologist John Davis argues that in times of suffering people strive hard to preserve their way of life and whatever is left from their culture. According to Davis maintaining the social order can work as a "response to uncertainty and dismay, when people do tend to rely on known and certain sources of strength, and partly a determination to preserve the characteristics of humanity, to continue to be what they understood as essentially civilized and human."[57] The political refugees' attempts to preserve their organized life in times of a lack of official status and incalculability of the next step of their journey can be taken as an attempt to rely on those "known and certain sources of strength." Accordingly, Azadeh and Behrouz from their very first stop in Van, Turkey, strived to maintain an organized life as opposed to a life based on mere waiting on transit. Their efforts to preserving their way of life were parallel to their attempt to keep a distance from the other Iranians in their hotel. They stated that the other guests of the hotel formed an "unusual group." There were three leftist guerrillas, draft evaders, and a woman with her son and a few other men around her. The woman had been deported several times and they thought "she was probably a prostitute." She used to curse and swear while speaking with her son of thirteen. Behrouz stated that although they "didn't have anything to do with them," their daughter, Aida, had started to use the very same words while they were in Van, which points to the "threat" of the abolition of boundaries.

To preserve the boundaries they used to have with that "unusual group," they gathered the youths and the leftists under a group to live communally. Because of their age, as they said, Azadeh was forty and Behrouz was thirty-four, they became responsible for planning the shopping and cooking with the collected money. They, by living a collective life with the people who belonged to "their life world," repaired the boundary that was destructed by the necessary cohabitation with the "unusual group." In line with what Davis states, theirs was an attempt to reclaim their identities as a response to the rule of uncertainty and dismay.

This attempt at leading an organized life involved taking morning walks and doing daily shopping and keeping a diary, visiting museums, and at times engaging in political activities. There were other forms of self-differentiation as well. Said stated that at the time he watched the movie, *The Guests of Hotel Astoria*, for the first time, the leftist militant's extramarital affair with a married woman, herself a transit migrant, seemed to be unbelievable for him. He had lived in Istanbul for eight months and had not thought of anything other than politics. He recalled Iranians who went to bars and brothels, showing the pictures of the girls they had affairs with. According to him, a leftist militant could not live that kind of a life.

The list of incomprehensible attitudes for a leftist militant was longer than having affairs with married women. Said recalled his conversation with another Iranian refugee who had passed through Turkey, after his arrival at Sweden. While in Turkey, Said had worked in construction and when he ran out of money, in his words, he had turned into a man of *çorba* (soup). For more than a month the only thing he had eaten was bread and soup. However, the man he met had told him that he had had a good time in Turkey and had not been deprived of anything; he stole whatever he wanted from supermarkets. He told Said that he used to have honey and butter every morning. Both for him and for Minoo, whom I met in our second meeting with Said, it was incomprehensible to steal as such. Minoo said, "I don't understand how people can steal. If you are hungry, I would understand if you steal bread. But of course not steak! There is a thick line between what is right and what is wrong; there are some principles!" Accordingly, the morality that we name as political morality is not morality in the realm of politics, but a set of referential rules related to the everyday life experiences of the political, revolutionary self that was seen to be the agent of the social change.

This was a wider, more structurally publicized, and international phenomenon that goes beyond the everyday life experiences of the transit refugees I interviewed. Its roots can be taken back to the politics of respectability formed in the workers' movement that shaped socialist movements from late 19th century to at least late 1970s, where instead of aiming for abolition of the classes altogether, the working-class identity was idealized and associated with pride differentiating itself from "the poor, the unwaged, the unemployed, or the nonworker."[58] As M. E. O'Brien brilliantly demonstrates in her book on family abolition, this socialist vision despised the "lumpenproletariat" seeing them as "shameful surplus of society."[59] The following chapter on differentiation politics among women will further explore this politics of respectability and its convergences with moral and sexual conformity.

Speaking to the Popular Front for the Liberation of Palestine (PFLA) weekly *Al Hadaf* in 1977, a Fadai guerrilla stated that the Iranian Revolution "is striving to build the new man. ... The revolution, based on the lessons it learned from the Vietnamese revolution, is concerned to concentrate on the human characteristics and the building of the revolutionary person."[60] Sevim Belli, a prominent Turkish revolutionary woman, provides further insight into a similar revolutionary rule of conduct in her memoirs. The Turkish Communist Party's Paris representative in the 1950s and the translator of the main texts of Marxism in Turkish, Belli goes beyond narrating her own experiences and describes, in a framework, how a revolutionary should behave in everyday life. Belli states that to be a revolutionary, one has to perceive "being revolutionary" (*devrimcilik*) as a lifestyle and should internalize its principles. According to her, one is not a revolutionary only in times of active struggle. To be a revolutionary, one has to take every step with consciousness (*bilinç*). Being revolutionary means being aware of your place, your targets, and your plans and taking a stance at every step irrespective of the conditions. To be determined and act according to the revolutionary consciousness at every moment, even while you are eating, drinking, sleeping, or having fun, is integral to the formation of the revolutionary self.[61] Examples from her personal life illuminate what she expects from a revolutionary in further detail:

> I have never spent all my money until the last penny. I think you should behave cautiously before you come to that point. Or, I will prefer to stay hungry. I don't purchase anything unless it is really necessary, especially for myself. I have some principles, some norms which I don't know the basis of.

They are quite tough. … A revolutionary of Turkey should not breach those norms that I define.⁶²

One of the required readings of the Fadai movement, *What a Revolutionary Should Know* written by Bijan Jazani,⁶³ after analyzing the Iranian political, social, and economic history and putting forward the arguments that render armed struggle necessary, depicts the "revolutionary individual" (*fard-e enqelabi*) and the revolutionary generation as well. The statements involve a number of direct practical advice on a wide range of subjects from guerrilla life in countryside, to what position to take while establishing international links and what to do in captivity.⁶⁴ There are a few general statements about everyday life such as the claim that the lifestyle of the revolutionary individual determines their revolutionary capacity⁶⁵ and that the revolutionary generation needs to forgo their welfare and leisure for the sake of true democracy.⁶⁶ Far from being a collection of cliché statements, the text is mostly directed to revolutionary cadres and underlines the importance of disciplinary measures and staying dedicated to the cause and the organization. The disciplinary measures and the level of sacrifice expected from the militants might not be exceptional taking into account that the organization at stake was an underground, armed guerrilla organization. It is argued that in the 1970s the average Fadai guerrilla lifespan was estimated to be six months.⁶⁷ Peyman Vahabzadeh depicts the daily life of a guerilla as such:

> The life of a cadre was filled with around-the-clock, minutely drafted tasks with rounds of meetings, rendezvous, surveillance, military training, physical fitness, team discussions, ideological training, making explosives, carrying out of operations, monitoring of police radio signals, guarding of bases, and smuggling of weapons, in addition to daily chores of cleaning, cooking and shopping.⁶⁸

Narratives of guerrillas attest to this minute scheduling and heavy workload.⁶⁹ Moreover, many continued this practice, as much as it was possible, also in prisons.⁷⁰ Parallels can be drawn between the prison experience of some political cadres and the transit refugee experience narrated in this book. Different from the experience in safe houses that were cohabitated by people of similar convictions, Fadai guerrillas created basic forms of communes with people coming from different backgrounds in prisons and in transit spaces. In a way both could be seen as places where cohabitation of people from different walks of lives was imposed rather than chosen.

Hammed Shahidian claimed the problem started when "the requirements of a guerrilla's life, such as self-denial and obliviousness regarding material, practical, and personal matters, were expanded, especially in post-revolutionary Iran, to dominate the life of any sympathetic person."[71] Shahidian argued that "high school students were expected to live by the same priorities as professional revolutionaries, and personal lives were overshadowed by political demands."[72]

While some of these practices can be specific to the Fadai movement or the Iranian left, we should not overlook some of the historical ideological roots of this "self-sacrificing revolutionary"[73] ideal, literally reflected in the name of the organization, Fadai, forming the core value of being a political—*siyasi*. Mainly it was an overinterpretation of "the primacy of the collective good over the individual interest," by taking everything that is personal to be individualistic. Moghissi argues:

> Self-sacrifice in the service of the proletariat, rejection of the individual interests and rights, and austerity and self-discipline in personal interests and desires were more rigorously and religiously respected by the Fedayeen than a great number of other leftist activists.[74]

A comparative analysis of various Iranian leftist groups' practices with respect to the way they handled the submission of the personal to the collective is way beyond the scope of this work. Moreover, memoirs and analyses written by ex-militants in the Iranian left centralize on their own subjective experience. Given the history of the Iranian left and the way it was crashed ruthlessly, this is often a bitter experience.

However, by 1978 Fadaiyan had turned into a movement. It being the most influential leftist organization on university campuses led to the foundation of the organization's student affiliate the *Pishgam* (Vanguard) Student Organization in 1979 and soon after the organization "came out" opening its first branch in a university campus.[75] While the influence of the organization's literature on this new generation of activists, to which many of my interviewees belonged, has been significant, we should not assume that the practices of the cadres were replicated by the thousands joining the movement. Neither overestimation of the impact of the culture of the organization nor ignoring this influence altogether can help us understand the attitude and behavior of political refugees in transit.

Furthermore, asserting political refugee identity and structuring daily lives in accordance with the principles it implied served as an empowering tactic for refugees navigating a prolonged period of transit characterized by uncertainty. It served as a means of giving purpose to a life primarily characterized by waiting. It also functioned as claiming a subjectivity, the particularity of which was not acknowledged by the state or other governing bodies. Thus, refugees' concern for maintaining their distinction from "others" can be taken as an act of protecting their existence in the symbolic realm. In the following chapter I will explore how this concern manifested itself among the women in transit.

4

"Not One of Those Women": Negotiating Womanhood in Transit

The interviewed women's remarkable effort to mark their difference from the other Iranian women in the hotel lobbies is closely linked with the set of ideas and value system defining what being political meant for post-1979 Iranian refugees. This effort should also be seen as a part of survival tactics in the material realm, which I discussed in the previous chapter. However, due to the multiplicity of the axes of oppression refugee women are faced with, the gendered dynamics of being in transit requires particular attention. At times, the differentiation tactics among women did not challenge the regimes of subordination, but rather reproduced them. The codes of political morality and gender normative, conservative social norms intersected when the subject was the sexuality of women. The most widespread discourse on self-differentiation among women was constructed around the phenomenon of decency. Women's narratives point to more visible differentiation tactics as well as stricter norms of self-control and adherence to a certain type of gender conformity, particularly in case of single mothers in transit.

In this chapter, I will first give an overview of the major concerns in gender dynamics of displacement as many of the issues the case of post-1979 Iranian women refugees presented are not singular cases but symptoms of a sociopolitical context shaped by overlapping and interdependent systems of oppression involving probably the oldest regime of subordination in history, namely gender-based oppression and its contextual and historical manifestations. Then, I will present the tropes on self-differentiation in the narratives of the Iranian refugee women I talked with. Their case, once again, sheds light on how gender-based oppression is ingrained even in the most subversive circles dedicated to change the society.

Gender Dynamics of Displacement

It is only since 2011 that the UNHCR has incorporated intersectionality in their research and policy papers, defining it as "the interaction of multiple identities and experiences of exclusion and subordination"[1] and is intentionally engaged in collecting and publishing relevant data and reports. According to the UNHCR reports, women compose half of the worldwide population of forcibly displaced people, which includes asylum seekers, refugees, and internally displaced people. These figures vary according to regions. There are proportionally more women and girls among refugee populations living in the West and Central Africa than Europe.[2] Reports on gender dimension of forced displacement demonstrate disproportionate effects of migration on women. Women and girls are the main recipients of sexual and gender-based violence, which ranges from sexual assault to rape, forced marriage, psychological abuse, physical assault, and denial of opportunities and resources. A 2017 UNHCR gender-based violence report registers that partners or ex-partners of survivors commit more than half of those violent acts.[3] However, as the report indicates, the low level of reporting other perpetrators including service providers and other officials can point to the lack of protection mechanisms for survivors who might refrain from reporting perpetrators in positions of power.[4] The World Bank's Gender Dimensions of Forced Displacement report based on research covering seventeen countries registers that "gender is a predictive factor in indicators of chronic deprivation."[5] Employing Women, Peace and Security (WPS) index assessing women's inclusion, justice, and security levels in five sub-Saharan countries, the report manifests that displaced women have worse WPS scores than host country women.[6]

Women do not fall into precarious living conditions just because they are displaced. The extent of gender-based oppression, or patriarchy in its common usage, is plain to see even when public statistics on gender inequality are reviewed. According to the UN's latest five-year World's Women report, women continue to be underrepresented in public and private decision mechanisms, have less access to education, less access to internet, lower literacy rates, and lower labor market participation, among others. When they work, they are overrepresented in informal jobs, thus have less access to employment-related social securities, and earn less. Moreover, one out of three women in the world have had experienced physical and sexual violence by an intimate partner.⁷ These figures might not be news to most of us. When compiled together, however, they present an alarming picture of the reality we live in.

In times of crises, these inequalities intensify and the marginalized segments of the population bear the effects of crises in disproportionate ways. Furthermore, these structural inequalities can have a domino effect, setting a chain of vulnerabilities. The referenced UN report on gender inequality highlights some of these combined vulnerabilities in the context of the recent Covid-19 pandemic. Three aspects registered in the report are significant. First, women were disproportionally hit with the pandemic, because they work in the sectors that were hit the most by pandemic lockdown measures, such as domestic work, service sector, and accommodation, among others. Second, 70 percent of workers in health sector are women. The pandemic meant not only more work for them but also higher risks of infections. Third, the worldwide lockdown measures and "stay-at-home" campaigns restrained women to their houses, which has not been a safe space for many.⁸ For a large number of women, home is the primary location where violence and oppression takes place. Another example of this domino effect of vulnerabilities is registered in the previously referenced World Bank report on the gendered dimensions of forced displacement. The report supports previous research showing that "experiencing sexual violence increases risk of future violence."⁹

While it is clear that displacement worsens the living conditions of people and in general crises deepen inequalities and create more risk for the marginalized, there is another side to this story, which indicates that an intersectional approach needs to go beyond a cumulative assessment of vulnerabilities. Displacement does not have the same effect on all refugee women. In addition to the specific reasons that placed them under the risk of persecution and thus made them refugees at the very first place, they might have more opportunities in their new country of residence depending on the norms and social conditions of their country of origin. Şimşek Ademi's work on Afghan refugee women in Iran and Syrian refugee women in Turkey highlights these diverse experiences of women in displacement. Escaping from the misogynistic Taliban regime and stricter patriarchal and religious norms in Afghanistan, Afghan women were able to have more social presence in Iran. They could go out by themselves and without wearing a *burqa*, could work, and have access to education. While many women had to live in extended families in Afghanistan due to social norms, economic problems, and war, among others, the composition of families changed as a result of migration. Many women narrated the positive impact of living with their nuclear family in Iran. Living with immediate family members meant not only less domestic labor and more privacy but also less social pressure from extended family members and mothers-in-law in particular.[10] This relative improvement in the lives of some Afghan women refugees in Iran should not blind us to the poverty, prejudice, racial discrimination, and social exclusion that have been constants in Afghan refugee lives in Iran for decades. Syrian women interviewed in Turkey did not report any positive changes in their lives when compared to their prewar living conditions. While generational differences were also observable among younger and older Afghan women, particularly in terms of younger women's easier integration to the society and having access to better jobs, in the case of Syrian women, these differences were severer due to their language barrier. The Syrian women interviewed in Şimşek Ademi's work complained about feeling infantilized because they did not speak Turkish. This not only makes them dependent on their children, but also hinders their possibilities to help their children in tasks that require Turkish knowledge, such as their homework, which has been detrimental on their identity as a competent parent. A 35-year-old university-graduated Syrian woman expressed the shame she feels when not being able to help her daughter's homework and how she thinks her daughter would not respect her anymore.[11]

Gender dynamics of displacement have many layers. Women's increased participation in labor market does not, at all times, point to a development in the displaced women's living conditions. Quite often displaced women work not because they want to but because they have to, despite the cultural norms they are accustomed to. Moreover, they work in precarious conditions and are underpaid. If they undertake some chores that make them get out of their homes and be more visible outside, it is not at all times a sign of emancipation either. Due to patriarchal norms at the host country, women can be more invisible to the mechanisms of surveillance that take men as agents and thus threatening.[12] If women apply to humanitarian organizations' cash benefits or other support tools, it is not at all times a sign of balanced gender distribution of help, but because men might find it degrading to ask for help due to normative gender roles. Gender-based oppression produces different symptoms in different contexts.

Minoo, Mahnaz, and Their Headscarves

Two women refugees I interviewed had fled Iran with their children and without any adult companion. Minoo had a young daughter and stayed first in Hotel Kanada in Aksaray and later in a shared apartment with other Iranian transit migrants. Mahnaz had two sons and a daughter staying with her in Hotel Tandoğan in Ankara. Minoo had arrived at Turkey by plane in 1985 and Mahnaz by bus in 1990. Minoo defined herself as political (refugee) and Mahnaz as the wife of a political (refugee). These two women, using different routes, passing through Turkey in different years, staying in different hotels, and even defining themselves in different ways said that they wore headscarves in Turkey at the beginning of their stay there. For Minoo, it took almost fifteen days to take off her headscarf, while Mahnaz wore it for six months.

Minoo stated that she had no reason for not taking off her headscarf in Turkey, as she had not worn it in Iran unless it was obligatory. She emphasized that she was neither traditional nor religious. However, she explained her behavior as an attempt of differentiating herself from the other women who had started to wear makeup on the plane to Turkey. She said:

> When we got out [from the plane], all the women took off their headscarves. I also put it on my shoulders. Then, when we landed, I saw that all those women went to the bathroom and when they came out they had been transformed completely into other people, it was as if they had put on masks. I think I wanted to keep away from them. I don't know why, but I did not take off my scarf for a period of time.[13]

Her account of a woman living with them in a shared apartment depicted that "other" from whom she wanted to differentiate, further:

> This woman was breastfeeding, she was really messy. The very first thing that I did every morning was to put her breasts in her shirt (laughs) … tak tak, I would put them in, and then I would go to make tea.[14]

In Minoo's narrative, the inappropriateness of nudity or sexual conspicuousness merges with the aforementioned morality of being political and points to her class position. She defines her difference and what it is based on as such:

> A guy had come there, they were gathering in the evenings, drinking alcohol. It was really annoying. Especially for me, as I had no familiarity at all with such a language. I mean the *lumpens'* language. I did not know them at all. I was shocked and wondering which part of Iran those people came from. I had not seen such people even in Iran … It was too strange for me. I did not know this part of Iranian society. Well, we had fallen to the line of politics at the age of fifteen or sixteen, with political people, people had some kind of principles in the gatherings we socialized at.[15] (Emphasis mine)

Hers is an illuminating example of the solidness of some boundaries even in times of necessary cohabitation. Her insistence on not having familiarity with the "kind of people" that she had to live with and her wearing headscarf can be taken as attempts to maintain the boundaries at risk. Her aversion to nudity or conspicuous sexuality was explicitly interwoven with her political subjectivity. However, the refugee women's obsession with restraining their sexuality or policing other women's is not at all times a direct effect of their political subjectivity. Mahnaz's story presents another version of "keeping the headscarf."

Mahnaz's whole story bore the stamp of pride, decency, and reputation. She had grown up in a conservative family, but she had not worn a headscarf unless it was legally obligatory. She stated that she was "the wife of a political" and her husband was a militant of the Marxist Fadaiyan. In her single-mother days in Ankara, wearing a headscarf was a way of self-assertion or rather "performing" as a devout mother. She spoke of her two years in Hotel Tandoğan with pride. She wore long sleeved shirts with trousers and spent her days looking after her children. On Monday afternoons, at late hours as it was cheaper then, she went to the market and kept what she bought in wet linens placed in the balcony, to keep them fresh, for a week. She bought chicken bones, which she claimed they used to call *cenaze* (corpse) and cooked soup with it. She used to knit pullovers for her children in her spare time and waited until four in the morning to be able to use the hotel's kitchen for cooking meals for them.

She was proud to state that she was a sister to the hotel employees. According to her, she was seen and protected as a sister due to her behavior. Being a sister brought both security and control. Mahnaz exemplified the extent of this as such:

> They were really nice to me. For example if a Turk came, or a bad [erotic] movie was shown; they, the waiters themselves or the receptionists, would point at me and tell me to go upstairs. I was like a sister to them, they were brothers, cause they saw my behavior … they were feeling so responsible for me that even if I wanted to go somewhere [late] they were looking in such a way that … I would go to a right place … really they were brothers.[16]

She clearly depicted the "other" women:

> I saw it with my very eyes. The girl had come; she wanted to get a Green Card to join her husband. All of a sudden we saw that she was wearing a mini skirt, make up, she had taken off her headscarf and things, and had sat at the end of the saloon with a guy, and a sexy film was being watched … Then at night she went to a disco with that guy.[17]

Mahnaz stated that the employees saw her difference from the other women who went to bars and discos. While her self-assertion as a devout mother and sister resulted in being policed by the employees, it also made her life easier at the hotel. For example, she did not pay for baths as she was allowed to use it and she was so trusted that the Iranians who were leaving would give her their belongings to share them among the ones in need. She was a "wife" to the political, "sister" to the receptionists, and was referred as the "mother" of her elder son in the hotel. Her compliance to the patriarchal rules of conduct had increased her life chance as a single mother in transit.

Haideh Moghissi's interviews with former Fadai sympathizers a decade before my interviews point to similar discussions on the norms of decency with respect to clothing among Fadai circles. She cites a woman activist's experience with "serious squabble with her 'superior comrade' over a pink shirt she wore while selling the newspaper." "Women were asked to wear simple dresses, not to wear bright colours, make-up or jewelry," she adds.[18]

Demarking difference through clothing and wearing symbolic pieces of clothing to convey a certain message is a not a rare everyday life practice. In some settings, such as current France or pre-AKP Turkey, clothing affiliated with religious concerns has been prohibited to be worn in schools or as state employees, with similar pretext. What makes the case of these two women

I interviewed particular was that they wore headscarf, which is widely affiliated with living one's life according to Islamic principles, while they did not live according to such principles. For none of them it was a conscious decision; they just felt wearing headscarf would make their lives easier in their context.

Aksu Bora, in her work on the relationship between domestic service providers and their employers, both being predominantly women, cites Beverly Skeggs's study on English working-class women and the importance of clothing in the making of their subjectivity. According to Skeggs, demarcating womanhood from sexuality has been the most widespread act of distinction among women and this has been made through appearance, which, in addition to behavior, has been the indicator of respectability. However, she adds, too much concentration on appearance might also be seen as an indicator of womanly seductiveness.[19] Thus, women had to make sure they care about their appearance but not so much to make them seem they want to look attractive as respectability was accepted to be at odds with "attractiveness."[20] Bora's interviewees also discussed what they thought was and was not the proper look for the other women: nail polish, dyed hair, headscarf, and so on. The interviews with headscarf-wearing women cleaners once again demonstrate that headscarf has more than one meaning and that it can be employed as a means in women's strategies of strengthening their positions, namely, as a strategy of women's differentiating themselves from other women.[21]

In Turkey, headscarf has been more than a piece of symbolic clothing for decades. A quick overview of the modern history of countries with majority Muslim populations, such as Iran and Turkey, will provide the reader with many instances of political struggle over headscarf. Until the rule of Erdoğan's AKP, headscarf-wearing women were marginalized in modern, urban life. Wearing it was banned in schools and universities (with some exceptions) and as employees working in state institutions.[22] The political discussion around the threat of political Islam in the 1990s introduced a top-down separation between different forms of headscarves. The "traditional" style that was associated with women in the countryside or older people was referred as headscarf, *başörtüsü*, and the more elaborate, modern version was referred as *türban*. Women wearing headscarf were not seen as a threat to the ideal of Turkish Republican woman, even if they were not seen as the true bearer of the ideal. Women wearing *türban* were labeled as agents of political Islam and a threat to the ideal of Turkish Republican woman. Headscarf was tolerated as long as it belonged to the old, the lower class, or the uneducated. When it was stylized and entered modern, urban life, it was seen as a threat.

The cleaners Bora interviewed not only acknowledged the politicization of the headscarf/*türban* distinction but also exposed the futility of it, as in as much as the political discussion suggested, styles were not as binary as were pushed for. Less and less people would wear a headscarf with a simple knot under the chin, which would be seen as the traditional way. However, a binary existed, not between different styles of headscarf but between women who wore headscarf and who did not, to the extent that in everyday usage women would be referred to as *açık-kapalı*, open-closed. One of Bora's interviewees, Fatma, working as a cleaner for eight years, underlined that she started to wear a headscarf to be able to differentiate herself from other women living in the working-class neighborhood she despised.[23] For some others, headscarf belonged to a lower-class, nonurban lifestyle.[24] It was "normal" that the cleaners wore it, or surprising if they did not.

The Turkish series *Ethos* aired on Netflix in 2020 brought these dynamics on screen. Starring a cleaner woman wearing headscarf working in middle-class neighborhoods, *Ethos* materialized the class dimension of headscarf and the division wearing and not wearing it created among Turkish women. However, the dynamics it presented were outdated. The last two decades of AKP's rule has changed these class dynamics significantly. It is no longer possible to take headscarf as a clothing piece associated with lower class or the marginalized. With the lift on the headscarf ban, more women wore headscarf publicly, making them present in universities and workplaces. The proportion of women wearing headscarf has significantly increased among the ruling class families, from the family of Erdoğan himself, to the richest business people in Turkey.[25] While it would be far-fetched to claim the binary between women wearing headscarf and those who do not wear it has disappeared, it is necessary to acknowledge the shift in these dynamics of differentiation. A historical and contextual analysis is indispensable in the art of interpreting cultural norms and the meanings of behaviors.

The historical discussions on "the ideal woman" have often linked the physical appearance of women and her sexuality with her values. The literature on body politics and sexuality is a vast domain to explore here; however, it is worthwhile to see the relevance of some main tropes in the said literature in analyzing parts of the discourse used by Iranian women in transit. Interpretation of actions and words cannot be separated from the historical and theoretical knowledge and the experience of the interpreted and the interpreter. As Ian Parker also argues in his discussion on historical materialism, we move "from abstract to concrete," "from things viewed separately, abstractly, to things in their context, concretely. When we grasp something in the world it includes our reflective thoughtful activity, and then we can step back and analyse it." Parker adds, "What we hold and discuss in our conscious awareness of the world is not merely a reflection of the world but is moulded by our interests in it, in what we want to do with it."[26]

Minoo's and Mahnaz's depiction of the other women around the hotels, from whom they tried to differentiate themselves from, can be interpreted with respect to their political ideology's norms of morality and the patriarchal norms of the time and place they lived in. However, the sexualization of women's bodies and the moral panic around it have a longer history than Iranian leftist movements' conservative sexual politics, and taking the latter as the main cause would be misleading and reductionist. Minoo's and Mahnaz's acts and discourse about other women and problematization of their sexuality are not isolated cases but linked with various historical discussions over morality, gender norms, and representation of the ideal woman.

Sister versus Prostitute

In addition to "not being like other women," the main trope of Mahnaz's narrative was that she was acknowledged as a sister by the hotel employees. It is very common to use names depicting family ties for unrelated people in Turkey. You call younger men and women *kardeş*—sibling, women *abla* or *bacı*—sister, older men *dayı, amca*—uncle, and so on. Also in the leftist discourse in the 1970s in Turkey, while some women were seen living with degenerated, bourgeois morality, others, the women in the struggle, were seen as "sisters," pointing to women without sexuality.[27] In her study on representations of women in Turkish media in the 1980s, Ayşe Saktanber argues that women were divided into two groups. As it was a legal and social norm for women to live under men's guardianship, the division worked as such: women who belong to the family and women who are "free." While the former was seen to be devoid of sexuality except within their monogamous, matrimonial relationships, the latter, "free" women were the ones whose sexuality was under scrutiny all the time.[28] Nilüfer Göle makes a similar argument. She says that as women, due to conservative societal norms, were not expected to be a part of the public life in early 20th century, taking titles based on family ties in public made them retain their respected status while being in public. To be free and yet protected, women had to give up their "threatening sexuality" and assume family ties to be a sister, a mother, or a daughter to the anonymous men on the street.[29] When Mahnaz was proudly explaining how she was seen as a sister to the hotel employees, she claimed the protection that the "other women" were not seen to be entitled to. Saktanber exemplifies the extent and impact of this sexual versus nonsexual women division in society by the material consequences of a known verdict in 1986 that flamed women's movement's fight for legal change in Turkey.[30] The article 438 of Turkish Penal Code made it possible for courts to reduce the sentence for sexual assault to one-third if the victim was a sex worker as the dignity of a sex worker and a woman with morality was argued not to be comparable. Thanks to the women's movement's resolute campaigns, the article was taken out of the penal code in 1990.

The rumors about prostitution among Iranian transit migrants in Turkey at that time should be contextualized in this discourse of sexual versus nonsexual women. Bauer states that "in Germany there was much talk and concern about the 'brothers and sisters' remaining in Turkey and particularly about the plight of women—were they forced to resort to prostitution?".[31] Such rumors were widespread among the interviewed refugees. While some claimed to have known Iranian women working as sex workers in Turkey, for most of the interviewed refugees it was not more than hearsay. Azadeh, Behrouz, Mahnaz, Said, and Hooman knew of Iranian women involved in prostitution in Turkey. Interviewees also argued that the prohibition of prostitution in Iran and the subsequent atrocities committed against sex workers in Iran, including burning alive, had led to the migration of Iranian sex workers to Turkey. However, some of the transit migrants stated that they had not seen anything, but had learned that it existed only when they arrived in Sweden. Prostitution is a hardly recordable activity, particularly in the case of undocumented women working in precarious conditions; thus it is hard to assess the validity of such rumors. However, our preoccupation with meaning more than the event necessitates elaborating on this rumor's meaning for the people participating in its dissemination and taking the cited women's aversion of conspicuous sexuality in the context of such rumors.

The interviewed women's assertive self-differentiation from "other" women within the context of the rumors of Iranian prostitution in Turkey can also be taken as testimonies of the precarious life conditions of the women in transit. The previously referenced movie, *The Guests of Hotel Astoria*, provides a striking hint at the relationship between the sexual abuse of women and the police threat upon transit migrants. In her interrogation by the Turkish police, the Iranian translator, who claims to be working with both regimes, threatens Pouri by implying to link her case with the arrested communist and offers her an escape way: to have sex with the police. In another scene, the same "translator" serves as the driver of a young girl who has become a sex worker in Turkey.

Melissa Gira Grant, in *Playing the Whore*, unpacks "the whore stigma" coined by Gail Pheterson and states that it is another reason to why a universal class of women does not exist.[32] Pheterson argued that the whore stigma "attaches not to femaleness alone, but to illegitimate or illicit femaleness."[33] Jill Nagle argued that whore stigma not only mandated that you should be virtuous but also that you should appear virtuous. As Grant skillfully puts it, "While only some women may be sex workers, all of us negotiate whore stigma."[34] The moral panic around the sexualization of other women does not translate into greater sexual agency for women but creates boundaries between women.[35] While being a sister to men has different consequences than sisterhood among women, the latter, as we also see from the examples earlier, is not that straightforward either. The question of sisterhood among women has been widely discussed in feminist literature. Bora points to the construction of different womanhoods in relation with each other, challenging each other and at times devaluating each other.[36] Therefore womanhood is a process that is not exempt from power relations, and tactics are employed by each woman participating actively in the construction of her own subjectivity, either in solidarity with other women or in differentiation from them.[37]

Women's Emancipation and the Left

Consistent with Minoo's and Mahnaz's narratives, there are also feminist critiques that link women's political subjectivity, of leftist orientation, with their aversion from conspicuous clothing or sexuality. However, contrary to what Minoo and Mahnaz stated, this aversion is taken to be linked with the leftist movements' constriction of women into traditional gender roles, thus to its restrictive role. Fatmagül Berktay states that the leftist movement in Turkey assumed that women are more prone to become bourgeois due to their gender and thus protecting the revolutionary self-required controlling women's behavior and clothing.[38] Berktay argues that taken in the same category as of drinking, gambling, and using drugs, women were seen as toxic substances in the leftist culture. This was more a reflection of the societal norms that the left accepted and did not challenge due to populist concerns.[39] In *One Era, Two Women*, Oya Baydar and Melek Ulagay, two women from Turkey who have been leftist militants since 1960s, point to similar references to "the people's values" mentioned by male revolutionaries while discussing proper clothing for women.[40] "The people" were seen to have conservative morality and to get their support, leftist militants had to avoid estranging them.

In the Iranian left, and particularly in the Fadai movement, on the one hand the conservative norms of the society were criticized and seen to belong to an ancient regime; on the other hand, sexual liberties and "feminine" clothing were seen to be linked with manipulation of sexuality through cultural imperialism to "displace young people's energy and distract them".[41] Shahidian argues that women militants were seen as "desexed revolutionaries" or "honorary men."[42] Their dress codes would involve baggy clothes and no cosmetics.[43] Shahidian's example of leftist woman activist and writer Qodsi Qazinur's commentary on the imposition of mandatory hijab in 1979 is illuminating in this aspect of "emancipation" through erasure of femininity:

> If by hijab is meant modesty, then why not doing something fundamental? Why not teaching women to dress simply—a baggy pair of pants, a long and loose blouse with hair tied behind the back with a rubber band ... Then womanhood will no longer be so problematic.[44]

A prominent Fadai leader, Ali Keshtgar, in an interview with Moghissi in 1990s said:

> Exactly like in Islamic Sharia where a women's beauty should be covered under a veil, from a guerrilla point of view a beautiful woman should cover her beauty. The more ugly-looking and the more lousily dressed, the more dedicated you appeared. This was the general feeling in the guerrilla movement.[45]

Moghissi argues that Fadai guerrillas, despite their formal stance for gender equality, were products of their own upbringing and socialization, which was heavily influenced by Iranian patriarchal norms and Shiite cultural norms. As it is widely known, the impact of Shiite culture on guerrilla culture is first and foremost manifested in the centrality of martyrdom. Moghissi claims that the impact of Shiite norms on the revolutionary left in Iran goes beyond this. The sexual purity and modesty of women, the glorification of motherhood, and guardianship and control over women's behaviors by male family members, Moghissi argues, were impactful on male militants' approach toward their female comrades.[46]

Fadai guerrilla narratives on their everyday life in 1970s underline the equality between male and female guerrillas in safe houses and during operations. All three narratives by Nahid Ajar, Roqiyeh Daneshgari, and Qorbanali Abdolrahimpour, published recently in one volume, underline that tasks and responsibilities of guerillas were divided according to skills and abilities and not according to gender.[47] However, reading more of their narratives reveals that these abilities and skills were not immune to gender normative assessments. Ajar states that "women were usually in charge of security and finances," "supervision and the security of the houses. They checked the appearance of comrades and carefully managed communication with the neighbours, maintaining an image of normalcy to prevent extra curiosity or sensitivity from the landlord and neighbours." [48] Abdolrahimpour argues that "women would also engage in better domestic management and discipline, hygiene and nutrition within safehouses."[49] Fadais knew that they were living in a traditional society organized around normative families. Each safe house was built around two guerillas disguised as a married couple and the rest of their comrades would be members of their extended families.

Wearing the *chador*, an overall cover from head to toe, was an ideal tool not only for disguise but also to hide and transport things. Living in a society shaped by gender-based oppression and discrimination, they were aware that women would be seen as less dangerous and would attract less attention performing tasks related to purchase of materials for operations. Therefore some of these tasks were gendered due to pragmatic reasons and was not necessarily due to conforming to gender norms. However, this does not hold for some of the gender-normative distribution of tasks. Being in charge of the safe house budget, checking the appearance of other comrades for security reasons, domestic management, hygiene, and nutrition-related matters reveal compliance with gender normative task distribution, which bestow mental, emotional, and care labor disproportionally on women.

The referenced women activists' narratives on gender relations in the revolutionary leftist groups in Turkey and Iran are illuminating to understand the interaction of social, cultural, and ideological dynamics in these cases. However, to argue that revolutionary left movement has at best no interest in sexual liberation if not obstructing it would be an a reductionist, ahistorical argument. Accordingly, Moghissi underlines that the theoretical backing to de-prioritizing the "women question" and anti-feminism of the Iranian left was a selective reading of Lenin's criticism to feminists, whom he thought paid "too much" attention to marriage and sex.[50] Holly Lewis points to another misreading of Marxism in the discourse against cosmetics in the leftist circles. Lewis argues that the disdain for fashion and cosmetics focused on women's clothing was based on a reductionist reading of Marxist political economy, focusing on consumerism instead of capitalist production.[51] As anti-consumerism does not target capitalism but the consumer, being disproportionally in charge of buying consumer goods, women got a disproportionate share of this blame.

Cinzia Aruzza, in her book on "the marriages and divorces of Marxism and Feminism," *Dangerous Liaisons*, gives a historical account of the relationship between the women's movement and Marxist movement since the late 19th century.[52] I do not intend to get into the details of the historical and theoretical discussions on the relationship between women's emancipation and Marxism or the position of women militants in the leftist movement. However, aversion from conspicuous sexuality, the moral panic about "other women," and claiming the role of a sister, a mother, and a wife that Minoo and Mahnaz's accounts involved are also related to those historical debates in the left on the family, the personal versus public realm, and the separation of the domestic sphere from the production sphere in capitalism, some of which has been mentioned before.

For example, according to the most globally influential example of a leftist movement, the Bolsheviks, family was where oppression was perpetuated.[53] For them, women's liberation involved women's liberation from domestic labor and independence from men.[54] In an attempt to abolish the bourgeois family, full proletarianization and collectivization of reproductive labor was envisioned.[55] Heading departments of social welfare and women's work in the early revolutionary Soviet government, Alexandra Kollontai advocated for integrating the social reproductive work that was previously seen to be a part of private realm into the national economy as a collectivized social responsibility.[56] In its early years, the October Revolution made divorce easier, abolished the attribution of "head of family" to the man, eliminated the distinction between legitimate and illegitimate children, made abortion legal and free, and abolished the classification of homosexuality as a crime.[57] It was in the 1930s that family, which was seen as a center of oppression before, was reestablished as the core of the society. In 1933 homosexuality was recriminalized, in 1936 abortion banned for the first pregnancy, a tax was imposed on single people, and free sexuality was condemned.[58] This Stalinist degeneration of the communist regime in the USSR set the line for the Third International, followed by other participating communist parties.[59]

It was the premise of "the personal/private is political" that brought another tension to the relationship between socialist politics and women's politics, in the late 1960s particularly in the Global North. More and more women problematized both their position and treatment in their revolutionary organizations and the perpetual postponement of discussing issues related to women's emancipation such as sexual violence, oppression, and discrimination. In Turkey, this shift happened after the 1980 coup, following the bloody repression of the revolutionary movement.[60] Earlier, "the women's question" was seen as a symptom of the capitalist regime, which would be resolved with the revolution. Arguing for different political interests of men and women was seen as creating division within class interests.[61] In addition to the challenges it brought to the practices of some socialist men, at a more theoretical level, "the personal is political" was seen problematic both because it was seen to prioritize the individual over the society and that it accentuated the singular experience over structural mechanisms. Thus, in the former case, the gendered discrimination and oppression could be seen as secondary to the class's unified interests, and on the latter, they could be seen as symptoms of the current political-economic system.

However, being a part of the leftist movement was an empowering process for a great number of women as well. Women's narratives of revolutionary Iran in 1979 quoted in Ghorashi's *Ways to Survive, Battles to Win* highlight the effect of being political in their daily lives:

> I felt for the first time that I was someone. I was always studying but when I became a member of a political organization, I was satisfied with the fact that I was someone. I was then 19 years old. Before that I was not responsible for anything, but all of a sudden I became a person who was in charge of some people and there was a person who was in charge of me. ... I did not have to stay at home and wait until someone entered the door. It was really like that, before I became politically active.[62]
>
> I can say that those years were the better years of my life. I think that I never in my life enjoyed life like that. I gained a lot of personal freedom at that time and socially all those restrictions were not there anymore. You could go wherever you wanted to go, you could do whatever you wanted to do.[63]
>
> That period felt like a paradise on earth, which was beautifully called the "spring of freedom." It was great; I became politically active in Fadaiyan organization and did my best to increase my revolutionary self-discipline. ... Everything was exciting and you felt that you were doing something important in life. I acquired a political identity, which was respected both socially and by my family.[64]

Therefore, for these women being a part of the leftist movement was more an empowering process than a restricting and controlling one. Accordingly, Mahnaz's and Minoo's rule of conduct needs to be interpreted by attending to the various layers contributing to those behaviors. From moralist reproduction of gendered roles to which leftists were not immune, to pragmatic and voluntary reproduction of them as a survival tactic, those layers were numerous.

John Davis, in his lecture on the anthropology of suffering, stresses that pains related to routine life and pains of external causes do not represent distinct phenomena. In addition, there are "continuities between the causes of exceptional suffering and routine suffering."[65] Giving the example of famine, he underlines that it is not famine, but hunger that kills. Or in other words, famine is in fact a part of daily life. Davis states that there is no rupture between ordinary social experience and the pains caused by suffering from war, famine, or, we may say, *exile*. Everyday experiences of women in transit, marked by sexual harassment, hunger, sense of unpredictability, suppression caused by the responsibility of children, threat of deportation, harassment of the police, and fear of state violence, among many others, cannot be taken apart. In fact they are the mortar of the precarious conditions in which the transit life takes place. In that light, rumors can be employed as "alarms" to state that they are or were in danger and—taking into account the case of my interviewees—had successfully overcome them.

The victimized portrait of refugees renders the tactics they employed in their life in transit unseen. Although Iranians' cohabitation in the same hotels and in shared apartments brings forth the assumption that in-group differences might have diminished in time, refugees' narratives point to concerns for self-differentiation for advancing their claims in the material and symbolic realms. As presented in the last two chapters, those everyday life tactics ranged from ways of dealing with bread and butter issues to the assertion of their subjective existence in a context, where they were not recognized as refugees but as tourists or illegal migrants.

5

The Collective Memory of Being in Transit in Turkey

In her contribution to the edited volume *Iranian Refugees and Exiles since Khomeini*, Janet Bauer records a poem by an anonymous Iranian refugee, which she states was widely circulated at the time: "and my hidden lover on the other side of the mountain range / Is awaiting the revelry / and I am here with the backpack of a wounded generation / I am waiting for her / she is my hopes and dreams / and Istanbul is the pain and depth of our separated love."[1]

Turkey has a distinguished place in the memories of Iranian refugees. Both the refugees who passed through Turkey and the refugees who have used different paths to reach Western countries have something to say about being in transit in Turkey. It is true that the Iranian refugees of the 1980s carried their, both enabling and disabling, baggage of experiences with them. However, it was also representations of Turkey accompanying them that seemed to foreshadow the conditions of their life in transit. This chapter reviews the meaning of living in Turkey as a refugee for Iranians through literary texts and films that were both the products of these representations and used in their reproduction.

"Why Did We Come Here?"

The majority of the refugees I interviewed assured me that it was quite easy to find refugees who had taken the Turkey route. However, finding such people was not as easy as it seemed to be. Being highly dependent on my interviewees, waiting for return calls tempted me to find alternative ways, such as strolling in the neighborhoods where Iranians lived or worked, which provided additional insight into the Iranian refugees' general perspective on Turkey.

It was hard to find such particular neighborhoods in Cologne, but Malmö and Stockholm were proper for such trials. There were Iranian supermarkets, butchers, bakeries, and several boutiques with Iranian names in Möllevångsgatan, Malmö. Some Iranians even called the neighborhood as "Malevan"'s-gatan—*malevan* meaning sailor in Persian. In Stockholm, a big shopping mall in Kista, in the north-east of the city, was known as a place where Iranians spent time especially in and around the Iranian restaurant Saffron. There was also an Iranian shop called Mahan selling literally everything coming from Iran: music albums, cheese, pickles, rice, biscuits, chewing gums, and even canned chickpeas. Mahan was in Rinkeby, the easternmost part of north Stockholm, where mostly Africans and later on Iraqis lived. Strolling in those neighborhoods might not have provided acquaintances for more interviewees, but provided insight into what people, particularly those who had not passed from Turkey, thought of passing through Turkey.

The people who had not passed through Turkey on their route to Sweden frequently responded to the question of whether they had used Turkey as a transit route by saying "unfortunately" (*moteasefaneh*), to be followed by "or fortunately" (*shayad ham khoshbakhtaneh*). The first answer was given for the sake of politeness as they would not be able to help, but the latter would follow to highlight that they felt fortunate not to have gone through Turkey. This short answer summarized the Iranian refugees' general approach to the idea of being in transit in Turkey. Turkey is used as a signifier of tough experiences by some of the refugees I talked to, especially by those who did not use the route, and in some literary texts with reference to this collective memory of the Iranian refugees. Mehri Yalfani's novel *Afsaneh's Moon* is an example of such literature. Yalfani narrates the story of four young Iranians (Afsaneh, Ramin, Bahram, and Negar) whose lives are intertwined in Canada.[2] It is a love story among those four people set in Canada; however, as Negar recounts her past, we learn that Negar and Ramin had been transit migrants in Turkey on their way to Canada:

> I talked about life in Turkey, where I was depressed and wanted to go back to Iran. I cried night and day and made Ramin sick of me. I called my parents and told them I wanted to return. … Life in Turkey was so terrible that sometimes I was tempted to throw myself out of the hotel window. I wasn't ready for *that kind of life*.[3] (Emphasis mine)

Although Negar asserts these words in the first part of the novel, it is not possible to find a clue of what "that kind of life" was in the next hundred pages of the novel. On page 135 we learn that she was not happy with the hotel, the people, or the Iranians living there from her dialogue with Ramin:

> It was a year since they had left Iran. They were still in Turkey and could not find a way to enter a European country or Canada. Ramin liked the idea of Canada, Negar still wasn't happy about leaving Iran. She was sullen most of the time, not eating meals, complaining.
>
> "Why did we come here?"
>
> "You know better than me. We had to." "I was very young. I knew nothing." ... "You wanted to marry me." ... "But this life, this disgusting hotel, these people, these Iranians! I want to go back. I'll die here. I miss Maman and Baba. I want to see Siamak."
>
> He had hidden Siamak's execution from her, suffered his death alone without talking about it to anyone, for fear the news would reach Negar. ... "You should be strong. For Siamek's sake you should be strong. He wanted you to leave Iran, to live in peace and study."
>
> *"I can't. I'm not made for this kind of life."*
>
> "When we get to Canada, all these hardships will be over. I promise you." ...
>
> *"I'll be dead before we get to Canada."*[4] (Emphasis mine)

These quoted parts are the only references in the novel to their lives as transit migrants in Turkey. Although in this second part the causes of Negar's sullenness are more explicit, yet we have only access to the objects of her feeling. It's the life, the "disgusting hotel," the people, and the Iranians that bother her. However, we still do not know *how* they rendered her life so unbearable. Perhaps, Yalfani does not feel the necessity of telling more. The phrase of "life in Turkey" is such a strong signifier that it connotes a set of experiences familiar to those who share the collective memory of being in transit in Turkey. Accordingly, the two objects of her suffering, the hotel and the Iranians around, are the key words of transit migrants' narratives.

Corruption and insecurity were the main themes of Iranian refugees' narratives on Turkey. Apart from the opportunities of education in the Western European countries, it was mainly the sense of being vulnerable to exploitation by the people who knew their situation that rendered them reluctant to even think of staying in Turkey. Despite its frequent statement, no instance of exploitation by local people, but police harassment for money, was repeatedly reported. Furthermore, the inability of calculating the next step in their journey, discussed in Chapter 2, weighed on them. Most of the time, the inability to assess the next step impelled the transit migrants to save more money than it was necessary, which deteriorated their life standards further. One of the interviewees, Sima, who had left Iran in the winter of 1985 at the age of seventeen with her cousin who was a few years older than her, said they had only eaten bread and *Rama*, a brand of margarine, for a couple of months as they had a common budget and her cousin was trying to save money. She stated that she had enough money to live a better life, but the incalculability of conditions had impelled her cousin to save and she could not object her.[5] Excess saving was not the only reason of deprivation. A majority of migrants were literally deprived of money the longer they stayed in Turkey. Whether they had money or not, most of the transit migrants found it necessary to save money, so they stayed in cheap hotels, which brought them together with other Iranians of different life worlds in terms of class and political opinion, as demonstrated in the previous chapters.

"Aksaray Is a Swamp"

Hotels are the main settings of refugee narratives and are recalled as sources of both grief and opportunity, just like what Aksaray as a neighborhood and Turkey as a transit country connote. Most of the refugees who had stayed in Istanbul had at least spent their first night in Aksaray or Laleli hotels. In the following days, according to their budget and the duration of their stay, they had rented a house or continued to live in Aksaray/Laleli hotels. Abbas Kazerooni's novel, *The Little Man*, claiming to be based on a true story, narrates how the Iranians found those hotels.[6]

The novel narrates the story of a seven-year-old boy (Kazerooni) who had lived in Istanbul as a transit migrant on his own. His story involves many shared attributes with other accounts of transit migrant experiences in Turkey, such as eating one meal a day, exchanging money on a daily basis as currency rates differed each day, and being accompanied by a taxi driver to find a cheap hotel. Given a list of cheap hotels at the airport by the man who was supposed to take care of him, "the little man" gets on a taxi and goes to check hotel prices. Telling him that there are many Iranians in Turkey, the taxi driver states that "the hotels—most Iranians come with similar list—these hotels are famous in Istanbul for Iranians. Taxi drivers know them very good."[7] None of the refugees I spoke with had a list of hotels when they arrived in Turkey, yet it was those hotels that were "famous in Istanbul for Iranians" in which they had settled in, and in most cases, taxi drivers had led them to those hotels. The others had either been given the name of a hotel by their smuggler or simply looked for a cheap hotel when they got off the bus at its last stop near Aksaray. Aksaray and its "famous for Iranians" hotels played an important part in the lives of transit migrants who were trying to leave Turkey for Western countries.

Laleli and Aksaray are two adjacent neighborhoods of Istanbul known as a center of trade and tourism. A prominent historian of architecture, Doğan Kuban, defined contemporary Aksaray as a *transit* space. Kuban argued the neighborhood is deprived of any in-city attributes due to the high number of underpasses and overpasses.[8] Before the late 1950s, the neighborhood was partially residential with a number of stores around Aksaray Square and a bazaar, which rendered it more dynamic than its eastern neighbor, Laleli.[9] Çağlar Keyder describes Laleli of that time as a "profoundly local world," where residents and shopkeepers were acquainted with each other.[10] During the government of the Democrat Party (1950–60), Prime Minister Menderes's endeavor at urban engineering resulted in the demolition of Aksaray and Beyazıt Squares (on the east and west sides of Laleli) and the construction of huge traffic circles in their place.[11] As the neighborhood lost its residential characteristics gradually, given its geographical proximity to the historical sites of the old city, the apartments in the neighborhood were converted into hotels especially for tourists on a limited budget.[12] In the 1980s, Laleli and Aksaray had completely been transformed into centers of informal commerce and tourism.

The opportunity of finding cheap accommodation and even a small amount of income within the circle of the informal economy has turned the neighborhood into an attraction point for migrants of various ethnicities. Because of its being home to many Iranians, Bangladeshis, Afghans, and Africans, as well as internally displaced Kurds, Behzad Yaghmaian calls

Aksaray a "migrant city within the larger metropolis of Istanbul."[13] Those hotels lost their "old role" in the 1990s with Turkey's stricter border controls.[14] However, the perception of Aksaray as the center of Istanbul and a key to the Western countries is hardly contestable for Iranians even today.

Aksaray has evolved to be a central part of Istanbul's representation for Iranians. For example, in a 2005 Iranian movie, *Aquarium*, a young racing driver gets on a bus to Istanbul to arrange his migration to the United States.[15] In this popular movie shown in Iranian movie theatres, there is no explicit reference to the young man's first destination until he is given the address of a hotel by phone. The man in the lobby says: "Write please, Aksaray." We don't even hear the rest of the address—as there is no need—and Aksaray is pronounced so loud that is impossible to miss. Being such a frequently referenced neighborhood, it signifies the center of the city, whatever that center may connote. It may represent the lack of security in Istanbul, as your purse can be grabbed the very moment that you put your step there[16] or used as an example of "rich neighborhoods where rich people dine in restaurants in front of which the poor beg."[17] The content of these statements is not relevant as Aksaray is miles away from being a rich neighborhood. It is the neighborhood's central place in the imagination of Turkey that gives an authority to the narrator who utters its name. Mentioning Aksaray evokes the meaning that the popular new phrase "if you know, you know" carries.

A majority of the interviewed refugees had stayed in Aksaray or Laleli hotels at least in their first days in Turkey. Many had heard the neighborhood's reputation already when they were in Iran. Sima said, "Istanbul was the escape hatch," while Sohrab stressed he had heard in Iran that it was only enough to step in Aksaray to make your way to the West. Aksaray was either a trampoline[18] or a hole that you got stuck in[19] for the transit migrants of Istanbul. Likewise, a human smuggler had told Yaghmaian that, "Aksaray is like a swamp: once in it, you cannot escape it."[20] Despite all the negative connotations of the neighborhood and its distrustful atmosphere, which former transit migrants frequently stressed, the main source of that distrustfulness, namely the Iranians' and smugglers' presence there, was at the same time a reason for the neighborhood's being a center of attraction for Iranian transit migrants. All the refugees interviewed had spent a great amount of their time in Aksaray hotels even after they moved to other parts of Istanbul. For example, Said, who after changing two hotels (Hotel Dünya in Taksim and Hotel Baran in Aksaray) had moved to a much more cheaper hotel in Taksim (Hotel Sivas), stated that every other day he would visit Hotel Dünya and stroll on the Aksaray streets. Khosrow had moved to a shared apartment with other waiting Iranians in Sarıyer; yet every day he had visited either Taksim or Aksaray hotels' lobbies. Mahrou used to visit two different smugglers in their hotels in Aksaray every week to compare conditions and price. The party professionals mentioned earlier, Hooman and Farhad, visited those hotels to meet with their comrades who had recently arrived. Therefore, Aksaray was not only a source of cheap accommodation for Iranian transit migrants but also a source of information. Its latter role was much more important for the Iranian transit migrants of the 1980s. Shahram Khosravi narrates similar experiences in Karachi, where a so-called migration market was established at the hotel lobbies and coffeehouses next to the hotels where smugglers, dealers, and newly arrived refugees would meet. As he points out, these nodes exist in many big cities on refugees' transit routes.[21]

In a world before cellphones and social media, the interviewees stressed that they had "gathered information" on the streets as a main activity on a daily basis. Going back to the classifications according to political affiliations in Chapters 2 and 3, it was mostly militants, and not professionals or sympathizers, who had not made travel plans before leaving Iran. Some had to leave as soon as they had been able as they had been told that they would be arrested in a short period of time and the others mostly did not know where was "better." Furthermore, leaving Iran was sufficient for most of the militants who wanted to pursue their political activities and thought that a regime change back home was near. The refugees interviewed, especially the militants, had mostly used smugglers in their flight from Iran. For the rest of their journey, they depended on the information that they gathered themselves on Aksaray streets or in hotel lobbies.

Nevertheless, it was not possible to attain coherent information from the streets and hotel lobbies. For the people whose destination was the United States, the International Catholic Migration Commission (ICMC) was the main address. However, the United States was not the preferred destination of any of the refugees I interviewed. This reluctance toward seeking asylum in the United States stemmed primarily from the geographical remoteness of the

United States. The same reason was frequently given for reluctance to go to Canada. Moreover, from the perception of leftist militants, the United States was a capitalist, imperialist state. Some leftist militants even stated that they had argued against US capitalism in the ICMC office and left the office without filling out the application. For the people who wanted to continue their journey to the Western European countries, there were more than one address and thus information was much more diversified. The most popular route until the second half of the 1980s was getting a transit visa for East Germany and then getting to the western side or taking a train to Sweden. But, none of the routes was without risk, so it was crucial to update the gathered information regularly. Plans were made in line with the general knowledge gathered in the Aksaray lobbies and modified in accordance with the updated information. Adaptation to altered conditions was vital for being able to keep track of the available travel routes. Hence, the incalculability of the next step, which had haunted the transit migrants since their flight from Iran, continued to be the main source of their grievance in Turkey.

Azadeh's and Behrouz's travel plans exemplify the extent of modifications in action. Fleeing Iran in 1983, Azadeh and her husband Behrouz had passports issued in the Pahlavi era that were legally invalid, but still accepted in the Western European countries. They were among the few people who had information about several Western countries, as both had studied in Sweden before revolution. Azadeh had lived in London for a short period as well. Due to their education in Sweden, they even had residence permits, which were no longer valid. Nevertheless, despite these perceived advantages they were not able to plan their next step better than the others. Sitting in a café at the Cultural Center of Stockholm (Kulturhusset) in 2007, Azadeh and Behrouz started to describe their plans in 1983 as such:

> The first thing that came to our minds was to change those dates and go with those dates [of the invalid Swedish visa]. When we changed the dates, it was quite obvious that they had been changed, our work wasn't really professional. Then we thought it wouldn't work, so let's go for a visa from somewhere else, for example, East Germany. East Germany was giving visas easily at that period; it didn't bother whether your passport was official or not official. They did this to put pressure on Western countries, in particular on Sweden. It was a politics of obstinacy. We went to Ankara and got our

visa. Then, we receded, they told us that it is hard there, that entering Sweden from there would be problematic.[22]

Azadeh stressed that it was ghastly (*vahshatnak*) to think about various routes all the time. It was the repetition of the same words: making a plan, changing it, and later returning to the former plan, which had rendered the discussion on routes unbearable. After receding from going to East Germany they took a Syrian visa from a smuggler and then got back to their first idea of using their invalid residence permit. For reaching Sweden, they flew to Yugoslavia and changed planes to Copenhagen.

Their story is a good example of the cacophony caused by the advice given in the lobbies of Aksaray hotels. The characters in the widely referenced movie, *The Guests of Hotel Astoria*, were also subject to such frequent modification of journey plans. The main characters of the movie, Pouri and her husband Karim, attempt to get a visa for the Netherlands with an invitation sent by Karim's brother, who lives there. After being rejected by the Dutch consulate, without being delivered with an explanation, they begin to "gather information" from other transit migrants sitting in the lobby. That's how they are introduced to a Turkish smuggler called Ali, who advises them to go to the Cuban consulate in Ankara and get a one-week visa. He promises to buy a ticket for Cuba that stops in Amsterdam where they would have enough time to claim asylum. Pouri and Karim act according to Ali's advice and succeed in arriving at the Amsterdam Airport. However, after seeking asylum officially, they are deported to Turkey without being given any information. Their flight plans are modified each day, according to the latest information available. Mrs. Ziai, an Iranian transit migrant sitting in the lobby of Hotel Astoria, tells the migration story of one of her acquaintances. The woman had escaped through the Pakistan route and got pregnant in Karachi. When her baby was seven months old, she got a tourist visa for Britain and delivered her baby there. Thus, the baby was a citizen of Britain and her parents were given permanent residence permit there. Being assured by this story, Pouri, who became pregnant in Istanbul, decides to give birth to her baby in the United States to a get residence permit there. She gets a visa for the United States with a forged Italian passport. However, when she arrives there, she learns that her claim has no legal basis.

"Gathering information" on the streets and lobbies involved both the routes that could be employed to reach the destination desired and the opportunities that asylum-granting countries provided. This was another complex axis. Most of the transit migrants in Istanbul had not traveled abroad before and did not have enough information to choose a destination. Choices were many. Canada, Sweden, and the Netherlands were among the most favorite destinations.[23] Various arguments were presented in favor of some destination countries. *The Guests of Hotel Astoria* presents a scene that underlines the absurdity of some of the assessments in this aspect. While all the guests of Hotel Astoria are sitting in the lobby having drinks and talking about their travel plans, Mr. Ziai comments on every country expressed. Pouri and Karim say that they are trying to go to the Netherlands and Ziai states that in the Netherlands, "they have roses [*gol-e mohammadi*] growing out of ice in the middle of the winter." His comment on France is much more detailed: "In France they have everything. It is true that the French are known best for their art and literature, but they are far ahead in everything compared to the rest. Cheese? Would you believe me if I told you French have 1700 kinds of cheese?"

"One Does Not Remember Alone": *The Guests of Hotel Astoria*

The publicity booklet of the film describes Hotel Astoria as such:

> *Hotel Astoria* is a small guesthouse in Istanbul where Iranians who have fled their homeland are residing while waiting to find refuge somewhere in Europe or America. This entrepot is used by an Iranian smuggler for stockpiling his human merchandise until it is dispatched to its final destination. It is the focal point of the shortlived hopes and the endless cares of people who are prepared to face any hardship and alienation. These travelers have packed their bags and set out without knowing who will be their host in the end. They have left behind the inferno of "Khomeini" while before them lies a foreign world about which they are completely uninformed.[24]

The film reifies the aura of transit migration narrated by Iranian refugees of the era. However, its impact on the Iranian refugee community once in transit in Turkey goes beyond that. Its widespread circulation among the refugee community gives it its particular place in the collective memory of being in transit in Turkey. In *Visual Methodologies*, Gillan Rose points to three sites at which the meaning of an image are made.[25] These are the sites of its production, the site of the image itself, and the sites of its audiences. I have referred to many scenes of this movie in previous chapters. *The Guests of Hotel Astoria* is not a documentary; however, its characters, plot, and dialogues are based on real life stories and has visualized the experience of being in transit in Turkey. The sites I will discuss in this chapter are the sites of its production and its audience, which are impactful to understand its significance.

My story of having access to the film exemplifies the site of its audience. The first time I heard about the film was in Malmö, Sweden, where Hossein (Mahnaz's husband) advised me to watch the movie to understand the atmosphere of those years. In every other interview the movie was recounted as a representation of transit life in Turkey. Traveling to Stockholm, I was repeatedly advised to watch the film, which I could not find in any of the multimedia shops I visited. Azadeh and Behrouz gave me the name of an Iranian publisher in Stockholm with whom, by coincidence, I had an appointment the very same day. He, Said, gave me the address of a bookstore, Ferdowsi, selling books on Iran and books by Iranian authors collected from various countries, mostly in Persian and English, as well as movies and music albums in Persian. However, they had run out of the copies of *The Guests of Hotel Astoria*. Finally, I copied Said's own DVD and watched it the very same evening with Khosrow. Therefore, the process of having access to the movie was totally collective.[26]

Fifteen years after this first acquaintance with the movie, while finalizing this book in the Netherlands, I finally met the director Allamezadeh in his house where we talked about the production of the movie and his own story of passing through Turkey as a transit refugee. Living as a political refugee in the Netherlands since 1983, Allamezadeh was imprisoned in the Pahlavi era along with other prominent political intellectuals and spent five years in jail until he was freed in 1978 with the start of the revolutionary period.[27]

Passing through a similar route as of Said's narrated in this book, Allamezadeh and Nassim Khaksar, a prominent Iranian writer, arrive in Turkey in 1983. They both carried semi-forged passports. Allamezadeh's passport was his real passport with a fake sticker and stamps, and Khaksar's passport belonged to someone else. Using the advantage of being older than many other activists, they pretended to be on a mission of looking for Allamezadeh's brother lost in the Iran-Iraq war in Turkey on their way to Istanbul. Once in Istanbul, they settled in a hotel similar to the depicted Hotel Astoria and searched for ways of leaving to Europe. Allamezadeh stayed in Istanbul only for three months but his short stay bears many similarities with the experiences of other transit refugees I interviewed before. In addition to using a similar route and ending up in a similar hotel, he had to do the *giriş-çıkış* (literally enter-exit) by traveling to Bulgaria to renew his three-month visa, did not have a clear plan of where to go even though he did not want to go to France, which was the center of Iranian political opposition, and ended up in Netherlands as they were able to get a visa on their semi-forged passports. While initially he did not want to apply for asylum, in the end, he kept his asylum passport for eleven years after settling in the Netherlands.[28] He made *The Guests of Hotel Astoria* in 1989, six years after his stay in Turkey as a transit migrant.

The movie was not only an interpretation of Allamezadeh's experience of being in transit in Turkey but could also be seen as his performance as an exilic filmmaker. Naficy argues that the selection of the cast, scenes, and the cut makes the filmmakers' explicit presence unnecessary in the movie to render it the performance of the filmmaker's identity.[29] According to the writer, "To perform by making films is to remember, to memorialize yourself (and your community), and to remind others that you were there—even if you were in disguise."[30]

Hamid Naficy's study of exilic and diasporic films[31] not only tells the problems faced in the distribution of films made in exile, but also discusses the previously cited inter-Iranian mistrust in exile, linking the two sites at stake: the production and the audience(s). Naficy provides an overview of Iranian exilic and diasporic filmmaking. In his 2001 book, he states that Iranian filmmakers have produced the greatest number of films (one-third) among other filmmakers from sixteen Middle Eastern and African countries living abroad mostly in Europe and North America.[32] However, their productivity has not led to the formation of a collectivity. Unlike Black and Asian film collectives in Britain and North African, South Asian, East Asian, and Caribbean filmmakers in France, Iranians have not created a formal, collective organization to deal with the production and distribution of their films.[33] Both the reasons for such a lack of collective action among the Iranian filmmakers and the result of this lack are useful for our analysis of the Iranian transit migrants of the 1980s.

Naficy indicates the difference between exiles from postcolonial countries and Iranians with respect to their experiences of exile. He argues that émigrés from formerly colonized states are familiar with the language and the culture of their colonizers and have a shared experience of colonialism, which emanates a collective identity among them, whereas Iranians have no experience of direct colonialism, but a tug of war first between Britain and Russia and second between the United States and the USSR.[34] The interventions of the imperialist states, the factional politics of the revolutionary era, and the Islamic regime's operations abroad have led to "a deep sense of deep paranoia, conspiracy thinking, and ambivalence, which compounded the general mistrust that comes with political exile." [35] The highly factional exilic politics had added up to those historical experiences of mistrust and has resulted in the aversion of collective action.

Apart from religious minorities and the supporters of the former regime, most of the exiles have been sent into exile as a result of the very revolution they fought for. This consolidates the exile's sense of mistrust toward their fellow citizens. This distinct exilic condition enlightens Negar's complaint of "these Iranians" in Yalfani's novel *Afsaneh's Moon* and the interviewed refugees' frequent statements on lack of communication among the transit migrants on the road and in Turkey.

When we take the site of the audiences, we see that the reverse of production criteria is in force. While the production is highly independent and individual, the target population is highly communal. Here the difference between postcolonial émigrés and Iranian exiles come into force again. While the former have greater access to the host country's language and mostly produce in that language, enabling their products even to be bestsellers, the latter mainly write and shoot films in Persian casting Iranian actors, and their products have access only to "exile outlets" where books on Iran or by Iranians, groceries from Iran, and Persian music are marketed (such as Ferdowsi Bookstore or Mahan Supermarket in Stockholm).[36] This communal consumption of exilic films renders them instrumental in the formation of a collective memory of exiles.

The term "collective memory" does not indicate that groups remember the very same things. However, it detaches memory from the pure realm of psychology, stressing the impact of social conditions and social relations on its formation. In his review of Maurice Halbwachs' *The Collective Memory*, Paul Ricoeur states that the text stresses the necessity of others for remembering.[37] Put in aphoristic terms, according to Halbwachs, "one does not remember alone."[38] This is both a reference to the social texture of the remembered experience and to its recollection afterward. Hence, memory is not a direct product of sensual experiences assessed in the physiology of the brain. It is always in making through communication with the "outer world," and it is alive as long as this communication continues.[39] Therefore, we can take *The Guests of Hotel Astoria* as functional in inflaming the political refugees' flight memories. By its very "tangible" form, the movie provides political refugees a medium of discussion or an opportunity to take position, which is functional in sustaining the collective "refugee subjectivity."

Said's account of his feelings when he first watched the movie mentioned in Chapter 3 illuminates this effect. The movie portrays a one-night affair between Pouri and a leftist militant staying at Hotel Astoria when Pouri's husband, Karim, is in Ankara applying for a visa for Cuba. Said stated that such a relationship had been inconceivable for him when he watched the movie the first time. "We were idealist," he said. "How could he have an affair with a married woman?"[40] His account rendered his communication with the movie visible. He compared himself with the leftist militant in the movie, who, according to him (at that time), had not behaved properly in terms of the revolutionary rules of conduct or (political) morality, discussed in Chapter 3.

During the eight months that he had spent between Taksim and Aksaray, he had not thought of anything except political struggle. He got in touch with the headquarters of his organization in France, which was depicted as the destination country of the leftist militant in the movie as well, in order to be introduced to his comrades in Turkey and engage in propaganda activities with them. He worked in copying propaganda leaflets delivered from France and distributing them among Iranian tourists mostly around the Blue Mosque and Hagia Sophia. He had started to think of not traveling to France and of going to Iraq instead to struggle against the regime. As a leftist militant, whose life was shaped by politics, engaging in an extramarital relationship, as shown in the movie, was inconceivable for him.

It is true that Turkey does not invoke positive memories for a great number of Iranian refugees. However, constituting the first step of a successful journey, all interviewed refugees had succeeded in getting asylum in Sweden or Germany, this "stop" embodied opportunities as much as suffering. Despite the lack of unity among the Iranian transit migrants due to the factional politics before and after the revolution, and the possibility of agents infiltrating their gatherings, spontaneous gatherings in the hotel lobbies and on Aksaray streets functioned as sources of information for the transit migrants who did not have any premade flight plan. Therefore, first being a necessity, being in Aksaray had evolved into a chosen action by refugees due to the very fact of the opportunities generated by the very people who were there out of necessity.

Concluding Remarks

This book depicts the experiences of Iranian refugees as they transited through Turkey following the 1979 revolution. It also closely examines their interactions with Turkey's sociopolitical environment and the significant influence of certain works and political ideologies on their perspectives and convictions. Through the examination of postrevolution Iranian transit refugees, a range of significant themes have been explored. These include the interactions between a host country's political dynamics and the identities of incoming refugees, the inefficiency of the international asylum system not only to protect and cater to the needs of the people in search of a safer space, but also in employing clear measures to identify those in need of international protection. Furthermore, the discrepancy between the homogenizing discourse on refugees and their actual diversity was explored by detailing refugees' identity formation and performativity as a survival strategy, the complex negotiation of womanhood during transit, and the profound influence of social memory and imagination in shaping both the lived experiences of refugees and their narratives.

As highlighted in prior sections, neither exile nor passing through Aksaray were isolated events; they were processes with roots that extended beyond their initiation in Turkey. Similarly, the political refugee identity could transcend EU citizenship or be acquired after fleeing. This does not imply that everything remains in a state of flux or that it is an insurmountable challenge to identify individuals with well-founded asylum claims. Instead, it underscores the necessity of adopting an intersectional perspective, one cultivated through a deep understanding of the prevailing social, economic, and political dynamics of the era. Furthermore, the approach to addressing the "refugee issue" must be reoriented, shifting the focus toward global inequalities and the paradox of borders that ease the functioning of global supply chains but restrict the movement of people.

In this concluding chapter, I will take a closer look at three issues that have previously appeared in the book. These discussions aim to shed light on the limitations of the prevailing approach and offer alternative perspectives. These issues involve the shift in the interpretation of the concept of autonomy when applied to refugees, the tendency to isolate refugees as a categorically distinct group, and transit migration as a challenging category to the existing asylum system. These issues are interconnected and stem from a common perspective that often confuses the effect with the cause.

Autonomy

Working as an interpreter for a refugee settlement organization, I have heard many bisexual asylum seekers or lesbians being asked why they had to come out if they could pass as straight. Baha'i and Christian converts were often queried about their decision to not conceal their conversion, especially when they were aware that doing so could endanger their lives. Therefore, while the fundamental basis of refugee status primarily centers on the fear of persecution due to factors such as race, religion, nationality, and affiliation with a specific social group, or political beliefs, in practice, refugees' awareness of the circumstances surrounding this persecution is often utilized to discredit the legitimacy of their asylum claims. The established asylum system, comprising national authorities and the UNHCR, fosters an environment in which individuals are encouraged to conceal their nonnormative or rebellious attributes to prevent persecution. Knowing the circumstances and not living in hiding because of the threat of persecution may, in fact, render you ineligible for legal protection.

A central argument explored in this book asserts that the hegemonic discourse on refugees negates their agency by exposing them to various litmus tests assessing the degree of choice in each aspect of their lives. As demonstrated in Chapter 3, expressing a preference for their destination is frequently met with resistance and skepticism regarding the sincerity of their asylum claims. Having and sharing the multiple reasons of leaving their country of origin can lead to the rejection of their asylum application. They can be labeled as "asylum shoppers" due to their unwillingness to stay in the first country of asylum. In short, asylum regulations penalize refugees' autonomy. The attack on refugees' autonomy has two aspects. On the one hand, as discussed in Chapter 1, flexible and pragmatic state-security-centered policies severe the precarious life conditions of refugees practically restricting their autonomy further. On the other hand, the limited areas where refugees assert their autonomy are met with skepticism and work to their detriment. The accounts of Iranian refugees making their way through Turkey following the 1979 revolution, a refugee group leaving a country in the midst of a turmoil of counterrevolution and war, a scenario that closely matches the conventional refugee archetype, contradicts the assumption that authenticity of asylum claims is synonymous with passivity and dependence.

People do not migrate in a vacuum but navigate through openings that are shaped by the current state of balance of forces. The recent historical shifts in policies related to the reception of migrants and border fortifications, as explored in this book, exemplify that when legal doors are sealed off, new pathways emerge. Even though nation-states assert their authority over regulating border crossings, many borders remain permeable for local residents and people and goods they choose to transport. The decisions refugees give on the route they choose, their destination country, or even the hotel they stay in temporarily are not made in a vacuum either. We all walk on a spectrum between choice and compulsion. The interplay between our individual agency and the societal structures shapes our lives. This holds true for refugees as well. However, even though we all recognize the inadequacy of reducing the complex relationship between free will and compulsion to a simplistic equation within our own lives, refugees are held to different standards.

Refugees as a Categorical Group

Refugees are often depicted in a simplified and stereotypical manner, a parallel drawn by Liisa Malkki to an "essentialized, anthropological tribe."[1] This results in the use of broad, generic terms like "the refugee identity," "the refugee experience," "the refugee mentality," and "the refugee psychology,"[2] which overlook their diversity. The term "refugee crisis," frequently employed since 2015, can be included in this category of oversimplifications.

Shahram Khosravi, himself an Iranian refugee from the 1980s, shares his observations in his work *"Illegal" Traveller: An Auto-Ethnography of Borders*, where he recounts an incident involving a lawyer representing a rejected asylum seeker, a young Kurdish woman in her early twenties. The lawyer had offered unsolicited comments on the woman's appearance, advising her to "wipe off her makeup and change from her miniskirt into jeans, because in her current condition 'she did not look like a refugee.'"[3] A similar mindset becomes evident when refugees are observed using smartphones or wearing branded clothing. The better their phones' quality, the more likely their status as a refugee is called into question, particularly in media commentaries or in casual, everyday conversations. The international asylum system is designed to respond to the specific consequences of social and political catastrophes on individuals and therefore claims to take each case separately demanding individual evidence of persecution risk. However, paradoxically, the moment people apply for asylum, their individual histories, including their class background, political convictions, or lifestyle, seem to be erased.

This erasure of individuality has many aspects. Edward Said, cited in Chapter 3, stated that the word refugee suggests "large herds of innocent and bewildered people requiring urgent international assistance."[4] Barbara Harrell-Bond, the founder of the Refugee Studies Center in Oxford University, also criticized this approach of taking refugees as undifferentiated masses, as if they "no longer comprise groups of individuals with personal histories, skills and aspirations, with varying capacities for strategic planning and decision-making, with different human needs or feelings such as hope, joy, despair and pain."[5] This perception of "uncountable," "excess", or "mass exodus" requires further unpacking.

This deindividualization of refugees is further accentuated by the images captured of them crammed in the back of trucks, squeezed onto boats, and left waiting in overcrowded cellars, among others. Humanitarian campaigns contribute to this narrative as well. Charity is based on perceiving the refugees as pure human beings, with no "contaminating" history. This approach extracts the history and politics embedded in their sufferings, rendering it a natural outcome of being a refugee. Plight is seen as a natural result of dislocation.

Neither the ineptness of the asylum system nor violent border regimes, particularly of the Global North, are taken as responsible. The experiences of refugees are depoliticized and dehistoricized.[6]

As Malkki argues, this act of erasing the refugees' histories also infantilizes them. The very moment they pass the borders of the country to which they are believed to belong, everything that has formed their identity is assumed to be lost.[7] Harrell-Bond points to publications of some humanitarian institutions, including the UNHCR, with its claim to give voice to refugees, to demonstrate this further. She argues that by overlooking language barriers and cultural differences, they present a childlike image of refugees, who use "simply worded, semantically flat expressions."[8] This picture of the pure, childlike, and helpless refugee, which at times refugees benefit from, is also sustained by juxtaposing it to the "other" refugee: the *bad* refugee that is thankless, ungrateful, cheating, and aggressive.[9]

The deindividualization of refugees coupled with the accompanying imagery described earlier fosters a narrative that there is an overwhelming number of refugees at present, exceeding the capacity of receiving countries. However, as it has been detailed throughout the book, it is not the number of refugees that shape the responses of states or international organizations. From the different responses Bulgarian and Kurdish refugees received in Turkey in the late 1980s to early 1990s explored in Chapter 1, to current attitudes toward African, Syrian, or Ukrainian refugees in the world, and the current experiences of Syrians and Afghans in Turkey, which will be detailed in the following epilogue, the "refugee crisis" is not about the number of refugees but the responding states' selective support toward the populations in move. As Khalid Koser also argues, there are not "too many asylum seekers," but more people arriving than states are willing to accept.[10] Therefore, the focus on the excessiveness of refugees not only distorts the reality, but also obscures the root causes of the problem. As I will discuss further in the epilogue, before Russia's war on Ukraine in 2022, there have been twenty-six million refugees in the world, 85 percent of whom were hosted in the countries of the Global South. Turkey, Jordan, Uganda, and Pakistan are the top four countries that host the largest number of refugees.[11] However, the panic-inducing news about arrival of refugees do not focus on the countries of the Global South but on the borders of the Global North.

The discussion on categorization of migrating people presented in this book is far from being only an academic debate either. Each day, people's reasons to leave their country of origin are delegitimized and tested by exposing them to various categories. On the one hand, undocumented people are criminalized by being labeled as illegal and people escaping horrid armed conflicts and its wider societal effects are seen as bogus refugees or *gelukszoeker* (fortune seeker) if they have not been directly involved in those conflicts. On the other hand, people's experiences of persecution are disregarded by either not seeing them a direct fit to the category as in "not gay enough" or its total opposite questioning whether they could "pass" as straight, as Muslim, as whatever the norm at stake is to avoid persecution. Stripping the problem from its political roots, migrating people are seen as a part of a technical debate and their struggles to pass borders or not being deported to avoid persecution are seen as mere legal matters. Instead of discussing the impact of global economic inequality, rise of political authoritarianism, neoliberal borders being porous for capital and commodities but rock hard for people of the Global South, and rising right-wing populism and racism in countries of destination, among others, we discuss who fits the existing legal framework to have basic rights in a territory.

Transit Migration as a Non-category

In the midst of this attack on the autonomy of people in move, the transit refugee category creates cracks in this hegemonic discourse. The stricter policies against the free movement of people are, the more people become transit migrants. The widely used description refers to transit migrants as "people who come to a country of destination with the intention of going to and staying in another country."[12] Not staying in the first country of asylum, which is a very common practice among transit refugees, highlights the existence of choice in refugees' flight plans. This is seen to be in contradiction with the conventional definition of the refugee as the person who has no other choice than to flee.

Özge Biner underlines that the term "transit migration" has been put into wider circulation with reports published by the International Organization of

Migration (IOM) in the 1990s. The IOM first started by publishing reports on transit migration involving Eastern European countries, such as Romania, Hungary, Bulgaria, Czech Republic, and Poland and later on adding the Russian Federation, Ukraine, and Turkey to the list. By the 2000s, the study of transit migration was extended to Egypt, Syria, Lebanon, and Yemen.[13] This coincides with the extension and fortification of European borders. Particularly with the Schengen treaty signed in 1995 rendering visa-free movement within European countries party to the agreement, the external borders of the EU got fortified. Formation of Frontex in 2005 as the main policing agent of these borders militarized the border control further.[14]

In Chapter 3, "'Their Categories and Ours': Politics of Differentiation," I discussed the inadequacy of the asylum system in recognizing refugees' actual reasons of flight contributing to the shift in their categorization at different junctures. In line with this argument, Aspasia Papadopoulou, a migration and asylum expert who currently serves as a UN policymaker on migration, described transit migration and smuggling as outcomes of the deficiencies of asylum policies in her article on transit migrants in Greece published just before Frontex was established.[15] The argument is that transit migration or irregular migration should not be seen as different types, but as different phases of migration. Temporary residence in the first host country is defined as a mechanism of negotiation with European structures of exclusion.[16] Elsewhere, discussing the migration-asylum nexus covered in Chapter 3, Papadopulou criticizes the established definition of transit migration that focuses on the transit migrants' intention of leaving to and settling in another country, by stating that such an intention might not exist at the beginning of the journey and that some migrants become transit migrants "by accident."[17] It is highlighted that transit migration is not a status, but a process that is negotiated in relation with the structural and individual factors.[18]

The category of transit migration is challenging to the hegemonic discourse on asylum and migration not only because it reveals a certain level of choice, but also because it is in fact a residual category or a non-category. People avoiding asylum application in the first country of asylum to be able to proceed to another country,[19] people not fitting the asylum framework identified in the 1951 Convention but are still in need of moving to another country, and people whose asylum claims have been rejected but are not in their country of origin can all be listed under the category of transit migrants. Thus, the very category of transit migrant points either to the inefficiency of the ideal categories to provide protection for the people who claim it or to the difficulties in having access to that protection.

However, the Iranian transit migrants and refugees of the 1980s mostly fit the criticized, conventional description of transit migration. That is, they fled to Turkey with the *intention* of going to some other country. It is true that the destination country and the route they would take were not thoroughly thought, but the intention was explicit. Only two out of the twenty-one refugees I interviewed considered settling in Turkey. These two were political militants who pursued political activities in Turkey, hoping that regime change in Iran would not take too long and they would return to Iran. Therefore, permanent settlement in Turkey was not seen as an option by any of the refugees I interviewed.

What's Home?

The UNHCR lists voluntary repatriation, resettlement, and integration as three solutions for refugees.[20] However, although repatriation is encouraged for the countries that are declared to be safe, examples refute this claim. The countries that are claimed to be safe continue to "produce" refugees, as the case of Afghanistan has shown for decades. The idea that "the best place for refugees is their country of origin" poses several issues, extending beyond overlooking the actual safety conditions in the country of origin. As the discussion on internal exile in Chapter 2, "When Does Exile Begin?", detailed, the fear of persecution that is essential to the definition of refugee refutes such a perception of peaceful belonging to the country of origin. In a similar vein, Liisa Malkki questions the portrayal of refugees as disoriented individuals trying to find their way in a foreign and consequently frightening country. She underlines that the refugee's own homeland can be just as frightening.[21] As demonstrated in Chapter 2, she suggests that "displacements occur precisely when one's own, accustomed society has become 'strange and frightening' because of war, massacres, political terror, or other forms of violence and uncertainty."[22]

Esmail Khoi, a prominent Iranian poet who passed away in exile in 2021, in his "What a Sense of Being Lost," underlined that he does not want to be a "bird of a rootless sigh," but a tree "that holds its umbrella on its head / and presses / its knowing roots / into the unquestioning earth."[23] This is not an exceptional reference to the "roots" of the refugee. Another prominent Iranian writer, Gholam-Hosein Sa'edi, who also passed away in exile in 1985, wrote about roots of refugee in his widely cited article "*Degardisi va Rahai-ye Avareh-ha*."[24]

> An *émigré* is hopeful. ... [He] takes vitamins and visits museums for the sake of maintaining his health and sanity. He is well integrated into the routine of life: he enjoys movies, wearing a tie and relaxing in a park. The *émigré* believes that he is deeply rooted and does not know that a pulled-out root will eventually rot, and cause the fall of even the haughtiest, largest tree.[25]
>
> An *avareh*, however, is a pessimist. He knows that he has been chopped up- not a portion of his body but a portion of his being. The *avareh* sees that his pulled out roots are rotting just as gangrene first blackens its victim's feet, works its way up his body and eventually, if not killing the patient, immobilizes him, uprootedness makes the *avareh* visibly see his own gradual death.[26]

These depictions are not confined to the realm of literature either. Richard Black, in his study on the fifty years of refugee studies, criticizes the policy-oriented researchers' uncritical employment of the term "refugee" in academic writings. He states that "indicating uprootedness and exile, it often implies a dependence on humanitarian intervention and a rupture of 'normal' social, economic and cultural relations."[27]

Perhaps it is primarily the belief of being rooted in the country in which one is born that needs to be questioned. It is this assumption that creates a problematic self out of the refugee. The refugee is a person who fears to live in their "own country," in the place that is thought to be the most suitable for them, the place to which it is assumed that they belong to. Therefore, they are seen to be "out of place"[28] and thus each act of solving the "problem" results in appointing the right place for the refugee.

Those "botanical metaphors"[29] of roots, being uprooted, rotten, or chopped, tend to naturalize the link between people and place, and render that relation unquestionable. Malkki starts with questioning this given relationship with reference to the critical literature on the formation of the nation (such as Geertz, Gellner, Giddens, and Hobsbawm).[30] As she argues, refugees are seen as a problem because they do not fit in the "national order of things." The naturalization of the territoriality of nation-states renders a refugee as a being "out of place" and thus ready for intervention. Furthermore, taking the refugee as a being who loses their identity when "uprooted" renders the refugee a being without history; thus the violence at home is left unseen although flight does not erase the traces of refugees' life at "home." Experiences of marginalized people, such as religious minorities and LGBTQI people, show that home is not always a safe place. The uncritical employment of concepts such as nation-state, nationality, borders, belonging, and even seeking refuge masks the given terminology's inability of generating fair and purposeful solutions.

In this book, I have used the term "refugee" to define the people leaving their countries due to well-founded fear of persecution. While this definition covers almost all Iranians who are the subject of this book, not everyone who has left their countries due to well-founded fear of persecution are given the legal protection that comes with the institutional recognition of the refugee status. Institutional recognition is not intrinsic to the definition of being a refugee, but fleeing due to threat of persecution is.

As we have seen throughout this book, even within a single, historically specific refugee community, such as the Iranian transit refugees in Turkey following the 1979 revolution, there exists a diversity in experiences, choices, class positions, aspirations, and exposure to threats. This diversity is shaped by their past and present experiences and their interactions with the social and political dynamics of the context they live. The disparities in how Bulgarian and Kurdish refugees were received in the late 1980s and early 1990s mentioned earlier, the differing terminology employed to characterize them, the vigilance of Iranian revolutionary leftists and Kurds regarding "forced repatriation" agreements in Turkey, the minors and youth escaping conscription, and women and LGBTQI individuals' lives under constant threat of gender-based oppression establish that we cannot talk about a single, uniform refugee experience.

We need to reorient the debate to focus on the inefficiencies of the asylum system and the incapability of nation-states to address the needs of millions of people while remembering how those policies have changed according to political dynamics and struggles of the time rather than contribute to myths around the number of refugees. It is the selective permeability of borders and increasing limitations on the mobility of people in the 21st century, rather than millions of people suspended and violated at borders that create a "crisis." Mobility of peoples predates national borders.

Epilogue: Turkey as a Transit Hub Today

As we have seen in the *Iranian Refugees in Transit*, the post-1979 Iranian refugees had ended up in a postcoup Turkey ruled by a nascent neoliberal regime. Democratic and political rights were suppressed, and Kurdish armed struggle was on its rise. A 1985 Amnesty International report on torture in Turkey recorded almost 180,000 people taken into custody for investigation during the first four years of this postcoup regime. Martial law was imposed in all major cities, with thousands participating in hunger strikes in prisons, and the state admitting the killing of 25 people under torture among 204 deaths in prison between September 1980 and March 1982.[1]

When I was writing these lines in November 2023, decades after this first mass wave of political refugees coming from a neighboring country, millions of Syrians escaping war had ended up in Turkey, ruled by another authoritarian, neoliberal regime. While in 1989, the estimate of political prisoners was 5,000 (of 50,000 prisoners),[2] in 2022 the number is estimated to be 45,000 to 60,000 (of 300,000 prisoners).[3] The rate of political prisoners to all prisoners was estimated to be 10 percent in 1989, while it rose to 15–20 percent in 2022. Building on one of the main arguments of the book, that is, the importance of the interplay between Turkey's sociopolitical dynamics and arriving refugees' identities on refugees' experiences, this epilogue expands the discussion to Turkey's current role in the international refugee regime and its impact on refugees' experiences.

According to the Ministry of Interior Presidency of Migration Management, the main center for migration affairs in Turkey, the biggest group of irregular migrants apprehended in Turkey between 2016 and 2023 comes from Afghanistan (half a million), to be followed by Pakistan, Syria, and Iraq.[4]

Applications from Afghans, Ukrainians, and Iraqis compose the majority of asylum applications in 2023.[5]

Syrians in Turkey

By the beginning of 2024, when *Iranian Refugees in Transit* was being finalized, there have been 3,200,000 Syrians under temporary protection in Turkey.[6] The temporary protection status covers Syrian citizens, refugees, and stateless persons coming from Syria since April 2011. Syrians, composing the biggest population of migrants in contemporary Turkey, are hard to be named as transit migrants anymore. However, according to the project director of the most comprehensive studies on Syrians in Turkey, the *Syrians Barometer Reports*,[7] Murat Erdoğan, more than half of Syrians want to leave Turkey for a third country and this figure is on rise.[8] Even though a majority of them have "temporary protection" status, a status that was created for dealing with the reality of Syrian refugees in Turkey in 2014, their stay in Turkey is no longer temporary. Together with Syrians who have residence permits and who got Turkish citizenship the number of Syrians living in Turkey amount to 4 million.[9]

Racism and hate speech targeting Syrians have turned into a mundane part of everyday life and political discourse in Turkey.[10] In times of crises such as the aftermath of the 2023 earthquake in Turkey or in moments of populist campaigns such as elections, the level of discriminatory discourse peaks.[11] Syrians were systematically accused of looting and theft in the earthquake zones that resulted in public lynching and police torture.[12] Amnesty International reports that Syrians in the earthquake zone were mistreated, insulted, and discriminated.[13] Taking into account that almost half of the Syrian population in Turkey lives in the earthquake zone exposes the gravity of these reports. Elections compose another moment that this collective hysteria against Syrians is articulated. In the last ten years, there have been four general elections and three presidency elections in Turkey. At each election, Syrians' fate becomes a key campaign issue. Speculations about millions of Syrians voting for the government party is followed by sharing of various plans of how to send them back to Syria. As I will elaborate later on, the governing party's position is slightly changing on this issue, while various segments of the opposition unite in their vehement discourse on "getting rid of" Syrians. While the far right parties build all their political campaign on deporting Syrians, the social democrats and parties on the left of the political spectrum suggest negotiations with the Assad regime and the EU for voluntary repatriation of refugees.[14] During campaigns for the last elections in May 2023, Erdoğan also expressed his commitment to the "safe and voluntary" repatriation of 1 million Syrians and fight against illegal migration.[15] However with 900,000 Syrian children born in Turkey in the last ten years,[16] millions working and studying in Turkey, relocation of Syrians is more a dystopian ideal than a realistic one.

The monthly report on hate speech in media by the Hrant Dink Association covering all national newspapers and 500 local papers in Turkey have repeatedly reported Syrians to be one of the top targets of hate speech together with Kurds, Armenians, Jews, and Greeks in Turkey between 2014 and 2019, when the last report was published.[17] According to 2019 report Syrians have been systematically associated with murder, theft, and sexual harassment, have been presented as potential criminals, have been associated with terrorism and security concerns, and have been presented to be responsible for the deteriorating economy and unemployment.[18] Even though studies point to miniscule effects of Syrians on unemployment figures,[19] the misinformation on Syrians in Turkey have no limits. The financial aid of the EU to Turkey to be spent on Syrians in temporary protection is seen by many in Turkey as money directly paid to Syrian refugees by the Turkish State. Many NGOs publish reports and information on how this is not the case. The Emergency Social Safety Net (ESSN) program, which provides for the social integration assistance paid to Syrians under temporary protection, is funded by the EU's European Civil Protection and Humanitarian Aid Operations (ECHO). This contribution is less than 10 euros per month per person.[20] From 2011 until 2016, the Turkish State used its own resources to temporarily shelter Syrian refugees and after that the EU has been paying the Turkish State on a project-by-project basis, which involves educational scholarships, the emergency social safety program, and migrant health centers, among others.[21]

The temporary protection status given to Syrians is not a privilege but a cover-up for Turkey's, previously explained, de jure nonexistent asylum regime. Only in 2013, Turkey's first asylum law was ratified. According to this new law, a new category, "the conditional refugee status," was introduced to cover the (non-Syrian) refugees excluded due to Turkey's geographical limitation to 1951 Geneva Convention. It took five years for the newly founded Directorate General of Migration Management (DGMM) to take over refugee registration from the UNHCR.[22] This new status does not cover internationally recognized refugee rights such as accommodation, access to health care, and measures of integration to social and economic structures but only gives temporary protection (without time limit) to non-Convention refugees.

Syrians under temporary protection have better access to social services than other noncitizens of Turkey. However, their access to work market is limited and the high interest in cheap labor pushes them into informality. According to figures published in 2023, only 30,000 Syrians have work permits and there are 15,000 companies in Turkey with at least one Syrian partner.[23] These statistics and qualitative studies done with Syrians in various cities demonstrate that most of Syrians work informally in precarious jobs.[24] 2020 ILO report *Syrian Refugees in The Turkish Labour Market* registers that 91 percent of Syrian refugees work informally, doing low-skill jobs. Almost one in every three Syrians work in textile, clothing, leather, and footwear industries[25] and three out of four earn less than minimum wage.[26] Average monthly salary of a Syrian worker falls under the hunger threshold defined by the Confederation of Turkish Trade Unions.[27] Child employment rises by age, peaking at 66 percent at the age of fifteen for Syrian boys.[28] Bureaucratic limitations and social discrimination are seen as major factors pushing Syrians to informality in Turkey.[29] The tendency to see Syrians as "temporary" adds to their precarity and discrimination, further limiting their societal integration.

All Those Afghan Men and Gendered Xenophobia

Just before United States withdrew from Afghanistan after twenty years of war and occupation in end August 2021, photographs of Afghan men walking through Iran-Turkey border were shared in Turkish media with panic inducing headlines. "Thousands of young Afghan men are marching into Turkey everyday," news channels reported. "Who's going to stop them?" One month later, we all saw people escaping Afghanistan that was left in the hands of Taliban, overflowing the Kabul airport. Turkish news commentaries were focusing on one point: "If these people are escaping Taliban why are they all men? If they are genuine refugees how can they leave their families, the women and children behind?". In times of moral panic, the most straightforward answers to these kinds of questions are often overseen in search for a more complicated one.

The panic around Afghan migrants in July 2021 was not based on facts. It was not correct that Afghan refugees were composed only of young men. While the majority of walking refugees were men, there were also families. Also, it was not correct that thousands of people marched through borders everyday in July 2021. Sibel Karadağ of GAR Migration Research Association states that the mass migration from Afghanistan to Turkey started in 2018 with the intensification of Taliban's control over Afghanistan and the worsening conditions in Iran for Afghan migrants.[30] The available statistics published by the Presidency of Migration Management in Turkey confirm this argument. In addition to the Syrians, Afghans have been the biggest group of irregular migrants in Turkey since at least 2014. The 2021 report, the year of the Afghan panic in Turkey, registers 70,000 apprehended irregular Afghan migrants. In 2019, this figure was more than 200,000.[31]

The straightforward answer to the foundational question on the Afghan panic lies at the material conditions of the migration itself and also goes beyond the reality of the Afghan case. Contrary to the chivalric sailors' motto "women and children first," irregular migratory routes are mostly led by young men. Physical endurance, having access to the pooling of family resources, and more potential to integrate in the informal economy of the receiving country are among main reasons why men take the lead in these routes.[32] Interviews with those young Afghan men on road reveal that their journey took almost forty-five days, involving days of walking ten hours a day and passing three borders.[33] Karadağ points to the deadly physical conditions of passing through Iran-Turkey border. In addition to many forms of interpersonal violence including sexual assault and robbery on the road, the natural habitat of the region with wild animals and extreme climate has caused death of many refugees. Karadağ notes that when snow melts, frozen dead bodies of migrants are exposed.[34] Not only the harsh conditions enable the survival of the physically fittest, but also the social status of men in society renders men taking the lead in irregular migration routes. Men are visible. Patriarchal norms establish men as active agents, while women are seen less capable and thus less threatening. Men's visibility makes them both a threat and target of recruitment by Taliban, and also entitles them to family resources more than women. In Chapter 4 that discusses the gender dynamics of displacement, I cited narratives of undocumented Afghan women in Iran on how women's visibility in public is seen as less risky for the family as the probability of undocumented men to be stopped by police is higher than women. Not seen as agents, being invisible, and nonthreatening had enabled women to be present in public more than their male family members. Gender-based oppression forms social and cultural norms that produce both enabling and endangering trajectories for people.

The panic created by Afghan men is not a unique event or unrelated with the general order of things in Turkey or in the world. Particularly after 9/11 and also predating it, unaccompanied men of presumably Muslim origins have been seen as a threat to national security in many countries. This perceived threat has ranged from a wide spectrum extending from violence to women in shape of sexual harassment, to violence against society and state in the shape of terrorism. I will first elaborate on the landmarks of the international manifestation of this symptom before delving in its Turkish variety.

The turning point following 9/11 (2001) was 2015. 2015 marked not only the so-called refugee crisis when more than 4 million people were in need for international protection,[35] but also the intensification of Islamophobic reactions to it. According to the UNHCR, more than 75 percent of those arriving in Europe in 2015 had escaped war and persecution in Syria, Afghanistan, or Iraq.[36] In 2015 more than 3,000 people died during crossing the Mediterranean Sea, including Alan Kurdi, the two-year-old Kurdish boy from Syria whose body was found on the Turkish coast and alarmed the world in September 2015. As discussed in the book, reinforcing the EU borders while establishing free travel within EU borders at the same time has a long history. Between 2007 and 2013, the EU spent almost 2 billion euros on surveillance systems fortifying its sea and land borders according to the estimations of Amnesty International.[37] Its expenditure for reception of refugees is estimated to be limited to a mere figure of 700 million euros.[38]

The humanitarian crisis in the eastern borders of the EU and in the Mediterranean Sea made it impossible to ignore the plight of refugees at the borders even though it was an expected result of the aforementioned Frontex policies. In early September 2015, Germany and Austria opened their borders to refugees coming from Hungary and later on in the same month the EU agreed to a quota scheme to relocate 160,000 refugees from Hungary, Italy, and Greece to other EU member states to "share the burden." The distribution was done according to criteria determined by the population of the EU member states, the GDP, average number of past asylum applications, and unemployment rate.[39] In 2015, almost 300,000 people were recognized as refugees in Europe and half a million others applied for asylum.[40] Almost half of these applications were received and accepted in Germany (140,000).[41] In 2015–16, more than a million people applied for asylum in Germany.[42]

In this climate, the mass sexual assaults in Germany, mainly in Cologne, in 2015 New Year's Eve, where over 1,200 women were reported to be sexually assaulted by men of "Arab or North African" origins, and the attack into a Christmas market in Berlin in 2016 were seen in mass media as reasons leading to a "paradigm shift" in the German society bringing the tightening of laws covering the right to asylum and making deportations easier and quicker.[43] The "opening" of German borders did not last long. However, while men of "Arab or North African" origin were reported to be the culprits of mass sexual assaults in Cologne, reports later on pointed to the lack of enough security measures in a public place that was expected to be crowded and the police's dismissal of complaints made at the site by women. The origins of the culprits were not confirmed either.[44] Instead of taking the complaints seriously, the police took the questionable measure of trapping hundreds of people inside the train station. Five years after the mass assaults only 2 of the 2,000 reported men were convicted.[45]

It was not only Germany where crimes committed by people of supposed Muslim origins made headlines in 2015 and 2016; the terrorist attacks of ISIS in Paris in 2015 and Belgium in 2016 were main landmarks instrumentalized by xenophobic outlets to feed the "Muslim scare." If men of non-European origin were not pictured as harassers or rapists due to "misinterpretation of cultural codes" or "lack of integration," they would be seen as targets of Islamist radicalization leading to terrorism. The updated anti-terror laws after the ISIS terrorist attacks in 2016 and 2017 in Western Europe rendered racial profiling of non-European men living in Europe a part of their everyday life.

Neighbors of asylum seekers in so-called integration projects are encouraged to report any "suspicious activity" to police in the Netherlands. An Amnesty International report on racial profiling in the Netherlands in 2022 notes that "racial/ethnic profiling is a standing practice of various Dutch authorities" and underlines that the coordinator for Counterterrorism and Security "deploys various means of surveillance in violation of international human rights law and standards" including secret and illegal visits to mosques and Muslim organizations and following people on social media.[46] A Human Rights Watch report in 2020 states that French police "use broad powers to stop and search Black and Arab youth even when there is no sign or evidence of wrongdoing."[47] "Black and Arab youth" univocally means Black and Arab boys and young men.

Halted shortly by a federal judge after its announcement, Trump's executive order banned travelers, including refugees, from seven Muslim-majority countries (Iran, Iraq, Libya, Somalia, Sudan, Syria, and Yemen) from entering the United States for ninety days in 2017.[48] However, the Visa Waiver Program Improvement and Terrorist Travel Prevention Act of 2015 signed by Obama, which exempts everyone born in Iraq, North Korea, Syria, Iran, Sudan, Libya, Somalia, and Yemen from a visa waiver program, is still in force in 2024. Both have made the travel of people from countries originating sizeable refugee communities harder.

This "Muslim men scare" predates the 2015 "refugee crisis." Shahram Khosravi in his work on Iranian men in Sweden points to the representation of the "immigrant man" as a threat to the Swedish society in the Swedish media through repeated coverage on rape and honor killings since late 1980s. Seen as a threat to his Muslim female partner and a "force that violates Swedish norms and values," the Muslim immigrant men have often been stigmatized as carriers of "primitive and savage masculinity."[49] Sara Farris, in her *In the Name of Women's Rights: The Rise of Femonationalism*, expands the case of vilified Muslim immigrant men to France, Netherlands, and Italy. Farris discusses the links of racism and sexism particularly in the case of femonationalist discourse against Muslim men and women, which she defines as "the exploitation of feminist themes by nationalists and neoliberals in anti-islam [and anti-immigration] campaigns" and "participation of certain feminists and femocrats in stigmatization of Muslim men under the banner of gender equality."[50] The main trope in this discourse is stigmatizing Muslim men as dangerous while registering the Muslim women as victims to be saved. Farris points to the colonial roots of this imagery, being part of racist techniques of domination used to justify imperialism as a civilizing mission.[51] Zuher Jazmati and Nina Studer also point to the continuity of colonial narratives on the North African men in particular and "oriental" men in general in their article on the media representations of the Cologne attacks. They argue that the magazine covers representing the non-white attack on the white women are built up on a preexisting colonial understanding of "how Muslim men function."[52]

The scare of Afghan and Syrian men in Turkey should be seen as a part of this global discourse against migrants, and particularly men, from presumably Muslim origins. However, Turkey's local flavor, which is being a Muslim majority country with a long history of social and political conflicts between secular and Islamists forces, makes the case even more complex. While in Europe the issue of Muslims or people presumed to be Muslims involves mainly migrants and refugees who represent a repressed, mostly precarious working-class minority, in Turkey it does not. This is not to say that there is no class-based discrimination in the case of Afghan and Syrian refugees and migrants in Turkey. There is no doubt that Afghans and Syrians are a part of the most precarious segment of the working class if not underclass in Turkey today. However, Muslims or people presenting as Muslims are not in minority or underrepresented in Turkey. Conversely, the two decades of AKP rule has popularized religious conservatism and has marginalized secular lifestyle.

Nevertheless, if we put aside the blatant anti-Arab racism among non-Arab populations of the Middle East, this "Muslim scare" has deeper roots and reflects aspects of Turkey's complicated history with secularism and its assumed symbols of modernity. The authoritarian modernism of the founders of the Turkish Republic was based on creating a nation previously organized according to traditions and religion into one based on citizenship, formal equality, and united interest.[53] So while many progressive steps were taken in the extension of secular education and other means of social infrastructure to the peripheries of the country, this "social engineering" was done in an authoritarian, homogenizing, and top-down manner. The "foundational revolutions," as they are named in the official Republican history, included not only the change of the political regime by the abolition of monarchy and caliphate, and establishing the Republic, but also new regulations for a comprehensive social change. Instituting a civil code separating religion and law, closing religious lodges and banning religious orders, establishing secularism, change in the alphabet, forced modernization of clothes including laws against traditional and religious headgear, and accompanying other "cultural reforms" established the symbolism that everything associated with the Arabic alphabet, measurement units, or religious clothing, among others, would be seen as a part of the "old regime," thus reactionary. Despite the so-called post-Kemalist trend in Turkish historiography and the rise of conservatism in the society, debates involving the symbols of these "foundational revolutions" are still highly polarizing in Turkey.

Moreover, gender-based oppression in Turkey has often manifested itself in the name of holding onto traditional Muslim values. Accordingly, secular concerns on individual rights and liberties have been articulated as oppositional to conservative Islamic norms in the society. Turkey's experience with Kemalism, post-Kemalism, and post-post Kemalism, as it is articulated recently, is a topic that needs to be taken into account while reviewing society's reactions to current migratory waves with their Muslim refugee population.[54] While Islamophobia is the right term to explain the "Muslim scare" in Europe, the concept loses its analytic power to explain the "Muslim scare" in Turkey. As Nisrine Chaer and Zuleikha Mirzazadeh, in their article "Doing Queer Politics between Islamophobia and Political Islam," also articulate, Islam does not occupy the same position of power in Europe as it does in the MENA region.[55] Defining the reactions given to refugees articulated on their presumed religious beliefs as "Muslim scare" does not mean negating that culprits of the aforementioned crimes were Muslims or that some did think they represent Muslims. It is also correct that social reforms by authoritarian modernists did liberate many people from traditional values and non-egalitarian ways of living and oppression. However, ahistorical interpretation of those reforms, forming the backbone of a ruling ideology focused on domination by establishing unity in the expense of religious and linguistic diversity, has given rise to structural undemocratic tendencies in Turkey. Thus while some facts can be correct, the causal links between two facts might not be as presented.

Taking into account Turkeys' geographical position and the legal framework presented earlier, the public reception of migrants in Turkey has always been entangled with this foundational ideology, as they almost unanimously come from countries with a Muslim majority population if not from a country officially named as Islamic. When Turkey was struggling with the rise of political Islam in mid-1990s, Turkish newspapers would publish pictures of conservative neighborhoods in Turkey with subtitles such as "this is not Iran." The infamous movie *Not without My Daughter* depicting an American woman trying to escape the Islamic Republic of Iran where her husband was from was shown fortnightly on TV in Turkey in late 1990s. The movie, with highly racist depiction of its Iranian characters, shaped the backbone of Iranian representation those days. What is tragic is that often people escaping Islamist authoritarianism are the same people racialized and discriminated based on Islamophobic or anti-political Islam attitudes in the receiving countries. The case of queer refugees from the MENA region residing in Europe, which Nisrine Chaer and Zuleikha Mirzazadeh discuss, exemplifies this clearly.[56] Racism and prejudice do not differentiate between secular, atheist, Muslim, or Islamist Iranians, Syrians, or Afghans.

Local Campism

Another particularity of local politics gives its color to the way refugees are received today in Turkey, which can be named as local campism. Primarily the Kurdish question and a decade of intense authoritarian rule have rendered Turkey a highly polarized country. Campism is a term used mostly to define reductionist political analyses that view the world divided into two camps on the primacy of one certain question or position. For example, a political analysis that prioritizes the role of US imperialism over anything else and formulates alliances first and foremost according to how actors position themselves vis-à-vis the United States may fall into a campist position, leading to being oblivious to the human right abuses in Iran or Putin's attack on Ukraine.[57] While historically used for analyzing global politics, it is a useful concept to understand the positions taken in contemporary Turkey on the refugee question and beyond.

The ruling party, Erdoğan's AKP, is in power since 2002. Its political journey from being a populist conservative party critical to the militaristic and authoritarian political legacy of the ruling class evolved to establishing a full-fledged neoliberal authoritarian regime in Turkey. From the official foreign policy attitude of "zero problems with neighbors"[58] as a defining part of the famous "Turkish model" in early days of AKP's rule to being an active party to the war and invasion in Syria, Turkey's foreign policy has been impactful on the public opinion on refugees.[59]

Turkey's historic tense relationship with Syria had improved in the beginning of Erdoğan's rule until the break of civil war in 2011. Before the war, Erdoğan and Assad families would visit each other often and present amicable relations, to the extent of spending vacations together.[60] When protests against corruption, inequality, and authoritarian rule started in Syria, the first reaction of Erdoğan's regime was to play the role of the mediator between the Assad regime and the Syrian Muslim brotherhood and to convince the former to schedule elections.[61] While still keeping ties with the Assad regime, Turkey gradually started to support the Islamist opposition forces by providing them platforms to organize.[62] In August 2011, the Turkish foreign minister Davutoğlu visited Damascus, delivering Erdoğan's message to end the violence and work with a Turkish sponsored peace plan.[63] After the rejection of this call by Assad, in September, the relations broke and Erdoğan publically called on Bashar Assad to step down.[64] It did not take long for Turkey to leave the mediator role to actively participate in the war. Joseph Daher, in *Syria after the Uprisings*, gives a detailed account of this process. As he registers, from 2012, arms bought by Saudi Arabia and Qatar were delivered to opposition groups through Turkey's Esenboğa Airport under the Turkish government's supervision. With Assad regime's withdrawal from northern Syria and the rise of Kurdish PYD's influence, Turkey facilitated the free movement of the Islamist fundamentalist and jihadists groups across the Syrian border and helped them develop their networks.[65] Until 2015, Turkey did not engage in any attacks against ISIS and did not let its military bases be used by the US-led coalition against ISIS.[66] By 2015, ISIS had extended its network in Turkey and engaged in a number of bombed attacks involving two major bombings, killing thirty-four young activists in July in Suruç and over a hundred people attending a peace and democracy rally in October in Ankara.[67] Stopping ISIS attacks in Turkey and containing the Kurds forming an autonomous region in Rojava became Turkey's priority in Syria. Particularly after 2014 with the official declaration of the autonomy of three cantons of Rojava at the border of Turkey and the world-renowned battle of Kobane against ISIS, Turkey's interventions in Syria moved from covert operations to direct assault. In 2016, Turkey launched its first military operation to Syria, Operation Euphrates Shield, on the basis of "self-defense," followed by other operations, which ended up in its occupation of territories in northern Syria that is currently home to 4 million people.[68] As Daher reports, Turkey's influence in Syria has expanded from engaging in security operations to controlling most aspects of political, economic, and civilian life in territories under its military operation.[69]

Turkey's involvement in Syria did not happen in a vacuum. In addition to the global repercussions of the Syrian war, its local politics went through many crises in the last ten years. 2013 Gezi protests and its suppression, the end of the Kurdish Peace Process in 2015, and the failed coup attempt of 2016 were the cornerstones of this internal turmoil. In 2013, a demonstration against the demolition of a public park in Istanbul turned into Turkey's largest contemporary anti-government uprising after Turkish State's nonproportional usage of violence and oppression to suppress it. Spreading to many parts in Turkey, the movement continued until the end of summer 2013 following three weeks of intense confrontation between protestors and police in June 2013. The Gezi trials that concluded in 2022 jailed seven human rights defenders as organizers of the nationwide protests, showcasing a most prominent example of political trials that have turned to be one of Erdoğan regime's tools of oppression. In 2015, the Peace Process between the Turkish State and the Kurdish armed resistance, the PKK, which had started officially in 2013 before the Gezi protests, ended in armed conflict in majority Kurdish cities. In January 2016 Amnesty International reported that more than 150 civilians were killed in the Kurdish cities under curfew and condemned the measures including the round-the-clock curfews and cuts to social services as collective punishment in the State's fight against PKK's youth wing.[70] The final nail in the coffin of the "Turkish model of democracy" was the 2016 military coup attempt by parts of military associated with Erdoğan regime's former partner, the Gülen movement. After the coup attempt, during which 250 people were killed, initially a three-month state of emergency was imposed, lasting for two years, during which political and civil liberties were suspended and Turkey was ruled by presidential decrees.[71] More than 170,000 people were removed from public sector jobs, and more than 50,000 people were imprisoned waiting for trials.[72]

Erdoğan's regime, in their own words, employed an "open door" policy with respect to Syrian refugees from the early days of the Syrian conflict.[73] However, this open door policy was neither planned nor managed properly. While in early 2012, the prime minister of the time pointed to 100,000 refugees as "the psychological limit" for the reception of Syrian refugees, there are almost four million Syrians now living in Turkey.[74] Combined with the high inflation and the current cost of living crisis in Turkey, the refugee population has turned to an easy target for large segments of the opposition. Also, the refugee population in Turkey is perceived to be a direct result of Erdoğan regime's active participation in the war. The organization and networking of Islamist groups in Turkey that resulted in a number of attacks in Turkey killing more than 200 people is taken as a consequence of this "open door" policy of the Erdoğan regime. Thus, according to this version of campism applied to national politics, opposition to Erdoğan's regime's authoritarian rule and irresponsible foreign policy can lead to opposition to Syrians' right of asylum in Turkey.

It would be naïve to ignore the impact of global campist analyses of the Syrian war on its Turkish national variant as well. From beginning of the uprisings in 2011, despite many reports by Syrian anti-regime activists, the war in Syria was seen as just a conflict between the Assad regime and its Islamist opposition by large segments of the population in Turkey. The pro-democracy forces in Syria, under years of Assad regime's suppression, was either totally ignored or seen as not a sizable force to be taken serious.[75] While a number of these Syrian pro-democracy activists resided in Turkey mostly as transit migrants and even established a cultural center in Istanbul such as *Hamisch*, the Istanbul Syrian Cultural House,[76] their connection with the broader left in Turkey has been limited. In addition to Erdoğan's "pro-refugee" stand with Islamic references, this lack of organic connection with the pro-democracy Syrian opposition has led to further homogenization of the Syrian refugees in public opinion. The opposition to AKP regime is not alone in its disdain for the Syrians' presence in Turkey. According to the research done by Social Democracy Foundation (SODEV) on the tenth year of Syrian migration to Turkey in 2021, 42.6 percent of the ruling AKP voters argued that Syrians should go back to their countries. The overall figure of people wanting Syrians to go back to their country was 55.4 percent.[77]

The Turkey-EU Deal

I discussed the hypocrisy of EU states in fortifying the external borders of the EU while enabling visa-free movement within European countries previously.

Frontex was established as the European Border and Coast Guard Agency, for which European countries pay more than they do for their reception of refugees. The EU's failure in providing safe asylum conditions for millions escaping war and persecution in the Middle East and beyond needs further attention. While cooperation of Turkey and Frontex has a longer history,[78] the 2016 pact with Turkey was a cornerstone in delegating the international responsibility of sheltering refugees to Turkey. Months before the coup attempt in Turkey, the EU signed a deal with Turkey to contain the migration flow to Greece. While the Dublin Regulation was already restricting the asylum request to be filled in the first European country that refugees arrived at, the 2016 deal aimed to extend the European borders to Turkey and stop refugees entering Greece and thus externalize its migration policies.

The original deal involved free travel for Turkish citizens in Europe in exchange of Turkey holding irregular migrants on their way to Greece, exchanging each apprehended irregular migrant with one recognized Syrian refugee from Turkey, and payment of 6 billion euros to the Turkish State to assist the refugee community stuck in Turkey. The payment was finalized four years later, after continuous complaints from the Turkish side claiming that the EU did not keep its promises.[79] There is yet no development on free movement of Turkish citizens within the EU territory. Reports presenting the balance sheet of the deal agree that the deal decreased the number of irregular migrants crossing to Greece.[80] However, the report prepared by Migratiedeals team at Utrecht University in December 2017 points to the increase in the fatality rate in the Mediterranean Sea from 1.4 percent in 2016 to 2 percent in 2017. Thus, while the overall number of people passing the borders decreased, relatively more people are drowning at the border. It is argued that people might be taking dangerous routes more than before, as there are fewer ways to leave Turkey after the deal.[81] The Turkey-EU deal, even if it were implemented as planned, would only cover the resettlement of 72,000 Syrians from Turkey to Europe.[82] Compared to 4 million Syrians in Turkey, this was far from being a solution. In addition to the faults from its inception, the Utrecht University report shows the problems of externalizing the refugee issue to a country with a poor track record of democracy. Interviews made with non-Syrian migrants readmitted to Turkey demonstrate that upon readmission, migrants were immediately detained to be deported to their countries of origin without access to asylum procedure. Migrants argued that their access to legal aid and means of communication was limited. Out of thirty-three interviewed non-Syrians, sixteen stated they were unable to apply for asylum and twenty-five stated they were intimidated and threatened.[83]

Asylum seekers got their share of the postcoup intensified authoritarian rule by presidential decrees as well. Turkey's first law on asylum made in 2013, the Law on Foreigners and International Protection, was amended by a presidential decree in October 2016, making it possible to halt and revoke asylum seekers' statuses without due process if it was confirmed that they had any terrorist affiliation.[84] Taking into account that almost all segments of the opposition have faced the threat of being linked with a terrorist organization after Gezi protests, the end of the Kurdish Peace Process, and the failed coup attempt that was discussed earlier, it is clear that this amendment will be detrimental on the asylum process of many refugees.

Turkey's four decades of experience with asylum and transit migration, with Iranians, Bulgarians, Kurds, Syrians, and Afghans constituting the most significant waves, demonstrate that its regulation of refugees and transit migrants is intertwined with the dynamics of its internal and foreign politics. Starting from the roots of the need of an asylum regulation in 1994, to arbitrary implementation of the existing rules and regulations including creating new categories when de facto situations render the existing regulations obsolete, Turkey's approach to asylum has never been rights-based, but pragmatic and securitized. Turkey's history with refugees is linked with its geopolitical situation and its deep-rooted, internal historical political conflicts. As long as the global economic inequality and crises of political representation manifested in authoritarian regimes in the Global South and the imperialist interests and restrictive, discriminatory border policies of the Global North remain, Turkey will continue to be a transit route for those seeking refuge from inequality and persecution, aspiring to reach security and welfare. As long as Turkey does not come to terms with its historical ethnic and political conflicts, the asylum issue will remain to be instrumentalized and abused for short-term political interests of the ruling elite. Access to safe routes of migration and asylum process is a right that cannot be left to individual nation-state's jurisdictions. While NGOs in the Netherlands campaigned for bringing 500 unaccompanied child refugees from Greek refugee camps in 2020, Turkey, Colombia, Pakistan, and Uganda are hosting more than 9 million refugees in 2024.[85] International institutions tasked with overseeing asylum processes must fulfill their responsibilities. Rather than passing off the "problem" to low- and middle-income countries with a poor track record of democracy, the countries of the Global North should take up their fair share of responsibility.

Notes

Introduction: Our Shared Pain

1 "Federal Almanya/İltica Hakkı: Mülteciye 'Domuz' Muamelesi," *Nokta*, October 5, 1986; "Söyleşi/Farah Diba'nın Kuaförü: Diba Saçı Lütfen," *Nokta*, November 2, 1986; "İranlı Kaçaklar/Anamur Burnu Komitesi: Denizden Mazlum Toplayanlar," *Nokta*, February 1, 1987; "Mülteciler/Türkiye'deki İranlılar: Coğrafyamız İzin Vermiyor," *Nokta*, May 31, 1987.
2 Except for Janet Bauer's illuminating study that focuses on women refugees and compares the refugees' lives in Germany and Turkey, the traces of Iranian refugees' temporary stay in Turkey are hardly covered in the literature. Among the studies conducted in Turkey, there is only one study, "A Fieldwork on the Post-1979 Iranian Migrants in İstanbul" conducted by Edman Nemati, which is mainly a graciously conducted questionnaire. Nemati presented the answers given to his survey with 104 Iranians, most of whom had left Iran between 1987 and 1989. The study is a collection of answers given to various questions ranging from the languages they know and the number of children they have, to their evaluation of the Islamic Regime's foreign policy, among others. See Janet Bauer, "A Long Way Home: Islam in the Adaptation of Iranian Women Refugees in Turkey and West Germany," in *Iranian Refugees and Exiles since Khomeini*, edited by Asghar Fathi (Costa Mesa: Mazda Publishers, 1991), 77–101 and Edman Nemati, "1979 Sonrası İstanbul'da Bulunan İranlı Göçmenler Üzerine Saha Çalışması" (MA diss., University of Istanbul, Istanbul, 1989).
3 See figures here at https://www.unhcr.org/refugee-statistics/ (accessed September 29, 2022).
4 İhsan D. Dağı, "Democratic Transition in Turkey, 1980–83: The Impact of European Diplomacy," *Middle Eastern Studies*, vol. 32, no. 2 (April 1996), 125.
5 İbrahim Sirkeci and Neli Esipova, "Turkish Migration in Europe and Desire to Migrate to and from Turkey," *Border Crossing*, vol. 3, no. 1301 (2013), 3. https://bordercrossing.uk/bc/article/view/522/515 (accessed February 22, 2024).
6 Aslı Didem Danış, "Yeni Göç Hareketleri ve Türkiye," *Birikim*, nos. 184–5 (2004), 216–24.
7 Sirkeci and Esipova, "Turkish Migration in Europe and Desire to Migrate to and from Turkey," 5.

8 In 2013, a new category of "conditional refugee" was introduced and in 2018 Turkish State institutions took over refugee registration from the UNHCR. However it is too early to evaluate this change in Turkey's asylum system.
9 Sweden and Germany were popular countries of destination for the postrevolutionary Iranian refugees. Hassan Hosseini-Kaladjahi points to the years between 1984 and 1988 for the initiation of Iranian refugee flow to Sweden. The number of Iranian citizens in Sweden grew from 8,342 in 1985 to 38,982 in 1990. See Hassan Hosseini-Kaladjahi, *Iranians in Sweden: Economic, Cultural and Social Integration* (Stockholm: Stockholm University, 1997), 184–5; Patrick R. Ireland states that Germany, particularly prior to its amendment of its asylum law in 1993, received three quarters of Europe's political refugees. See Patrick R. Ireland, "Socialism, Unification Policy and the Rise of Racism in Eastern Germany," *International Migration Review*, vol. 31, no. 3 (Fall 1997), 555.
10 Kobena Mercer, *Welcome to the Jungle: New Positions in Black Cultural Studies* (New York: Routledge, 1994), 21, 91–2, 214, 233–58.
11 Ibid., 82–3.
12 Ibid., 91.
13 Ibid.
14 "Men make their own history, but they do not make it as they please; they do not make it under self-selected circumstances, but under circumstances existing already, given and transmitted from the past" (Karl Marx, "The Eighteenth Brumaire of Louis Bonaparte, 1852." https://www.marxists.org/archive/marx/works/1852/18th-brumaire/ch01.htm) (accessed May 3, 2023).
15 Alessandro Portelli, *The Death of Luigi Trastulli and Other Stories* (New York: State University of New York State, 1991), 51.
16 Ibid., 47.
17 Ibid., 50.
18 Ibid., 52.
19 See Aksu Bora, *Kadınların Sınıfı: Ücretli Ev Emeği ve Kadın Öznelliğinin İnşası* (İstanbul: İletişim Yayınları, 2005), 32–3.
20 Alessandro Portelli, *The Battle of Vale Giulia: Oral History and the Art of Dialogue* (Wisconsin: University of Wisconsin Press, 1997), xi.
21 Ibid., 11.
22 Alessandro Portelli. "Oral History as Genre," in *Narrative and Genre*, edited by M. Chamberlain and P. R. Thompson (London: Routledge, 1998), 30.
23 Portelli states: "What the interviewer reveals about him or herself is ultimately relevant in orienting the interview toward monologue or self-reflexive thick dialogue" (Portelli, *The Battle of Vale Giulia*, 12).
24 Ahmad Shamlu, " 'Eshq-e Umumi" (originally published in *Hava-ye Tazeh*, 1957), in *Majmu'e Asare Ahmad Shamlu, Volume One*, edited by Niyaz

Yaghubshahi (Tehran: Zamaneh, 1999), 233. Translated by the author. "dard-e moshtarak" is generally translated as "common pain." I chose to use "shared," both are correct.

25 Cited in Şebnem Köşer-Akçapar, "Conversion as a Migration Strategy in a Transit Country: Iranian Shiites becoming Christians in Turkey," *International Migration Review*, vol. 40, no. 4 (Winter 2006), 822.

26 Bauer, "A Long Way Home," 97.

1 Flexible or Precarious? "One and a Half Million Iranians" in Turkey

1 Kemal Kirişçi, "UNHCR and Turkey: Cooperating for Improved Implementation of the 1951 Convention Relating to the State of Refugees," *International Journal of Refugee Law*, vol. 13, no. 1/2 (January 2001), 76.

2 United Nations High Commissioner for Refugees, "Text of the 1951 Convention Relating to the Status of Refugees," *Convention and Protocol Relating to the Status of Refugees*, http://www.unhcr.org/protect/PROTECTION/3b66c2aa10.pdf (accessed September 9, 2021).

3 Ahmet İçduygu, *Irregular Migration in Turkey* (Geneva: International Organization for Migration, February 2003), 20.

4 Kirişçi, "UNHCR and Turkey," 71.

5 Ibid., 76.

6 Ahmet İçduygu, *Transit Migration in Turkey: Trends, Patters, Issues*, European University Institute, Robert Schuman Centre for Advanced Studies, 2005, 6–7, https://cadmus.eui.eu/handle/1814/6277 (accessed May 3, 2023).

7 Halleh Ghorashi names this period as "the spring of freedom" that was put to an end with the consolidation of the Islamic Regime. She underlines that for those associated with the Pahlavi regime, "spring of freedom" referred to a period of horror. See Halleh Ghorashi, *Ways to Survive, Battles to Win: Iranian Women Exiles in the Netherlands and the United States* (New York: Nova Science Publishers, 2003), 7.

8 Ervand Abrahamian, *A History of Modern Iran* (New York: Cambridge University Press, 2008), 181.

9 Fereshteh Ahmadi Lewin, "Identity Crisis and Integration: The Divergent Attitudes of Iranian Immigrant Men and Women towards Integration into Swedish Society," *International Migration*, vol. 39, no. 3 (2001), 122.

10 Mehdi Bozorgmehr and Georges Sabagh, "High Status Immigrants: A Statistical Profile of Iranians in the United States," *Iranian Studies*, vol. 21, no. 3 (1988), 34.

11 Köşer-Akçapar, "Conversion as a Migration Strategy in a Transit Country," 822.
12 Lewin, "Identity Crisis and Integration," 122.
13 Abrahamian, *A History of Modern Iran*, 181.
14 Ayse Parla, *Precarious Hope: Migration and Limits of Belonging in Turkey* (Stanford: Stanford University Press, 2019), 9–11.
15 Ibid., 7.
16 For the figures, see İçduygu, *Irregular Migration in Turkey*, 21.
17 Ibid.
18 Human Rights Watch Report, *Whatever Happened to the Iraqi Kurds?*, March 11, 1991, https://www.hrw.org/reports/1991/iraq/ (accessed June 23, 2022).
19 Kemal Kirişçi, "Disaggregating Turkish Citizenship and Immigration Practices," *Middle Eastern Studies*, vol. 36, no. 3 (July 2000), 12.
20 Ibid., 13.
21 Ibid.
22 Ibid., 14.
23 Ibid.
24 Ibid.
25 Deniz Sert, "Elements of Uncertainty in Turkey's Refugee System," *Turkish Policy Quarterly*, vol. 13, no. 1 (2014), 163.
26 Kemal Kirişçi, "Reconciling Refugee Protection with Combating Irregular Migration: The Experience of Turkey," Paper presented at the Council of Europe Regional Conference on Migrants in Transit Countries: Sharing Responsibility for Management and Protection, Istanbul, September 30–October 1, 2004, Proceedings, 148, http://www.coe.int/t/dg3/migration/Regional_Conferences/MG-RCONF_2004_9e_Istanbul_conference_Proceedings_en.pdf (accessed September 9, 2021).
27 Kemal Kirişçi, "The Question of Asylum and Illegal Migration in European Union-Turkish Relations," *Turkish Studies*, vol. 4, no. 1 (2003), 86.
28 Ibid.
29 Ministry of the Interior in Turkey, *Türkiyeye İltica Eden veya Başka Bir Ülkeye İltica Etmek Üzere Türkiyeden İkamet İzni Talep Eden Münferit Yabancılar ile Topluca Sığınma Amacıyla Sınırlarımıza Gelen Yabancılara ve Olabilecek Nüfus Hareketlerine Uygulanacak Usul ve Esaslar Hakkında Yönetmelik*, https://www.multeci.org.tr/wp-content/uploads/2016/12/1994-Yonetmeligi.pdf (accessed September 9, 2021).
30 Ahmet İçduygu and Fuat E. Keyman, "Globalization, Security and Migration: The Case of Turkey," *Global Governance*, vol. 6, no. 3 (July–September 2000), 385.
31 Kirişçi, "Reconciling Refugee Protection with Combating Irregular Migration," 148–9. Both cases were of Iranians who had entered Turkey illegally in 1996 and

whose resettlements were arranged by the UNHCR (the first to the United States and the second to Finland).
32 Kirişci, "The Question of Asylum and Illegal Migration," 87.
33 "Iranian Refugees at Risk," *Iranian Refugees Alliance Quarterly Newsletter*, Summer/Fall 1997, IISH Archives, Amsterdam.
34 Ibid.
35 Kirişci, "UNHCR and Turkey," 72.
36 Ibid., 86–7.
37 Ibid., 87.
38 Ibid., 88.
39 *Söz*, August 12, 1995, IISH Archives, Amsterdam.
40 The Iranian Refugees' Alliance, "About Iranian Refugees' Alliance," https://www.irainc.org/aboutus.php (accessed September 9, 2022).
41 Iranian Refugees' Alliance, "Update on the Iranian Sit-In Protest in Turkey," *Iranian Refugees at Risk Spring 96/Summer 96*, https://irainc.org/nletter/sp96su96/sp96su96.html (accessed September 9, 2022) and Iranian Refugees' Alliance, "Turkey's Refugee Machination," *Iranian Refugees at Risk Fall 95/Winter 96*, https://irainc.org/nletter/f95w96/f95w96.html (accessed September 9, 2022).
42 Kemal Kirişci, "Is Turkey Lifting the 'Geographical Limitation'?—the November 1994 Regulation on Asylum in Turkey," *International Journal of Refugee Law*, vol. 8, no. 3 (1996), 294–318.
43 Ibid.
44 Ahmet Güder, UNHCR National Resettlement Officer, interview by the author, tape recording, Ankara, Turkey, April 21, 2008.
45 Kirişci, "UNHCR and Turkey," 72, 86–7.
46 Helsinki Citizens' Assembly, *Information for People Applying for Refugee Status in Turkey* (İstanbul: Helsinki Citizens' Assembly, August 2007), 3.
47 See 1994 Regulation at https://www.multeci.org.tr/wp-content/uploads/2016/12/1994-Yonetmeligi.pdf (accessed May 3, 2023).
48 Nadir Özbek, "Alternatif Tarih Tahayyülleri: Siyaset, İdeoloji ve Osmanlı-Türkiye Tarihi," *Toplum ve Bilim*, no. 98 (Fall 2003), 243.
49 I was repeatedly told by the interviewees that there was a lawyer of Iranian origin who had an office with a signboard on which it was written *"ikamet düzenlenir"* (we arrange residence) around Aksaray.
50 These are the most active human rights NGOs that formed the Human Rights Joint Platform (IHOP) in 2005, except the Association for Solidarity with Asylum-Seekers and Migrants.
51 IHD's president Akın Birdal visited the site of the protest.
52 Kirişci, "Reconciling Refugee Protection with Combating Irregular Migration: The Experience of Turkey," 149.

53 İçduygu brings forward the estimations of "nearly one and a half million Iranians," "half to one million," and "nearly one million" in the IOM reports of *Transit Migration in Turkey* (IOM (International Organization for Migration), *Transit Migration in Turkey* (Budapest: International Organization for Migration, 1996)), *Irregular Migration in Turkey* (2003), and "Globalization, Security, and Migration: The Case of Turkey" (İçduygu, Ahmet, and Fuat E. Keyman, "Globalization, Security and Migration: The Case of Turkey," *Global Governance*, vol. 6, no. 3 (July–September 2000), 383–98), respectively.

54 Nilüfer Narlı, "Transit Migration and Human Smuggling in Turkey: Preliminary Findings from the Field Work," *Turkish Review of Middle East Studies*, no. 3 (2002), 159.

55 Stéphane De Tapia, "Introduction to the Debate: Identification of Issues and Current and Future Trends of Irregular Migration in Transit Countries," Report presented at the Council of Europe Regional Conference on Migrants in Transit Countries: Sharing Responsibility for Management and Protection, Istanbul, September 30–October 1, 2004, Proceedings, 114.

56 State Institute of Statistics, *Statistical Yearbook of Turkey 1990* (Ankara: State Institute of Statistics, 1991); State Institute of Statistics, *Statistical Yearbook of Turkey 1994* (Ankara: State Institute of Statistics, 1995); State Institute of Statistics, *Statistical Yearbook of Turkey 2000* (Ankara: State Institute of Statistics, 2001).

57 Cited in De Tapia, "Introduction to the Debate," 114.

58 Güder, interview by the author.

59 Ibid.

60 Celia Mannaert, "Irregular Migration and Asylum in Turkey," *New Issues in Refugee Research*, Working Paper No. 89 (May 2003), 9.

61 "Mülteciler/Türkiye'deki İranlılar: Coğrafyamız İzin Vermiyor," *Nokta*, May 31, 1987, 20–1.

62 Farhad, interview by the author, tape recording, Cologne, Germany, August 9, 2007.

63 Amnesty International, *Türkiye Dosyası* (Istanbul: Alan, 1988).

64 Amnesty International, *Amnesty International Report 1997—Iran*, January 1, 1997, https://www.refworld.org/docid/3ae6aa0a78.html (accessed November 16, 2023).

65 Human Rights Watch, *Human Rights Watch World Report 1993—Iran*, January 1, 1993, https://www.refworld.org/docid/467fca731e.html (accessed November 16, 2023).

66 "Eski uzman, gizli tanık oldu: 40 mülteciyi öldürüp gömdük," *Sabah*, May 11, 2011, https://www.sabah.com.tr/gundem/2010/05/11/eski_uzman_gizli_tanik_oldu_40_multeciyi_oldurup_gomduk (accessed November 16, 2023).

67 Reza Allamehzadeh, *The Guests of Hotel Astoria*, Netherlands, 1989.
68 Roland Barthes, *Mythologies* (London: Vintage, 1993), 143.
69 Ibid., 142.
70 Bauer, "A Long Way Home," 80.
71 Ibid.
72 Ibid.
73 Ibid., 81.
74 Sabine Hess, "De-naturalising Transit Migration. Theory and Methods of an Ethnographic Regime Analysis," *Population, Space, and Place*, vol. 18, no. 4, Special Issue: Critical Approaches to Transit Migration (July/August 2012), 435.
75 See Chapter 5, "The Collective Memory of Being in Transit in Turkey."
76 Guy Standing, *The Precariat: The New Dangerous Class* (London: Bloomsbury, 2011), 11–21.
77 Guy Standing, "The Precariat and Class Struggle." *RCCS Annual Review, a Selection from the Portuguese Journal Revista Crítica de Ciências Sociais*, no. 7 (2015), 6.
78 Ibid., 13.
79 Ibid., 4.
80 Ibid., 6.
81 Thessa Lageman, "Remembering Mohamed Bouazizi: The Man Who Sparked the Arab Spring," December 17, 2020, https://www.aljazeera.com/featu res/2020/12/17/remembering-mohamed-bouazizi-his-death-triggered-the-arab (accessed May 3, 2023).
82 Joseph Daher, "An Unfinished Epoch of Revolution: 10 Years after the 'Arab' Revolutions," *Spectre Journal*, January 26, 2021, https://spectrejournal.com/an-unfinished-epoch-of-revolution/ (accessed May 3, 2023).
83 Marcel van der Linden, "San Precario: A New Inspiration for Labor Historians," *Labor*, vol. 11, no. 1 (2014), 11.
84 Ibid., 9.
85 Catarina Principe, "From Mobilisation to Resistance: Portugal's Struggle against Austerity," *International Socialism*, no. 138 (2013), http://isj.org.uk/from-mobil isation-to-resistance-portugals-struggle-against-austerity/#138principe_1 (accessed May 3, 2023).
86 International Labour Organization, *Global Estimates of Modern Slavery: Forced Labour and Forced Marriage*, September 2022, 37. https://www.ilo.org/wcmsp5/groups/public/---ed_norm/---ipec/documents/publication/wcms_854733.pdf (accessed May 3, 2023).
87 International Labour Organization, *Equality at Work: The Continuing Challenge*, Global Report under the Follow-Up to the ILO Declaration on Fundamental Principles and Rights at Work, April 27, 2017, 21, https://www.ilo.org/ilc/ILCS

essions/previous-sessions/100thSession/reports/reports-submitted/WCMS_154779/lang--en/index.htm (accessed May 3, 2023).
88 International Labour Organization, *Global Estimates of Modern Slavery*, 4.
89 International Labour Organization, *Women at Work Trends 2016*, https://www.ilo.org/gender/Informationresources/Publications/WCMS_457317/lang--en/index.htm (accessed May 3, 2023).
90 Parla, *Precarious Hope*, 104.
91 Ibid., 104–5.
92 Ibid., 107.
93 Ibid., 136.
94 Judith Butler, *Frames of War: When Is Life Grievable* (London: Verso: 2016), 24.
95 Ibid., 26.

2 When Does Exile Begin?

1 For example, see the accounts of Albert Banza-Bodika and Cemal. "I am one of the first seven Africans who arrived in Konya. In this city the locals asked me several questions. Where am I from? Where is Congo? Why and how did I come to Turkey, How long will I stay here? So many questions, but because of the language barrier the conversation was short." Albert Banza-Bodika, "A Refugee in Konya," *Refugee Voices*, vol. 3 (Fall 2007), 6; "People are sometimes too curious, they don't refrain from asking questions. They would not ask about your parents' occupations in Ghana." Cemal, cited in "Türkiye'deki Afrikalı Göçmenler: Bir Yiğit Gurbete Gitse," *Express*, no. 52 (August 2005), 42.
2 Ghorashi, *Ways to Survive, Battles to Win*, 72, 101–18.
3 Ibid., 110.
4 Maziar Behrooz, *Nasıl Yapılamadı: İran'da Solun Yenilgisi*, trans. Ercüment Özkaya (Ankara: Epos Yayınları, 2006), 193, 196. (*Rebels with a Cause: The Failure of the Left in Iran*. London: I.B. Tauris, 1999).
5 Ibid., 187–208.
6 Nikki R. Keddie, *Modern Iran: Roots and Results of Revolution* (New Haven: Yale University Press, 2006), 254.
7 Ghorashi, *Ways to Survive, Battles to Win*, 72.
8 Referring to the preexile years in Iran, Hammed Shahidian states that many militants had experienced "internal exile" in Abu-Lughod's terms. According to Shahidian, the social estrangement in an environment dominated by traditionalist and Islamists shaped the internal exile of the leftist militants. However, he argues that it was not only social estrangement but also the secret

life that most of the militants had to undergo that made their preexile experience in Iran an "internal exile." See Hammed Shahidian, "Iranian Exiles and Sexual Politics: Issues of Gender Relations and Identity," *Journal of Refugee Studies*, vol. 9, no. 1 (1996), 43–72.

9 Khodetun keh az kuh umadin, midunin. Anja az kasi entezar nemisheh dasht, har kasi beh fekre khodesheh. Rahpeymayi, bikhabi, az hameh badtar tars. … Hatta qachaqchiha-ye herfei ro az pa miandazad. Digar cheh bereseh be adamha-ye tip-e ma. An ham tu an sarma-ye Kordestan. Pustemun dasht az saremun miterekid. La'nat beh shabha-ye zemestun! Khargusho az yeh farsakhi misheh did, digar cheh bereseh beh panzdah, bist nafar adamo, asbo, qaṭero. (Pouri in *The Guests of Hotel Astoria*)

10 Esmail Fasih, "Excerpt from Sorraya in a Coma," in *Strange Times My Dear: The Pen Anthology of Contemporary Iranian Literature*, edited by Nahid Mozaffari and Ahmad Karimi Hakkak (New York: Arcade Publishing, 2005), 71.

11 Özge Biner, *Türkiye'de Mültecilik: İltica, Geçicilik ve Yasallık, "Van Uydu Şehir Örneği"* (İstanbul: İstanbul Bilgi Üniversitesi Yayınları, 2016), 9.

12 Those numbers were codes that would be added with a certain number to attain the telephone number.

13 Farhad, interview by the author, tape recording, Cologne, Germany, August 9, 2007.

14 Hooman, interview by the author, tape recording, Cologne, Germany, August 16, 2007.

15 According to the UN description, refugee's fear of persecution should stem from their political opinion, race, religion, ethnicity, or membership of a particular social group.

16 Nahid Qajar, "My Beloved Organization," in *Fada'i Guerilla Praxis in Iran 1970–1979*, edited by Touraj Atabaki, Naser Mohajer, and Siavush Randj-bar Daemi (London: I.B. Tauris, 2023), 124.

17 Ghorashi, *Ways to Survive, Battles to Win*, 117.

18 Sal-e 65 kheyli digeh bad shodeh bud. Migereftan, e'dam mikardan, kheyli az dustamo gerefteh budan, yeh seri ra gerefteh budan, kheyliha ra e'dam kardeh budan, nazdik dashtan mishodan behem. … Ma tu Iran rah miraftim, tu yeh khiyabun hamisheh bayad poshtemun ra negah mikardim. Masalan mirim az sare kar be khuneh hamisheh motma'en mishodim keh poshtemun kasi ma ro taqib nemikonad. … Nunvayi mikhastim berim negah mikardim, ke hichki donbalemun rah nayofteh khunemun ra peyda konad. Her ja, her ja miraftim bayad poshtesaremun ra negah mikardim. Do bar check mikardim. Un dard-e me'deh-yi ke man tu Iran dashtam bekhatereh inha bud hamash. Tarso, vahshato, yeh pastar mididam, yeh basiji mididam, hamisheh fekr mikardam daran ta'qibam mikonan. Nazdik ham mishodan khob, kheyli az dustamro

gerefteh budan. Torkiyeh anchenan tars nadashtam. Balad budim injur chizharo. [laughs] Be khatereh inha ham, vaqti keh umadim karemun ro zudtar rah endakhtim, bekhatere balad budaneh in chizha. Rahattar midunestim koja bayad jush bokhorim, koja bayad khodemun ra dur bokonim. Avvalan bachcheha-yi ke siyasi budan, saritar kareshun rah oftad. ... Saritar tunestan khodeshun ra jamo jur bokonan. (Sohrab, 48, interview by the author, tape recording, Cologne, Germany, August 9, 2007)

19 Shahidian, "Iranian Exiles and Sexual Politics."
20 Janet Abu-Lughod, "Palestinians: Exiles at Home and Abroad," *Current Sociology*, vol. 36, no. 2 (1988), 61–9, cited in Shahidian, "Iranian Exiles and Sexual Politics," 45.
21 Ibid., 44–6.
22 Ghorashi, *Ways to Survive, Battles to Win*, 116.
23 Yassin Al-Haj Saleh, "On the Exiles of Syrians and Syria as Exile," June 7, 2017. (Accessed February 21, 2024). https://yassinhs.com/?s=on+the+exiles (accessed February 21, 2024).
24 Shahidian, "Iranian Exiles and Sexual Politics," 47.
25 Said, 47, interview by the author, tape recording, Stockholm, Sweden, August 30, 2007; Khosrow, 43, interview by the author, tape recording, Stockholm, August 28, 2007.
26 Azadeh, 65, interview by the author, tape recording, Stockholm, Sweden, August 30, 2007.
27 Pasportharo dashtan pakhsh mikardan. ... Akharin lahzeh esmamro khund o pasamo dad. Baz man nemifahmidam chi shodeh bud. Faqat in sak dastam bud, sakamro gereftam keh dar beram. Dar-e utubus ham baz bud. Ke biam payin ... belakhareh yeh juri mitunestam khodam ra beresunam Khoy. Ziad ham faseleh nadasht Bazargan o Khoy. ... Umadim vasateh dota mileh. Yeh taraf Iran bud yeh taraf Torkiyeh. ... Vaqti keh un vasat budam, hess-e ajibi dashtam. ... Fekr mikardam kasi mano nemituneh bebareh un taraf. Ba'dan fahmidam keh beh Torka nemisheh etminan kard. (Mahmoud, 59, interview by the author, tape recording, Cologne, Germany, August 14, 2007)

3 "Their Categories and Ours": Politics of Differentiation

1 Kadir Ay in response to Didem Danış in "Türkiye'ye olan Uluslararası Göçün Yönleri: Toplumsal Şartlar ve Kişisel Yaşam Dünyaları," Orient Institut, Istanbul and Goethe Institut, Istanbul, March 7–10, 2007.

2 UNHCR, *Protecting Refugees and the Role of UNHCR 2007–2008*, 7. https://www.unhcr.org/media/protecting-refugees-and-role-unhcr-2007-2008 (accessed February 18, 2024).
3 Audre Lorde, "Learning from the 60s," Talk delivered at the Malcolm X Weekend, Harvard University, February 1982, https://www.blackpast.org/african-american-history/1982-audre-lorde-learning-60s/ (accessed May 3, 2023).
4 Khalid Koser, "New Approaches to Asylum?," *International Migration*, vol. 39, no. 6 (2001), 85.
5 Ibid., 88.
6 For figures, see https://watson.brown.edu/costsofwar/costs/human/refugees/afghan (accessed May 3, 2023).
7 Jeremy Harding, *Border Vigils: Keeping Migrants Out of the Rich World* (London: Verso, 2012), 66.
8 Ibid., 67.
9 Behzad Yaghmaian, *Embracing the Infidel: Stories of Muslim Migrants on the Journey West* (New York: Bantam Dell, 2006), 216–8.
10 This convergence is conceptualized as "the migration-asylum nexus." See Koser, "New Approaches to Asylum?," 87–9.
11 Ibid., 88.
12 Mehdi Bozorgmehr and Georges Sabagh, "Iranian Exiles and Immigrants in Los Angeles," in *Iranian Refugees and Exiles since Khomeini*, edited by Asghar Fathi (Costa Mesa: Mazda Publishers, 1991), 121–2.
13 Ibid., 125.
14 For "Cultural Revolution," see Keddie, *Modern Iran: Roots and Results of Revolution*, 250, 257, 290, 305.
15 I use the term "revolutionary political refugees" to be able to differentiate them from monarchist political refugees.
16 Janet L. Bauer, "Desiring Place: Iranian 'Refugee' Women and the Cultural Politics of Self and Community," *Comparative Studies of South Asia, Africa and the Middle East*, vol. 20, nos. 1–2 (2000), 196.
17 Köşer-Akçapar, "Conversion as a Migration Strategy in a Transit Country," 820.
18 Kathryn Spellman, *Religion and Nation: Iranian local and Transnational Networks in Britain* (New York: Berghahn Books, 2004), 185–8.
19 For UNHCR evaluation of Dublin Regulation, see https://www.unhcr.org/media/28986 (accessed May 3, 2023).
20 For Dublin Brothers, see https://www.facebook.com/dublinbrothersamsterdam, https://www.waytostay.nu/de-dublin-verordening/ (accessed May 16, 2022). For a detailed analysis of the Italian case and problems of the implementation of Dublin Regulations, see Maryellen Fullerton, "Asylum Crisis Italian Style: The Dublin Regulation Collides With European Human Rights Law," *Harvard*

      Human Rights Journal, vol. 29 (2016).https://journals.law.harvard.edu/hrj/wp-content/uploads/sites/83/2016/09/Fullerton-Asylum-Crisis.pdf (accessed February 19, 2024).

21 Mina Agha, "The Biographical Significance of Flight and Exile," *Comparative Studies of South Asia, Africa and the Middle East*, vol. 20, nos. 1–2 (2000), 165.

22 Ibid., 168.

23 Ibid., 169.

24 Ibid.

25 Agha, "The Biographical Significance of Flight and Exile," 207.

26 Vida Nassehy-Behnam, "Iranian Immigrants in France," *Iranian Refugees and Exiles since Khomeini*, edited by Asghar Fathi (Costa Mesa: Mazda Publishers, 1991), 104.

27 Ibid., 112–13.

28 Edward Said, "Reflections on Exile," in *Reflections on Exile and Other Essays* (London: Granta Books, 2001), 181.

29 Yassin Al-Haj Saleh, *The Impossible Revolution: Making Sense of the Syrian Tragedy* (London: Hurst, 2017), 1–2.

30 Shahidian, "Iranian Exiles and Sexual Politics."

31 Annabelle Sreberny and Ali Mohammadi, "Iranian Exiles as Opposition: Some Theses on the Dilemmas of Political Communication Inside and Outside Iran," in *Iranian Refugees and Exiles since Khomeini*, edited by Asghar Fathi (Costa Mesa: Mazda Publishers, 1991), 206.

32 Necmi Erdoğan, "Garibanların Dünyası Türkiye'de Yoksulların Kültürel Temsilleri Üzerine İlk Notlar," in *Yoksulluk Halleri*, edited by Necmi Erdoğan (İstanbul: İletişim Yayınları, 2007), 29–46; Necmi Erdoğan, "Yok-Sanma: Yoksulluk-Mâduniyet ve 'Fark Yaraları,'" in *Yoksulluk Halleri*, edited by Necmi Erdoğan (İstanbul: İletişim Yayınları, 2007), 47–95; Aksu Bora, "Kadınlar ve Hane: 'Olmayanın Nesini İdare Edeceksin?'," in *Yoksulluk Halleri*, edited by Necmi Erdoğan (İstanbul: İletişim Yayınları, 2007), 97–133.

33 Erdoğan, "Yok-Sanma: Yoksulluk-Mâduniyet ve 'Fark Yaraları,'" 77.

34 Erdoğan, "Garibanların Dünyası Türkiye'de Yoksulların Kültürel Temsilleri Üzerine İlk Notlar," 40–1.

35 Erdoğan, "Yok-Sanma: Yoksulluk-Mâduniyet ve 'Fark Yaraları,'" 77.

36 Erdoğan, "Garibanların Dünyası Türkiye'de Yoksulların Kültürel Temsilleri Üzerine İlk Notlar," 40.

37 Ibid., 41.

38 James C. Scott, *Weapons of the Weak: Everyday Forms of Peasant Resistance* (New Haven: Yale University Press, 1985).

39 James C. Scott. "Everyday Forms of Resistance," *The Copenhagen Journal of Asian Studies*, vol. 4 (1989), 33, https://rauli.cbs.dk/index.php/cjas/article/view/1765 (accessed May 3, 2023).
40 Ibid., 34.
41 Ibid., 36, 53.
42 Ibid., 38.
43 Gaim Kibreab, "Pulling the Wool Over the Eyes of the Strangers: Refugee Deceit and Trickery in Institutionalized Settings," *Journal of Refugee Studies*, vol. 17, no. 1 (2004), 2–8, 10–11, 24.
44 Khosrow, 43, tape recording, Stockholm, Sweden, August 28, 2007.
45 Sreberny-Mohammadi and Mohammadi, "Iranian Exiles as Opposition: Some Theses on the Dilemmas of Political Communication Inside and Outside Iran," 223.
46 Reproduction of E. P. Thompson's statement on the making of the English working class: "The working class did not rise like the sun at an appointed time. It was present at its own making." In "Preface," *The Making of the English Working Class* (New York: Vintage Books, 1966), 9.
47 Ibid.
48 Judith Butler, "Preface (1999)," in *Gender Trouble* (New York: Routledge, 2006), xv.
49 Ibid.
50 Judith Butler, "Performative Acts and Gender Constitution: An Essay in Phenomenology and Feminist Theory," *Theatre Journal*, vol. 40, no. 4 (December 1988), 526.
51 Nahid Qajar, "My Beloved Organization," in *Fada'i Guerilla Praxis in Iran, 1970–1979: Narratives and Reflections on Everyday Life*, edited by Touraj Atabaki, Nasser Mohajer, and Siavush Randjbar-Daemi (London: I.B. Tauris, 2023), 139.
52 Benedict Anderson, *Imagined Communities: Reflections on the Origin and Spread of Nationalism* (London: Verso, 2006); Eric Hobsbawm, "Introduction: Inventing Traditions," in *The Invention of Tradition*, edited by Eric Hobsbawm and Terence Ranger (Cambridge: Cambridge University Press, 1997), 1–14.
53 Bauer, "A Long Way Home," 85.
54 "Tu Hotelesh faqat Iruniha budan … Hameh ham montazer, hameh ham telefon beheshun mishod, inha telefon mizadan … aslan tori bud keh inha hameh-ye ruz mikhabidan, shabha ta sobh bidar mimundan. Varaq bazi mikardan … ba'dan bachcheha az in otaq be un otaq midavidand … Vahshatnak bud!" (Azadeh).

55 Vaqti keh ma umadim hotel, yek khanevadeh-yi bud keh ma mishnakhtimeshun az Iran bar hasb-e hadeseh unja didimeshun. Ettefaqan. Bad hamun ruz-e avval dovvom keh ma unja budim beh in e'teraz kardim in cheh zendegi hast, yeh bachcheh-ye kuchik ham dashtan, in cheh zendegi hast keh shoma darin. Ta nesfeh shab bidarin, mishinin tu dudo, takhteh bazio, mashrub mikhoreno … Bad mirin mikhabin ta zohr, ta yek, ta do, dobareh barmigardin be hamin dastan … In dust-e ma bergasht goft keh hala shoma yeh yeki do hafteh bemunin shoma ham injuri mishin … Ma do maho khurdeh-yi unja budim, unjuri ham nashodim … Ma injuri fekr kardim keh chetor vaqtemun ra mofid konim, sobh boland mishodim, baraye khodemun barnameh gozashteh budim … Miraftim bazar, ziad dur nabud, kharid-e ruzemun ra mikardim, miumadim hotel, yeh ghaza-yi dorost mikardim—in daf'eh yeh ojaq-e barqi kharideh budim … ghazamunro mikhordimo miumadim birun gardesh. (Behrouz)

56 "Ma sa'y mikardim keh ma ham dochar-e un vaz nashim. Baraye hamin nazm dadeh budim beh zendegimun … Beh vaqt mikhabidim, beh vaqt boland mishodim, miraftim qadam mizadim" (Behrouz).

57 John Davis, "The Anthropology of Suffering," *Journal of Refugee Studies*, vol. 5, no. 2 (1992), 156.

58 M. E. O'Brien, *Family Abolition, Capitalism and the Communizing of Care* (London: Pluto Press, 2023), 112–13.

59 Ibid.

60 Cited in Sazman-i Chirikha-yi Fada'i-yi Khalq-i Iran, *Iran's People's Struggle: Theory and Practice*, 1977, 45.

61 İnsanın devrimci olduğuna inanması başka şeydir; devrimciliği bir yaşam biçimi olarak algılamak ve özümsemek başka şey. Ben devrimciliği düzenin değişmesinden yana olmak, sosyalist devrime geçilmesi için savaşım vermek biçiminde anlıyorum. Devrimci olmakla da, her an silah elde olmayı kastetmiyorum sadece, isterse bu silah mecaz anlamda herhangi bir mücadele aracı olsun. Hayır. Ama devrimcilik, her an, nerede olduğunu, nasıl bir ortamda bulunduğunu, orada ne için bulunduğunu, nereye doğru baktığını, o gün nereye gideceğini, ertesi gün için neyi hedeflediğini, gittiği yerde ne yapacağını, yürüdüğü yollarda kimlerle nereye kadar yürüyeceğini, kime karşı duracağını, karşılaştıklarını nasıl ve hangi hedefe yönelik olarak etkileyeceğini, kime ve nasıl bilinç katacağını, kimden nasıl ve ne öğreneceğini, yerken, içerken, çalışırken; gezerken ve de eğlenirken, hatta uyurken bilinçle bilmek ve her an tavır belirlemek demekti; belirlediğin tavrı davranışınla, eyleminle ortaya koymak demektir; bu bilinçle oturup kalkmak, bu bilinçle mutlu ya da mutsuz olmak demektir; bireysel sevinci ve mutluluğu da bu açıdan görmek demektir, bunun dışında başka br ölçütü olmamak demektir. Ve de her zaman kendi kendisi ile

tutarlı ve kendi kendisi ile barışık olabilmek demektir. (Sevim Belli, *Boşuna mı Çiğnedik?* (İstanbul: Belge Yayınları, 2004), 639–40).
62 "Paramı son kuruşuna kadar harcadığım asla vaki değildir. O duruma gelmeden önlem alınmalıdır bence. Yoksa aç gezmeyi yeğ tutarım. Mutlaka gerekli olmayan hiçbirşey satın almam, hele kendim için. Kendime göre ilkelerim, neye göre ayarladığım belli olmayan normlarım vardır. Hem de oldukça katı. … Bir Türkiye devrimcisi bu benim koyduğum normların üzerine çıkmamalıdır" (Ibid., 399).
63 Ali Rahnema, *Call to Arms: Iran's Marxist Revolutionaries: Formation and Evolution of the Fada'is, 1964–1976* (London: Oneworld, 2021), 370.
64 Ali Akbar Safaii-Farahani (Bijan Jazani), *Anche yek Enghelabi Bayad Bedanad* (1970), 31, https://iran-archive.com/sites/default/files/2021-08/safaii-farahani-anche-yek-enghelabi-bayad-bedanad.pdf?fbclid=IwAR0y1FSmrtRHSV0jKE1ydSDpn8NZEKfjl7xxDJIodYaLaO314vsH9pM4VmU (accessed April 15, 2023).
65 Ibid.
66 Rahnema, *Call to Arms*, 59.
67 Peyman Vahabzadeh, *A Guerrilla Odyssey: Modernization, Secularism, Democracy, and the Fadai Period of National Liberation in Iran, 1971–1979* (Syracuse: Syracuse University Press, 2010), 237. Vahabzadeh is not the only one referring to six months for the lifespan of a guerilla. A former guerilla, Marziyeh Tohidast Shafi states that she had understood that the average life expectancy of a guerilla was not much more than six months when she went underground. Marziyeh Tohidast Shafi, "From School to Safehouse: A Woman Fada'i's account," in *Fada'i Guerilla Praxis in Iran, 1970–1979: Narratives and Reflections on Everyday Life*, edited by Touraj Atabaki, Nasser Mohajer, and Siavush Randjbar-Daemi (London: I.B. Tauris, 2023), 106.
68 Vahabzadeh, *A Guerrilla Odyssey*, 237.
69 See, for example, Shafi, "From School to Safehouse: A Woman Fada'i's Account," 107; Qajar, "My Beloved Organization", 132; Roqiyeh Daneshgari, "Female Prison," in *Fada'i Guerilla Praxis in Iran, 1970–1979: Narratives and Reflections on Everyday Life*, edited by Touraj Atabaki, Nasser Mohajer, and Siavush Randjbar-Daemi (London: I.B. Tauris, 2023), 156.
70 See Daneshgari, "Female Prison," 154–5; Nasser Rahimkhani and Nasser Mohajer, "The Organization of Iranian Peoples Fada'i Guerrillas' prison organization," in *Fada'i Guerilla Praxis in Iran, 1970–1979: Narratives and Reflections on Everyday Life*, edited by Touraj Atabaki, Nasser Mohajer, and Siavush Randjbar-Daemi (London: I.B. Tauris, 2023), 169.
71 Hammed Shahidian, "Women and Clandestine Politics in Iran, 1970–1985," *Feminist Studies*, vol. 23, no. 1 (Spring 1997), 28.
72 Ibid.

73 Vahabzadeh, *A Guerrilla Odyssey*, 43.
74 Haideh Moghissi, *Populism and Feminism in Iran: Women's Struggle in a Male-Defined Revolutionary Movement* (Basingstoke: Macmillan Press, 1996), 130.
75 Vahabzadeh, *A Guerrilla Odyssey*, 56–7.

4 "Not One of Those Women": Negotiating Womanhood in Transit

1 UNHCR, *Age, Gender and Diversity Accountability Report 2018–2019*, 16, https://www.unhcr.org/5f04946d4/unhcr-age-gender-diversity-accountability-report-2018-2019 (accessed April 15, 2023).
2 UNHCR, *Global Trends Report 2021*, 15, https://www.unhcr.org/62a9d1494/global-trends-report-2021 (accessed April 15, 2023).
3 UNHCR. *Gender-Based Violence Information Management System 2017 Report Jordan*, https://data.unhcr.org/ar/documents/download/66315 (accessed May 4, 2023).
4 UNHCR, *Gender-Based Violence Information Management System (GBVIMS) Annual Report 2016*, 6, https://data.unhcr.org/en/documents/download/62067 (accessed May 4, 2023).
5 Jeni Klugman, *The Gender Dimensions of Forced Displacement: A Synthesis of New Research.* (Washington, DC: World Bank Group, January 26, 2022), 3. http://documents.worldbank.org/curated/en/895601643214591612/The-Gender-Dimensions-of-Forced-Displacement-A-Synthesis-of-New-Research (accessed April 15, 2023).
6 Ibid., 7.
7 UN, *The World's Women 2020, Trends and Statistics*, https://unstats.un.org/unsd/demographic-social/products/worldswomen/documents/WW2020_ExecutiveSummary.pdf (accessed April 15, 2023).
8 Ibid.
9 Klugman, *The Gender Dimensions of Forced Displacement*, 7–8.
10 Asiye Şimşek Ademi, *"Afgan Suriyeli" Göçmen Kadınlar: Kaynanalardan Terör Örgütlerine Uluslararası Zorunlu Göçün Nedenleri-Sonuçları* (Ankara: Nobel Bilimsel Eserler, 2021), 105–32.
11 Ibid., 173.
12 Ibid., 109.
13 "Umadim birun hameh khanumha rusarishun ra bardashtan. Man ham rusarim ra endakhtam ru shunam. Ba'dan umadam payin, didam in khanuma hameshun raftan dastshuyi umadan birun aslan, masalan adamha-ye digeh-yi shodeh

budan, yeh mask zadeh budan. Engar mikhastam yeh faseleh-yi begiram. Nemidunam delilesh chi bud vali ta moddatha rusarim ra hefz kardeh budam." (Minoo, interview by the author of the thesis, tape recording, Stockholm, Sweden, September 1, 2007)

14 "In khanum bachcheh shir midad, akheh kheyli ham shalakhteh bud. Man sobha keh boland mishodam avval sineha-ye ino mikardam tu [laughs] … tak tak mikardam tu, bad masalan miraftam chayi mizashtam." (Ibid.)

15 Yeh aqai umadeh bud anja ba ina shabha jam' mishoden, mashrub mikhordan, kheyli azar dahandeh bud, aslan vaqti ke mast mikardan sohbathashun kheyli azar dahandeh bud. Un ham baraye man keh aslan ba in adabiyat ashenayi nadashtam, adabiyat-e foqola'deh lompani. Man aslan inharo nemishnakhtam. Mundeh budam masalan inha az koja-ye Iran umadeh budan. Keh man tu Iran ham injur adamha ro nemishnakhtam. … Kheyli baram gharib bud. In faz az jam'iyat Iranro man nashnakhteh budam, khob masalan az punzdah shunzdah salegi oftadeh budim be khat-te siyaset ba bachchehha-ye siyasi va yek khordeh prinsiphayi keh adamha dashtan tu jahayi keh sohbat mikardim. (Ibid.)

16 Kheyli ba man khub budan. Ya'ni agar yeh torki miumad hotel ya yeh filmi badi dasht midad, aslan khodeh garsonha va resepshinha esharehe mikardan keh to boro bala. Man digeh yeh khahar budam barashun, anha baradar budan, chon mididan raftaramro … unqadr ru man hesab mikardan, ageh khodam mikhastam yeh jayi beram yeh juri negah mikardan. Man yeh jaye dorost masalan dashtam miraftam … vaqe'an baradaram budan. (Mahnaz, interview by the author of the thesis, tape recording, Malmö, Sweden, August 24, 2007)

17 "Man ba cheshmha-ye khodam mididam. Dokhtare umadeh bud, mikhast *greencard* begireh, bereh pisheh shohareh. Bad yeho didim daman-e kutah pushideh o arayesh; rusari pusari hamasho dar avordeh, bad rafteh tahe salon ham neshasteh, film-e seksi ham neshun mideh, ba yeh pesareh … bad shab ba un miraft disko." (Ibid.)

18 Moghissi, *Populism and Feminism in Iran*, 132.

19 Beverly Skeggs, *Formations of Class and Gender/Becoming Respectable* (London: Sage Smith Dorothy, 1998), cited in Bora, *Kadınların Sınıfı*, 57.

20 Bora, *Kadınların Sınıfı*, 94.

21 Ibid., 89.

22 For further reading on the topic, see Sevgi Adak, *Anti-Veiling Campaigns in Turkey: State, Society and Gender in the Early Republic* (London: I.B. Tauris, 2022); Nilüfer Göle, *The Forbidden Modern, Civilization and Veiling* (Michigan: University of Michigan Press, 1997).

23 Bora, *Kadınların Sınıfı*, 89.

24 Ibid., 89–90.

25 Murat Ülker is listed as the richest businessman in Turkey in 2022 by Forbes, cited in "Türkiye'nin en zengin insanları kimlerdir? Türkiye'nin en zengin aileleri ve insanları listesi," https://www.dunya.com/is-dunyasi/turkiyenin-en-zengin-insanlari-kimlerdir-turkiyenin-en-zengin-aileleri-ve-insanlari-listesi-haberi-685310 (accessed May 4, 2023).

26 Ian Parker, Lecture notes, IIRE Youth School, August 2023.

27 Fatmagül Berktay, "Türkiye Solu'nun Kadına Bakışı: Değişen Bir Şey Var Mı?", in *Kadın Bakış Açısından 1980'ler Türkiye'sinde Kadın*, edited by Şirin Tekeli (Istanbul: İletişim Yayınları, 1990), 291.

28 Ayşe Saktanber, "Türkiye'de Medyada Kadın: Serbest Müsait Kadın veya İyi Eş, Fedakar Anne," in *Kadın Bakış Açısından 1980'ler Türkiye'sinde Kadın*, edited by Şirin Tekeli (Istanbul: İletişim Yayınları, 1990), 198.

29 Nilüfer Göle, *Modern Mahrem* (Istanbul: Metis Yayınları, 1992), 109.

30 Saktanber, "Türkiye'de Medyada Kadın," 230–2.

31 Bauer, "A Long Way Home," 89.

32 Melissa Gira Grant, *Playing the Whore: The Work of Sex Work* (London: Verso, 2014), 75.

33 Ibid.

34 Ibid., 76.

35 Ibid., 86.

36 Bora, *Kadınların Sınıfı*, 58.

37 Ibid., 22.

38 Berktay, "Türkiye Solu'nun Kadına Bakışı," 291.

39 Ibid., 292.

40 Oya Baydar and Melek Ulagay, *Bir Dönem İki Kadın: Birbirimizin Aynasında* (Istanbul: Can Yayınları, 2011), 391–2.

41 Hammed Shahidian, "The Iranian Left and the 'Woman Question' in the Revolution of 1978–79," *International Journal of Middle East Studies*, vol. 26, no. 2 (May 1994), 230, 241.

42 Shahidian, "Women and Clandestine Politics in Iran," 9, 27.

43 Shahidian, "The Iranian Left and the 'Woman Question,'" 234.

44 Ibid.

45 Moghissi, *Populism and Feminism in Iran*, 131.

46 Ibid., 2, 13, 78, 102, 129.

47 Qajar, "My Beloved Organization," 129; Qorbanali 'Abdolrahimpour, "A Glance at the Organization of Iranian People's Fada'i Guerrillas (1976–9)," in *Fada'i Guerilla Praxis in Iran, 1970–1979: Narratives and Reflections on Everyday Life*, edited by Touraj Atabaki, Nasser Mohajer, and Siavush Randjbar-Daemi (London: I.B. Tauris, 2023), 78; Daneshgari, "Female Prison," 155.

48 Qajar, "My Beloved Organization," 130.

49 'Abdolrahimpour, "A Glance at the Organization of Iranian People's Fada'i Guerrillas (1976–9)," 78.
50 Moghissi, *Populism and Feminism in Iran*, 88.
51 Holly Lewis, *The Politics of Everybody: Feminism, Queer Theory, and Marxism at the Intersection* (London: Zed Books, 2016), 94–5.
52 Cinzia Arruzza, *Dangerous Liaisons: The Marriages and Divorces of Marxism and Feminism* (London: Merlin Press, 2013).
53 Ibid., 38.
54 Ibid.
55 See M. E. O' Brien, *Family Abolition: Capitalism and the Communizing of Care* (London: Pluto Press, 2023), 123.
56 Ibid., 124–5.
57 Arruzza, *Dangerous Liaisons*, 41, 62.
58 Ibid., 62.
59 Ibid., 64.
60 Berktay, "Türkiye Solu'nun Kadına Bakışı," 289, 293.
61 Ibid., 294.
62 Samira, cited in Ghorashi, *Ways to Survive, Battles to Win*, 84.
63 Nahid, cited in Ghorashi, *Ways to Survive, Battles to Win*, 83.
64 Ghorashi, *Ways to Survive, Battles to Win*, 79.
65 Davis, "The Anthropology of Suffering," 150.

5 The Collective Memory of Being in Transit in Turkey

1 Bauer, "A Long Way Home."
2 Mehri Yalfani, *Afsaneh's Moon* (Ontario: McGilligan Books, 2002).
3 Ibid., 27.
4 Ibid., 135.
5 Sima, 40, interview by the author, tape recording, Stockholm, Sweden, August 31, 2007.
6 Abbas Kazerooni, *The Little Man* (Mustang: Tate Publishing, 2005).
7 Ibid., 48.
8 Doğan Kuban, "Aksaray," in *Dünden Bugüne İstanbul Ansiklopedisi*, volume 1 (İstanbul: Tarih Vakfı, 1993), 161–5.
9 Ibid.
10 Çağlar Keyder, "A Tale of Two Neighborhoods," *Istanbul: between the Global and the Local*, edited by Çağlar Keyder (Lanham, MD: Rowman & Littlefield Publishers, 1999), 174.

11 Ibid., 175.
12 Ibid., 176–7.
13 Yaghmaian, *Embracing the Infidel*, 13.
14 Ibid., 14.
15 *Aquarium*, directed by Iraj Ghaderi, Iran, 2005.
16 Ibid.
17 From an interview with the late economist Dr. Fariborz Raisdana. Fariborz Raisdana, interview by the author, tape recording, Tehran, Iran, August 2004.
18 Farhad, interview by the author, tape recording, Cologne, Germany, August 9, 2007.
19 Sohrab, interview by the author, tape recording, Cologne, Germany, August 9, 2007.
20 Yaghmaian, *Embracing the Infidel*, 15.
21 Shahram Khosravi, *'Illegal' Traveller: An Auto-Ethnography of Borders* (Basingstoke: Palgrave Macmillan, 2010), 31.
22 Avvalin fekri keh beh khateremun resid in bud keh in tarikharo avaz konim, ba in tarikha berim. Tarikharo keh dast kari kardim, ma'lum shod keh, kheyli moshakhkhaseh keh dast khordeh ya'ni ziad maheraneh nabud. Bad fekr kardim khob in nemisheh, pas berim donbale chiz, in keh yeh viza begirim az yeh jayi masalan alman-e sharqi keh un moqe' rahat viza midad, kari ham nadasht keh to aslan pasportet qanuniyeh, qanuni nist, makhsusan bekhatere in keh Suedo betore moshakhkhas, va keshvarha-ye gharbi ra that-e feshar qarar bedeh in karo mikard. Yek siyasat-e lajbazi dasht. Raftim Ankara viza gereftim. Ba'd pashiman shodim. Be ma ettela'at dadan keh anja sakhteh, moshkeleh, az anja vared shodan be Sued moshkel ijad mikonad. (Behrouz, interview by the author, tape recording, Stockholm, Sweden, August 30, 2007)
23 Hamid Naficy recounts France, Germany, the Netherlands, and Sweden as European countries that had receptive immigration policies toward Iranians in the postrevolution era. See Naficy, *An Accented Cinema* (New Jersey: Princeton University Press, 2001), 18.
24 Cited in Naficy, *An Accented Cinema*, 250.
25 Gillian Rose, "Researching Visual Materials," *Visual Methodologies* (London: Sage, 2001), 16.
26 The movie is now available on its director Reza Allamezadeh's YouTube channel, https://www.youtube.com/watch?v=hfEMgKszsOQ&ab_channel=RezaAllamehzadeh (accessed October 31, 2023).
27 See Behrooz, *Nasıl Yapılamadı: İran'da Solun Yenilgisi*, 129–30.
28 Reza Allamezadeh, interview by the author, tape recording, Netherlands, July 22, 2022.
29 Naficy, *An Accented Cinema*, 282.

30 Ibid.
31 Hamid Naficy names the films made by exilic and diasporic subjects as accented cinema vis-à-vis the dominant cinema that is taken as universal and without accent. He states that the accent of those films emerges not from the accented speech employed in the film but from the "displacement of filmmakers and their artisanal productions." See Naficy, *An Accented Cinema*, 4.
32 Ibid., 18. Naficy stresses that it is hard to keep track of the history of many Middle Eastern filmmakers living abroad because of both the objective conditions of their shifting status of exile/immigrant and their diversified claims of identity. See Naficy, *An Accented Cinema*, 295.
33 Ibid., 74.
34 Ibid., 74–5.
35 Ibid., 75.
36 Ibid., 74–80.
37 Paul Riceour, *Memory, History, Forgetting* (Chicago: University of Chicago Press, 2004), 120.
38 Ibid., 121.
39 Halbwachs cited in Mithat Sancar, *Geçmişle Hesaplaşma* (İstanbul: İletişim Yayınları 2007), 41–2.
40 Said, interview by the author, tape recording, Stockholm, Sweden, August 30, 2007.

Concluding Remarks

1 Liisa Malkki, "Refugees and Exile: From "Refugee Studies" to the National Order of Things," *Annual Review of Anthropology*, vol. 24 (1995), 511.
2 Malkki, *Purity and Exile* (Chicago: University of Chicago Press, 1995), 8.
3 Shahram Khosravi, *'Illegal' Traveller: An Auto-Ethnography of Borders* (Basingstoke: Palgrave Macmillan, 2010), 72.
4 Said, "Reflections on Exile," 181.
5 Barbara Harrell-Bond, "Repatriation: Under What Conditions Is It the Most Desirable Solution for Refugees? An Agenda for Research," *African Studies Review*, vol. 32, no. 1 (April 1989), 48.
6 Malkki, *Purity and Exile*, 13, 26.
7 Ibid., 11.
8 Barbara Harrell-Bond, "Can Humanitarian Work with Refugees Be Humane?" *Human Rights Quarterly*, vol. 24 (2002), 60.
9 Ibid., 58.

10 Koser, "New Approaches to Asylum?", 89. Also see Cuny and Stein cited in Harrell-Bond, "Repatriation: Under What Conditions Is It the Most Desirable Solution for Refugees?," 48.
11 For figures, see https://www.amnesty.org/en/what-we-do/refugees-asylum-seekers-and-migrants/global-refugee-crisis-statistics-and-facts/ and https://worldpopulationreview.com/country-rankings/refugees-by-country (accessed May 17, 2022).
12 Ahmet İçduygu, "Transit Migrants and Turkey," *Boğaziçi Journal: Review of Social, Economics and Administrative Studies*, vol. 10, nos. 1–2 (1996), 127.
13 Özge Biner, *Türkiye'de Mültecilik: İltica, Geçicilik ve Yasallık, "Van Uydu Şehir Örneği"* (İstanbul: İstanbul Bilgi Üniversitesi Yayınları, 2016), 13.
14 Reece Jones, *Violent Borders: Refugees and the Right to Move* (London: Verso, 2016), 16–17.
15 Aspasia Papadopoulou, "Smuggling into Europe: Transit Migrants in Greece," *Journal of Refugee Studies*, vol. 17, no. 2 (2004), 168.
16 Ibid.
17 Aspasia Papadopoulou, "Exploring the Asylum-Migration Nexus: A Case Study of Transit Migrants in Europe," *Global Migration Perspectives*, no. 23 (January 2005), 4.
18 Papadopoulou, "Smuggling into Europe," 175.
19 According to the 1991 Dublin Convention, the asylum determination process should take place in the first country of asylum in Europe.
20 See https://www.unhcr.org/solutions.html (accessed October 31, 2022).
21 Malkki criticizing Taylor and Nathan, in Malkki, "Refugees and Exile: From 'Refugee Studies' to the National Order of Things," 508.
22 Ibid., 509.
23 Esma'il Kho'i, "Time and Displacement: Three Poems by Esma'il Kho'i," trans. Ahmed Karimi-Hakkak and Michael Beard, *Iranian Studies*, vol. 30, no. 3 (1997), 333–4.
24 Translated as "Metamorphosis and Emancipation of the *Avareh*," trans. Hammed Shahidian, *Journal of Refugee Studies*, vol. 7, no. 4 (1994).
25 Ibid., 414.
26 Ibid.
27 Richard Black, "Fifty Years of Refugee Studies: From Theory to Policy," *International Migration Review*, vol. 35, no. 1, Special Issue: UNHCR at 50: Past, Present and Future of Refugee Assistance (Spring 2001), 63.
28 Mary Douglas cited in Liisa Malkki, "National Geographic: The Rooting of Peoples and the Territorialization of National Identity among Scholars and Refugees," *Cultural Anthropology*, vol. 7, no. 1 (February 1992), 34.
29 Malkki, "National Geographic," 26.
30 Ibid.

Epilogue: Turkey as a Transit Hub Today

1. Amnesty International, Turkey: Testimony on Torture. "Introduction," 1985, 6. https://www.amnesty.org/en/wp-content/uploads/2021/06/eur440231985en.pdf (accessed April 15, 2023).
2. Ömer Karasapan and Joe Stork, "Prison Conditions in Turkey," *Middle East Report*, no. 160 (September/October 1989), https://merip.org/1989/09/prison-conditions-in-turkey/ (accessed April 15, 2023).
3. The Human Rights Association (İHD) İstanbul Branch Prisons Commission. "End Violations of Rights against Political Prisoners in Turkey," Press release, March 18, 2022, https://m.bianet.org/english/law/259278-end-violations-of-rights-against-political-prisoners-in-turkey (accessed February 17, 2024).
4. For Ministry of Interior Presidency of Migration Management figures, see https://www.goc.gov.tr/duzensiz-goc-istatistikler (accessed August 2, 2022).
5. For Ministry of Interior Presidency of Migration Management figures, see https://www.goc.gov.tr/uluslararasi-koruma-istatistikler (accessed May 2, 2023).
6. For Ministry of Interior Presidency of Migration Management figures, see https://www.goc.gov.tr/gecici-koruma5638 (accessed March 5, 2024).
7. For Syrians Barometer Reports, see M. Murat Erdoğan, *Syrians Barometer 2021* (Ankara: Ankara University, 2021), https://www.unhcr.org/tr/wp-content/uploads/sites/14/2022/12/SB-2021-English-01122022.pdf and https://en.mmuraterdogan.com/raporlar (accessed April 25, 2023).
8. Elmas Topçu. "Turkey Elections: Refugees Are a Top Political Issue," Deutsche Welle (DW), https://www.dw.com/en/turkey-elections-refugees-are-a-top-political-issue/a-65374605 (accessed April 25, 2023) . There are many reports stating similar figures for Turkish citizens wanting to leave Turkey.
9. *Milliyet*, "174 bin Suriyeli Türk vatandaşı oldu," https://www.cnnturk.com/turkiye/174-bin-suriyeli-turk-vatandasi-oldu (accessed April 25, 2023).
10. There are many graduate theses written on hate speech against Syrians in Turkey. For example, see Mehmet Toprak, *Hate Discourses against Syrian Refugees on Social Media*, http://abakus.inonu.edu.tr/xmlui/bitstream/handle/11616/11332/514132.pdf?sequence=1&isAllowed=y (accessed February 17, 2024); İlayda Kurt, *Hate Speech and Others: Syrian Women in Turkey*, https://gcris.pau.edu.tr/bitstream/11499/50217/1/10519301.pdf (accessed February 17, 2024); Deniz Erdoğan, *Hate Speech in Local Media: Representation of Syrian Refugees in Local Press of Kilis*, http://www.openaccess.hacettepe.edu.tr:8080/xmlui/bitstream/handle/11655/4519/10190171.pdf?sequence=1&isAllowed=y (accessed February 17, 2024); Ilaf Rahmani, *Hate Speech against the Asylum Seekers from Syria (Refugees from Syria) in the Turkish Media*, https://dspace.

ankara.edu.tr/xmlui/bitstream/handle/20.500.12575/73046/633241.pdf?sequence=1&isAllowed=y (accessed February 17, 2024).

11 *Avlaremoz*, "Deprem sonrası nefret söylemi mültecileri ve göçmenleri hedef alıyor," March 10, 2023, https://www.avlaremoz.com/2023/03/10/deprem-sonrasi-nefret-soylemi-multecileri-ve-gocmenleri-hedef-aliyor/ (accessed April 25, 2023).

12 *Yeşil Gazete*, "Avukatlar deprem bölgesinde işkence iddialarıyla ilgili harekete geçti: Ümit Özdağ için suç duyurusu," February 13, 2023, https://yesilgazete.org/avukatlar-deprem-bolgesinde-iskence-iddialariyla-ilgili-harekete-gecti-umit-ozdag-icin-suc-duyurusu/ (accessed April 25, 2023).

13 Amnesty International, "Türkiye: Deprem bölgesinde polis ve jandarma ihlalleri—İşkence ve diğer türde kötü muamele yapıldı, şiddetli saldırılar önlenmedi," Press release, https://www.amnesty.org.tr/icerik/turkiye-deprem-bolgesinde-polis-ve-jandarma-ihlalleri-iskence-ve-diger-turde-kotu-muamele-yapildi-siddetli-saldirilar-onlenmedi (accessed April 25, 2023).

14 Topçu, "Turkey Elections: Refugees Are a Top Political Issue."

15 *Le Monde*, "Syrian Refugees Have Become an Electoral Issue in Turkey," January 26, 2023, https://www.lemonde.fr/en/international/article/2023/01/26/syrian-refugees-have-become-an-electoral-issue-in-turkey_6013207_4.html (accessed April 26, 2023).

16 Topçu, "Turkey Elections: Refugees Are a Top Political Issue."

17 Hrant Dink Vakfı, *Medyada Nefret Söylemi İzleme Raporu*, https://hrantdink.org/tr/asulis/yayinlar/72-medyada-nefret-soylemi-raporlari?start=0 (accessed April 25, 2023).

18 Ibid.

19 Ibid.

20 November 2023 figures. 230 TL. Also see Emergency Social Safety Net Programme (ESSN), https://platform.kizilaykart.org/en/suy.html (accessed May 3, 2023).

21 For more info on the monetary support Syrian refugees' receive, see "Avrupa Birliğinin Suriyeliler İçin Türkiye'ye Ödediği Para," https://multeciler.org.tr/avrupa-birliginin-suriyeliler-icin-turkiyeye-odedigi-para/ (accessed May 3, 2023).

22 UNHCR, "Moving On: Authorities in Turkey Take-over Refugee Registration," September 19, 2018, https://www.unhcr.org/blogs/moving-on-authorities-in-turkey-take-over-refugee-registration/ (accessed May 3, 2023).

23 For figures, see https://multeciler.org.tr/turkiyedeki-suriyeli-sayisi/ (accessed May 4, 2023).

24 Şeyda Nur Koca, "Suriyeli Sığınmacıların Türk Emek Piyasasına Katılım Süreçlerinin Toplumsal Boyutları," *Göç Araştırmaları Dergisi*, vol. 5, no. 2 (2019), 334–41.

25 Luis Pinedo Caro, *Syrian Refugees in the Turkish Labour Market*, International Labour Organization, February 9, 2020, 13, https://www.ilo.org/wcmsp5/groups/public/---europe/---ro-geneva/---ilo-ankara/documents/publication/wcms_738 602.pdf (accessed April 25, 2023).
26 Ibid., 19.
27 Ibid., 21.
28 Ibid., 10.
29 Koca, "Suriyeli Sığınmacıların Türk Emek Piyasasına Katılım Süreçlerinin Toplumsal Boyutları," 349–51.
30 Karadağ cited in Duygu Ayber Gültekin, "10 soruda Afganistan'dan göç gerçeği. Kim, neden geliyor, geri dönecekler mi?" *Evrensel*, August 14, 2022, https://www.evrensel.net/haber/440254/10-soruda-afganistandan-goc-gercegi-kim-neden-geliyor-geri-donecekler-mi (accessed July 29, 2022).
31 Ministry of Interior Presidency of Migration Management, "Yıllara göre yakalanan düzensiz göçmenlerin uyruklara göre dağılımı," https://www.goc.gov.tr/duzensiz-goc-istatistikler (accessed July 29, 2022).
32 Maral Jefroudi, "Afgan göçmenler neden hep erkek?," *İmdat Freni*, July 31, 2021, http://imdatfreni.org/afgan-gocmenler-neden-hep-erkek-maral-jefroudi/ (accessed May 3, 2023).
33 BBC News, "Escaping the Taliban: Fleeing Afghans struggle to enter Turkey," https://www.youtube.com/watch?v=thaijXHudOQ&ab_channel=BBCNews (accessed July 29, 2022).
34 Karadağ cited in Gültekin, "10 soruda Afganistan'dan göç gerçeği. Kim, neden geliyor, geri dönecekler mi?."
35 UNHCR Global Trends, https://www.unhcr.org/global-trends (accessed November 17, 2023).
36 William Spindler. "2015: The Year of Europe's Refugee Crisis," UNHCR, https://www.unhcr.org/news/stories/2015-year-europes-refugee-crisis (accessed May 3, 2023).
37 Daniel Trilling, "Five Myths about the Refugee Crisis," *The Guardian*, June 5, 2018, https://www.theguardian.com/news/2018/jun/05/five-myths-about-the-refugee-crisis (accessed May 3, 2023).
38 Ibid.
39 European Commission, "Refugee Crisis: European Commission Takes Decisive Action," Press release, September 9, 2015, https://ec.europa.eu/commission/presscorner/detail/en/IP_15_5596 (accessed May 3, 2023).
40 BBC News. "Migrant Crisis: Migration to Europe Explained in Seven Charts," March 4, 2016, https://www.bbc.com/news/world-europe-34131911 (accessed May 3, 2023).
41 Ibid.

42 Sekou Keita and Helen Dempster, "Five Years Later, One Million Refugees Are Thriving in Germany," Center For Global Development, December 4, 2020, https://www.cgdev.org/blog/five-years-later-one-million-refugees-are-thriving-germany (accessed April 25, 2023).

43 Ralf Bosen, "New Year's Eve in Cologne: 5 Years after the Mass Assaults," Deutsche Welle (DW), https://www.dw.com/en/new-years-eve-in-cologne-5-years-after-the-mass-assaults/a-56073007 (accessed August 1, 2022).

44 *The Guardian*, "Cologne Police 'Struggled to Gain Control during Mass Sexual Assaults,'" January 7, 2016, https://www.theguardian.com/world/2016/jan/07/cologne-police-struggled-to-gain-control-of-mass-sexual-assaults-new-years-eve (accessed April 26, 2023).

45 Bosen, "New Year's Eve in Cologne: 5 Years after the Mass Assaults."

46 Amnesty International, "The Netherlands: Racial Profiling, Corporate Crimes and Detention of Migrants," Submission to the 41st Session of the UPR Working Group, November 2022, https://www.amnesty.org/en/documents/eur35/5404/2022/en/ (accessed August 12, 2022).

47 Human Rights Watch, "'They Talk to Us Like We're Dogs' Abusive Police Stops in France," https://www.hrw.org/report/2020/06/18/they-talk-us-were-dogs/abusive-police-stops-france (accessed August 12, 2022).

48 Amnesty International UK, "A Licence to Discriminate: Trump's Muslim & Refugee Ban," https://www.amnesty.org.uk/licence-discriminate-trumps-muslim-refugee-ban (accessed May 3, 2023).

49 Shahram Khosravi, "Displaced Masculinity: Gender and Ethnicity among Iranian men in Sweden," *Iranian Studies*, vol. 42, no. 4 (2009), 597–8.

50 Sara R. Farris, *In the Name of Women's Rights: The Rise of Femonationalism* (Durham: Duke University Press, 2017), 4.

51 Ibid., 76.

52 Zuher Jazmati and Nina Studer, "Racializing 'Oriental' Manliness: From Colonial Contexts to Cologne," *Islamophobia Studies Journal*, vol. 4, no. 1 (Fall 2017), 89.

53 For authoritarian modernization, see Touraj Atabaki and Erik J. Zürcher, *Men of Order: Authoritarian Modernization under Atatürk and Reza Shah* (London: I.B. Tauris, 2004).

54 For post-post-Kemalism, see İlker Aytürk and Berk Esen, eds., *Post-Post-Kemalism: Türkiye Çalışmalarında Yeni Arayışlar* (Istanbul: İletişim Yayınları, 2023).

55 Nisrine Chaer and Zuleikha Mirzazadeh, "Doing Queer Politics between Islamophobia and Political Islam," *Crisis Magazine*, issue 3, August 5, 2022, https://crisismag.net/2022/08/05/doing-queer-politics-between-islamophobia-and-political-islam/ (accessed May 3, 2023).

56 Ibid.
57 For further reading on campism, see Dan La Botz, "Internationalism, Anti-imperialism, and the Origins of Campism," *New Politics*, vol. 18, no. 4 (Winter 2022), https://newpol.org/issue_post/internationalism-anti-imperialism-and-the-origins-of-campism/ (accessed April 25, 2023).
58 Ahmet Davutoglu, "Zero Problems in a New Era," March 21, 2013, https://foreignpolicy.com/2013/03/21/zero-problems-in-a-new-era/ (accessed April 25, 2023).
59 For "Turkish model," see Cihan Tugal, *The Fall of the Turkish Model: How the Arab Uprisings Brought Down Islamic Liberalism* (London: Verso, 2016).
60 Joseph Daher, *Syria after the Uprisings: The Political Economy of State Resilience* (London: Pluto Press, 2019).
61 Tugal, *The Fall of the Turkish Model*, 182.
62 Ibid., 183.
63 Daher, *Syria after the Uprisings*, 223–4.
64 Ibid.
65 Ibid., 224.
66 Ibid., 224–5.
67 BBC News Türkçe, "Türkiye'de son 10 yılda düzenlenen büyük saldırılar," November 14, 2022, https://www.bbc.com/turkce/articles/clmgndprxg8o (accessed May 3, 2023).
68 *The Economist*, "The Effects on Turkey of Syria's Civil War," *Erdogan's Empire-Special Report*, January 21, 2023, https://www.economist.com/special-report/2023/01/16/the-effects-on-turkey-of-syrias-civil-war (accessed May 3, 2023).
69 Daher, *Syria after the Uprisings*, 226–7.
70 Amnesty International, "Turkey: Onslaught on Kurdish Areas Putting Tens of Thousands of Lives at Risk," January 21, 2016, https://www.amnesty.org/en/latest/news/2016/01/turkey-onslaught-on-kurdish-areas-putting-tens-of-thousands-of-lives-at-risk/ (accessed May 4, 2023). In the same month, 264 academics from over 50 universities, known later on as Academics for Peace, signed a statement focusing on the human right violations in majority Kurdish areas and "demanded an immediate end to the violence perpetrated by the state." See "We Will Not be a Party to This Crime!," January 10, 2016, https://barisicinakademisyenler.net/node/63 (accessed May 3, 2023). Most of those academics were tried on the charges of "terrorist propaganda" and lost their jobs without due process irrespective of the legal process. In 2019, Turkey's Constitutional Court concluded that the conviction of Academics for Peace was a violation of their freedom of expression. See Amnesty International, "Turkey: Constitutional Court Clears Academics from Spurious 'Terrorism Propaganda' Charges," July 26, 2019, https://www.amnesty.org/en/latest/press-release/2019/07/turkey-constit

71. BBC News, "Turkey Ends State of Emergency after Two Years," July 18, 2018, https://www.bbc.com/news/world-europe-44881328 (accessed May 3, 2023).
72. Ibid.
73. AKP, *Bir İnsan hakkı Olarak Sığınma Hakkı. Suriyeli Sığınmacılarla İlgili Doğru Bilinen Yanlışlar*, https://www.akparti.org.tr/media/275669/suriyeliler-kitapcik-1.pdf (accessed April 26, 2023).
74. CNN Türk, "Davutoğlu: 'Sığınmacılar konusunda kırmızı çizgi aşıldı'," https://www.cnnturk.com/dunya/davutoglu-siginmacilar-konusunda-kirmizi-cizgi-asildi (accessed April 26, 2023).
75. See the Alliance of Middle Eastern and North African Socialists, https://allianceofmesocialists.org/, and "Third Anniversary of the Syrian Revolution: Creating the 'People's Liberation Factions' that Upholds the Program of the Original Popular Revolution" https://www.europe-solidaire.org/spip.php?article31382 (accessed April 26, 2023).
76. See https://www.facebook.com/profile.php?id=100068834110546 (accessed April 26, 2023).
77. SODEV, *Suriye Göçünün 10. Yılında Türkiye'de Suriyeli Göçmenler*, Istanbul, 2021, https://sodev.org.tr/sodev-suriye-gocunun-10-yilinda-turkiyede-suriyeli-gocmenler/ (accessed April 26, 2023).
78. See Nurcan Özgür Baklacıoğlu. " 'Open' Borders, Shifting Walls, at the Southeastern Borders of the EU," in *Turkey: Beyond the Fortress Paradigm at the Southeastern Borders of the EU*, edited by Nurcan Özgür Baklacıoğlu and Yeşim Özer (Lewiston: Edwin Edgar Melen Press, 2013), 410.
79. Emma Wallis, "EU Concludes €6 Billion Contract for Refugees in Turkey," December 18, 2023, https://www.infomigrants.net/en/post/29205/eu-concludes-%E2%82%AC6-billion-contract-for-refugees-in-turkey (accessed May 4, 2023).
80. TRT, "EU-Turkey Refugee Deal: Five Years On," https://www.trtworld.com/magazine/eu-turkey-refugee-deal-five-years-on-45126 (accessed May 4, 2023); Kyilah Terry, *The EU-Turkey Deal, Five Years On: A Frayed and Controversial but Enduring Blueprint*, Migration Policy Institute, April 8, 2021, https://www.migrationpolicy.org/article/eu-turkey-deal-five-years-on (accessed May 4, 2023); I. van Liempt, M. J. Alpes, S. Hassan, S. Tunaboylu, O. Ulusoy, and A. Zoomers, *Evidence-Based Assessment of Migration Deals: The Case of the EU Turkey Statement* (Utrecht: Universiteit Utrecht, 2017).
81. Liempt, Alpes, Hassan, Tunaboylu, Ulusoy, and Zoomers, *Evidence-Based Assessment of Migration Deals*, 8.
82. Terry, *The EU-Turkey Deal, Five Years On*.

83 Liempt, Alpes, Hassan, Tunaboylu, Ulusoy, and Zoomers, *Evidence-Based Assessment of Migration Deals*, 20–2.
84 Ibid., 20.
85 For figures, see https://www.unhcr.org/refugee-statistics/ (accessed May 4, 2024).

Bibliography

Interviews

Ali. Tape recording, Stockholm, Sweden, August 31, 2007.
Azadeh. Tape recording, Stockholm, Sweden, August 30, 2007.
Behrouz. Tape recording, Stockholm, Sweden, August 30, 2007.
Davoud. Tape recording, Stockholm, Sweden, September 1–2, 2007.
Farhad. Tape recording, Cologne, Germany, August 9, 2007.
Hasan. Tape recording, Malmö, Sweden, August 23, 2007.
Hooman. Tape recording, Cologne, Germany, August 16, 2007.
Khosrow. Tape recording, Stockholm, Sweden, August 28, 2007.
Mahin. Tape recording, Malmö, Sweden, August 3, 2007.
Mahmoud. Tape recording, Cologne, Germany, August 14, 2007.
Mahnaz. Tape recording, Malmö, Sweden, August 24, 2007.
Minoo. Tape recording, Stockholm, Sweden, September 1, 2007.
Mohammad. Tape recording, Malmö, Sweden, August 21, 2007.
Mostafa. Tape recording, Lund, Sweden, August 24, 2007.
Omeed. Tape recording, Cologne, Germany, August 19, 2007.
Roya. Tape recording, Stockholm, Sweden, September 2, 2007.
Said. Tape recording, Stockholm, Sweden, August 30, 2007.
Samad. Tape recording, Stockholm, Sweden, August 31, 2007
Sima. Tape recording, Stockholm, Sweden, August 31, 2007.
Sirous. Tape recording, Cologne, Germany, August 13, 2007.
Sohrab. Tape recording, Cologne, Germany, August 9, 2007.

Other

Allamezadeh, Reza. Tape recording, Netherlands, July 22, 2022.
Güder, Ahmet, UNHCR National Resettlement Officer, Tape recording, Ankara, Turkey, April 21, 2008.
Raisdana, Fariborz, Professor of Economy. Tape recording, Tehran, Iran, August 2004.

Movies

Allamezadeh, Reza. *The Guests of Hotel Astoria*. Netherlands, 1989.
Ghaderi, Iraj. *Aquarium*. Tehran, 2005.

Books, Articles, and Reports

'Abdolrahimpour, Qorbanali. "A Glance at the Organization of Iranian People's Fada'i Guerrillas (1976–9)." In *Fada'i Guerilla Praxis in Iran, 1970–1979: Narratives and Reflections on Everyday Life*, edited by Touraj Atabaki, Nasser Mohajer, and Siavush Randjbar-Daemi, 69–82. London: I.B. Tauris, 2023.

Abrahamian, Ervand. *A History of Modern Iran*. New York: Cambridge University Press, 2008.

Adak, Sevgi. *Anti-Veiling Campaigns in Turkey: State, Society and Gender in the Early Republic*. London: I.B. Tauris, 2022.

Agha, Mina. "The Biographical Significance of Flight and Exile." *Comparative Studies of South Asia, Africa and the Middle East*, vol. 20, nos. 1–2 (2000): 165–70.

Ahmadi Lewin, Fereshteh. "Identity Crisis and Integration: The Divergent Attitudes of Iranian Immigrant Men and Women towards Integration into Swedish Society." *International Migration*, vol. 39, no. 3 (2001): 121–35.

Al-Haj Saleh, Yassin. *The Impossible Revolution: Making Sense of the Syrian Tragedy*. London: Hurst, 2017.

Al-Haj Saleh, Yassin. "On the Exiles of Syrians and Syria as Exile." June 7, 2017. https://yassinhs.com/?s=on+the+exiles (accessed February 21, 2024).

Amnesty International. *Amnesty International Report 1997—Iran*. January 1, 1997. https://www.refworld.org/docid/3ae6aa0a78.html (accessed November 16, 2023).

Amnesty International. *The Netherlands: Racial Profiling, Corporate Crimes and Detention of Migrants: Amnesty International Submission to the 41st Session of the UPR Working Group*. November 2022. https://www.amnesty.org/en/documents/eur35/5404/2022/en/ (accessed August 12, 2022).

Amnesty International. *Turkey: Testimony on Torture*. 1985. https://www.amnesty.org/en/wp-content/uploads/2021/06/eur440231985en.pdf (accessed April 15, 2023).

Amnesty International. *Türkiye Dosyası*. Istanbul: Alan, 1988.

Anderson, Benedict. *Imagined Communities: Reflections on the Origin and Spread of Nationalism*. London: Verso, 2006.

Arruzza, Cinzia. *Dangerous Liaisons: The Marriages and Divorces of Marxism and Feminism*. London: Merlin Press, 2013.

Atabaki, Touraj, and Erik J. Zürcher. *Men of Order: Authoritarian Modernization under Atatürk and Reza Shah*. London: I.B.Tauris, 2004.

Ayber Gültekin, Duygu. "10 soruda Afganistan'dan göç gerçeği. Kim, neden geliyor, geri dönecekler mi?". *Evrensel*, August 14, 2022. https://www.evrensel.net/haber/440254/10-soruda-afganistandan-goc-gercegi-kim-neden-geliyor-geri-donecekler-mi (accessed July 29, 2022).

Aytürk, İlker, and Berk Esen. *Post-Post-Kemalism: Türkiye Çalışmalarında Yeni Arayışlar*. Istanbul: İletişim Yayınları, 2023.

Banza-Bodika, Albert. "A Refugee in Konya." *Refugee Voices*, vol. 3 (Fall 2007): 6.

Barthes, Roland. *Mythologies*. London: Vintage, 1993.

Bauer, Janet L. "Desiring Place: Iranian 'Refugee' Women and the Cultural Politics of Self and Community." *Comparative Studies of South Asia, Africa and the Middle East*, vol. 20, nos. 1–2 (2000): 180–99.

Bauer, Janet L. "A Long Way Home: Islam in the Adaptation of Iranian Women Refugees in Turkey and West Germany." In *Iranian Refugees and Exiles since Khomeini*, edited by Asghar Fathi, 77–101. Costa Mesa: Mazda Publishers, 1991.

Baydar, Oya, and Melek Ulagay. *Bir Dönem İki Kadın: Birbirimizin Aynasında*. Istanbul: Can Yayınları, 2011.

Behrooz, Maziar. *Nasıl Yapılamadı: İran'da Solun Yenilgisi*. Translated by Ercüment Özkaya. Ankara: Epos Yayınları, 2006. (*Rebels with a Cause: The Failure of the Left in Iran*. London, New York: I.B. Tauris, 1999).

Belli, Sevim. *Boşuna mı Çiğnedik?* Istanbul: Belge Yayınları, 2004.

Berktay, Fatmagül. "Türkiye Solu'nun Kadına Bakışı: Değişen Bir Şey Var Mı?." In *Kadın Bakış Açısından 1980'ler Türkiye'sinde Kadın*, edited by Şirin Tekeli, 289–300. Istanbul: İletişim Yayınları, 1990.

Biner, Özge. *Türkiye'de Mültecilik: İltica, Geçicilik ve Yasallık, "Van Uydu Şehir Örneği."* İstanbul: İstanbul Bilgi Üniversitesi Yayınları, 2016.

Black, Richard. "Fifty Years of Refugee Studies: From Theory to Policy." *International Migration Review*, vol. 35, no. 1, Special Issue: UNHCR at 50: Past, Present and Future of Refugee Assistance (Spring, 2001): 57–78.

Bora, Aksu. *Kadınların Sınıfı*. İstanbul: İletişim Yayınları, 2005.

Bora, Aksu. "Kadınlar ve Hane: 'Olmayanın Nesini İdare Edeceksin?'". In *Yoksulluk Halleri*, edited by Necmi Erdoğan, 97–133. Istanbul: İletişim Yayınları, 2007.

Bozorgmehr, Mehdi, and Georges Sabagh. "High Status Immigrants: A Statistical Profile of Iranians in the United States." *Iranian Studies*, vol. 21, no. 3 (1988): 5–36.

Bozorgmehr, Mehdi, and Georges Sabagh. "Iranian Exiles and Immigrants in Los Angeles." In *Iranian Refugees and Exiles since Khomeini*, edited by Asghar Fathi, 121–44. Costa Mesa: Mazda Publishers, 1991.

Butler, Judith. *Frames of War: When Is Life Grievable*. London: Verso, 2016.

Butler, Judith. *Gender Trouble*. New York: Routledge, 2006.

Butler, Judith. "Performative Acts and Gender Constitution: An Essay in Phenomenology and Feminist Theory." *Theatre Journal*, vol. 40, no. 4 (December 1988): 519–31.

Chaer, Nisrine, and Zuleikha Mirzazadeh, "Doing Queer Politics between Islamophobia and Political Islam," *Crisis Magazine*, issue 3 (2022). https://crisismag.net/2022/08/05/doing-queer-politics-between-islamophobia-and-political-islam/ (accessed May 3, 2023).

Dağı, İhsan D. "Democratic Transition in Turkey, 1980–83: The Impact of European Diplomacy." *Middle Eastern Studies*, vol. 32, no. 2 (1996): 124–41.

Daher, Joseph. *Syria after the Uprisings: The Political Economy of State Resilience*. London: Pluto Press, 2019.

Daher, Joseph. "An Unfinished Epoch of Revolution: 10 Years after the "Arab" Revolutions." *Spectre Journal*, January 26, 2021. https://spectrejournal.com/an-unfinished-epoch-of-revolution/ (accessed May 3, 2023).

Danış, Aslı Didem. "Yeni Göç Hareketleri ve Türkiye." *Birikim*, nos. 184–185 (2004): 216–24.

Davis, John. "The Anthropology of Suffering," *Journal of Refugee Studies*, vol. 5, no. 2 (1992): 149–61.

Davutoglu, Ahmet. "Zero Problems in a New Era." March 21, 2013. https://foreignpolicy.com/2013/03/21/zero-problems-in-a-new-era/ (accessed April 25, 2023).

De Tapia, Stéphane. "Introduction to the Debate: Identification of Issues and Current and Future Trends of Irregular Migration in Transit Countries." Report presented at the Council of Europe, "Regional Conference on Migrants in Transit Countries: Sharing Responsibility for Management and Protection," Istanbul, September 30–October 1, 2004, Proceedings. http://www.coe.int/t/dg3/migration/Regional_Conferences/MG-RCONF_2004_9e_Istanbul_conference_Proceedings_en.pdf (accessed September 9, 2021).

Erdoğan, M. Murat. *Syrians Barometer 2021*. Ankara: Ankara University, 2021. https://www.unhcr.org/tr/wp-content/uploads/sites/14/2022/12/SB-2021-English-01122022.pdf (accessed April 25, 2023).

Erdoğan, Necmi. "Garibanların Dünyası Türkiye'de Yoksulların Kültürel Temsilleri Üzerine İlk Notlar." In *Yoksulluk Halleri*, edited by Necmi Erdoğan, 29–46. İstanbul: İletişim Yayınları, 2007.

Erdoğan, Necmi. "Yok-Sanma: Yoksulluk-Mâduniyet ve 'Fark Yaraları.'" In *Yoksulluk Halleri*, edited by Necmi Erdoğan, 47–95. İstanbul: İletişim Yayınları, 2007.

Farris, Sara R. *In the Name of Women's Rights: The Rise of Femonationalism*. Durham: Duke University Press, 2017.

Fasih, Esmail. "Sorraya in a Coma." In *Strange Times My Dear: The Pen Anthology of Contemporary Iranian Literature*, edited by Nahid Mozaffari and Ahmad Karimi Hakkak, 61–80. New York: Arcade Publishing, 2005.

Fullerton, Maryellen. "Asylum Crisis Italian Style: The Dublin Regulation Collides with European Human Rights Law," *Harvard Human Rights Journal*, vol. 29 (2016). https://journals.law.harvard.edu/hrj/wp-content/uploads/sites/83/2016/09/Fullerton-Asylum-Crisis.pdf (accessed February 19, 2024).

Ghorashi, Halleh. *Ways to Survive, Battles to Win: Iranian Women Exiles in the Netherlands and the United States*. New York: Nova Science Publishers, 2003.

Gira Grant, Melissa. *Playing the Whore: The Work of Sex Work*. London: Verso, 2014.

Göle, Nilüfer. *The Forbidden Modern, Civilization and Veiling*. Michigan: University of Michigan Press, 1997.

Göle, Nilüfer. *Modern Mahrem*. İstanbul: Metis Yayınları, 1992.

Harding, Jeremy. *Border Vigils: Keeping Migrants Out of the Rich World*. London: Verso, 2012.

Harrell-Bond, Barbara. "Can Humanitarian Work with Refugees be Humane?". *Human Rights Quarterly*, vol. 24 (2002): 51–85.

Harrell-Bond, Barbara. "Repatriation: Under What Conditions Is It the Most Desirable Solution for Refugees? An Agenda for Research," *African Studies Review*, vol. 32, no. 1 (April 1989): 41–69.

Hess, Sabine. "De-naturalising Transit Migration. Theory and Methods of an Ethnographic Regime Analysis." *Population, Space, and Place*, vol. 18, issue 4, Special Issue: Critical Approaches to Transit Migration (July/August 2012), 428–40.

Hobsbawm, Eric. "Introduction: Inventing Traditions." In *The Invention of Tradition*, edited by Eric Hobsbawm and Terence Ranger, 1–14. Cambridge: Cambridge University Press, 1997.

Hosseini-Kaladjahi, Hassan. *Iranians in Sweden: Economic, Cultural and Social Integration*. Stockholm: Stockholm University, 1997.

Hrant Dink Vakfı. *Medyada Nefret Söylemi İzleme Raporu*. https://hrantdink.org/tr/asulis/yayinlar/72-medyada-nefret-soylemi-raporlari?start=0 (accessed April 25, 2023)

Human Rights Watch. *Human Rights Watch World Report 1993—Iran*. January 1, 1993. https://www.refworld.org/docid/467fca731e.html (accessed November 16, 2023).

Human Rights Watch. *"They Talk to Us Like We're Dogs": Abusive Police Stops in France*. June 18, 2020. https://www.hrw.org/report/2020/06/18/they-talk-us-were-dogs/abusive-police-stops-france (accessed August 12, 2022).

Human Rights Watch. *Whatever Happened to the Iraqi Kurds?* March 11, 1991. https://www.hrw.org/reports/1991/iraq/ (accessed June 23, 2022).

İçduygu, Ahmet. *Irregular Migration in Turkey*. Geneva: International Organization for Migration, February 2003.

İçduygu, Ahmet. "Transit Migrants and Turkey." *Boğaziçi Journal: Review of Social, Economics and Administrative Studies*, vol. 10, nos. 1–2 (1996): 127–42.

İçduygu, Ahmet. *Transit Migration in Turkey: Trends, Patterns, Issues*. European University Institute, Robert Schuman Centre for Advanced Studies, Florence, Italy, 2005, 6–7. https://cadmus.eui.eu/handle/1814/6277 (accessed May 3, 2023).

İçduygu, Ahmet, and Fuat E. Keyman "Globalization, Security and Migration: The Case of Turkey." *Global Governance*, vol. 6, no. 3 (July–September 2000): 383–98.

International Labour Organization. *Equality at Work: The Continuing Challenge*. Global report under the follow-up to the ILO Declaration on Fundamental Principles and Rights at Work. April 27, 2017. https://www.ilo.org/ilc/ILCSessions/previous-sessions/100thSession/reports/reports-submitted/WCMS_154779/lang--en/index.htm (accessed May 3, 2023).

International Labour Organization. *Global Estimates of Modern Slavery: Forced Labour and Forced Marriage*. September 2022. https://www.ilo.org/wcmsp5/groups/public/---ed_norm/---ipec/documents/publication/wcms_854733.pdf (accessed May 3, 2023).

International Labour Organization. *Women at Work Trends 2016*. https://www.ilo.org/gender/Informationresources/Publications/WCMS_457317/lang--en/index.htm (accessed May 3, 2023).

IOM (International Organization for Migration). *Transit Migration in Turkey*. Budapest: International Organization for Migration, 1996.

Iranian Refugees at Risk. *Iranian Refugees Alliance Quarterly Newsletter*. Summer/Fall 1997, IISG archives.

Iranian Refugees' Alliance. "Turkey's Refugee Machination." *Iranian Refugees at Risk Fall 95/Winter 96*. https://irainc.org/nletter/f95w96/f95w96.html (accessed September 9, 2022).

Iranian Refugees' Alliance. "Update on the Iranian Sit-in Protest in Turkey." *Iranian Refugees at Risk Spring 96/Summer 96*. https://irainc.org/nletter/sp96su96/sp96su96.html (accessed September 9, 2022).

Ireland, Patrick R. "Socialism, Unification Policy and the Rise of Racism in Eastern Germany," *The International Migration Review*, vol. 31, no. 3 (Fall 1997): 541–68.

Jazmati, Zuher, and Nina Studer. "Racializing "Oriental" Manliness: From Colonial Contexts to Cologne," *Islamophobia Studies Journal*, vol. 4, issue 1 (Fall 2017): 87–100.

Jefroudi, Maral. "Afgan göçmenler neden hep erkek?". *İmdat Freni*, July 31, 2021. http://imdatfreni.org/afgan-gocmenler-neden-hep-erkek-maral-jefroudi/ (accessed May 3, 2023).

Jefroudi, Maral. "Migration across the Turkish-Iranian Border." In *Migration, Asylum, and Refugees in Turkey: Studies in the Control of Population at the Southeastern Borders of the EU*, edited by Nurcan Ozgur Baklacioglu and Yesim Ozer, 305–7. Lewiston, NY: Edwin Edgar Melen Press, 2014.

Jones, Reece. *Violent Borders: Refugees and the Right to Move*. London: Verso, 2016.

Karasapan, Ömer, and Joe Stork. "Prison Conditions in Turkey," *Middle East Report*, no. 160 (September/October 1989). https://merip.org/1989/09/prison-conditions-in-turkey/.

Kazerooni, Abbas. *The Little Man*. Mustang: Tate Publishing, 2005.

Keddie, Nikki R. *Modern Iran: Roots and Results of Revolution*. New Haven: Yale University Press, 2006.

Keita, Sekou, and Helen Dempster. "Five Years Later, One Million Refugees Are Thriving in Germany." Center for Global Development. December 4, 2020. https://www.cgdev.org/blog/five-years-later-one-million-refugees-are-thriving-germany (accessed April 25, 2023).

Keyder, Çağlar. "A Tale of Two Neighborhoods." In *Istanbul: Between the Global and the Local*, edited by Çağlar Keyder, 173–86. Lanham, MD: Rowman & Littlefield Publishers, 1999.

Kho'i, Esma'il. "Time and Displacement: Three Poems by Esma'il Kho'i." Translated by Ahmed Karimi-Hakkak and Michael Beard, *Iranian Studies*, vol. 30, no. 3 (1997): 327–34.

Khosravi, Shahram. "Displaced Masculinity: Gender and Ethnicity among Iranian Men in Sweden," *Iranian Studies*, vol. 42, issue 4 (2009): 591–609.

Khosravi, Shahram. *"Illegal" Traveller: An Auto-Ethnography of Borders*. Basingstoke: Palgrave Macmillan, 2010.

Kibreab, Gaim. "Pulling the Wool Over the Eyes of the Strangers: Refugee Deceit and Trickery in Institutionalized Settings," *Journal of Refugee Studies*, vol. 17, no. 1 (2004): 1–26.

Kirişçi, Kemal. "Disaggregating Turkish Citizenship and Immigration Practices," *Middle Eastern Studies*, vol. 36, no. 3 (July 2000): 1–22.

Kirişçi, Kemal. "Is Turkey Lifting the "Geographical Limitation"?—the November 1994 Regulation on Asylum in Turkey," *International Journal of Refugee Law*, vol. 8, no. 3 (1996): 293–318.

Kirişçi, Kemal. "Reconciling Refugee Protection with Combating Irregular Migration: The Experience of Turkey." Paper presented at the Council of Europe Regional Conference on Migrants in Transit Countries: Sharing Responsibility for Management and Protection," Istanbul, September 30–October 1, 2004. Proceedings. http://www.coe.int/t/dg3/migration/Regional_Conferences/MG-RCONF_2004_9e_Istanbul_conference_Proceedings_en.pdf (accessed September 9, 2021).

Kirişçi, Kemal. "The Question of Asylum and Illegal Migration in European Union-Turkish Relations," *Turkish Studies*, vol. 4, no. 1 (2003): 79–106.

Kirişçi, Kemal. "UNHCR and Turkey: Cooperating for Improved Implementation of the 1951 Convention Relating to the State of Refugees," *International Journal of Refugee Law*, vol. 13, no. 1/2 (January 2001): 71–97.

Klugman, Jeni. *The Gender Dimensions of Forced Displacement: A Synthesis of New Research*. Washington, DC: World Bank Group, January 26, 2022. http://documents.worldbank.org/curated/en/895601643214591612/The-Gender-Dimensions-of-Forced-Displacement-A-Synthesis-of-New-Research (accessed April 15, 2023).

Koca, Şeyda Nur. "Suriyeli Sığınmacıların Türk Emek Piyasasına Katılım Süreçlerinin Toplumsal Boyutları." *Göç Araştırmaları Dergisi*, vol. 5, no. 2 (2019): 314–57.

Köşer-Akçapar, Şebnem. "Conversion as a Migration Strategy in a Transit Country: Iranian Shiites Becoming Christians in Turkey." *The International Migration Review*, vol. 40. no. 4 (Winter 2006): 817–53.

Köşer-Akçapar, Şebnem. "Iranian Transit Migrants in Turkey: Just a 'Waiting Room' before Entering the 'Paradise?'". Paper presented at the Fifth Mediterranean Social and Political Research Meeting of the Mediterranean Programme of the Robert Schuman Centre for Advanced Studies at the European University Institute, Montecatini Terme, March 24–28, 2004.

Köşer-Akçapar, Şebnem. "What's God Got to Do with It? The Role of Religion in the Internal Dynamics of Migrants' Networks in Turkey," *REMMM, Revue des Mondes Musulmans et de la Mediterranee*, nos. 119–120 (2007): 81–100.

Koser, Khalid. "New Approaches to Asylum?". *International Migration*, vol. 39, no. 6 (2001): 85–101.

Kuban, Doğan. "Aksaray." In *Dünden Bugüne İstanbul Ansiklopedisi*, volume 1, 161–5. İstanbul: Tarih Vakfı, 1993.

La Botz, Dan. "Internationalism, Anti-Imperialism, and the Origins of Campism." *New Politics*, vol. 18, no. 4 (Winter 2022). https://newpol.org/issue_post/internationalism-anti-imperialism-and-the-origins-of-campism/ (accessed April 25, 2023).

Levitan, Rachel, Esra Kaytaz, and Oktay Durukan, "Unwelcome Guests: The Detention of Refugees in Turkey's 'Foreigners' Guesthouses.'" *Refuge: Canada's Journal on Refugees/Refuge: Revue canadienne sur les réfugiés*, vol. 26, no. 1, Sanctuary in Context (Spring 2009): 77–90. https://refuge.journals.yorku.ca/index.php/refuge/article/download/30609/28119/31437.

Lewis, Holly. *The Politics of Everybody: Feminism, Queer Theory, and Marxism at the Intersection*. London: Zed Books, 2016.

Liempt, I. van, M. J. Alpes, S. Hassan, S. Tunaboylu, O. Ulusoy, and A. Zoomers, *Evidence-Based Assessment of Migration Deals: The Case of the EU Turkey Statement*. Utrecht: Universiteit Utrecht, 2017.

Lorde, Audre. "Learning from the 60s." Talk delivered at the Malcolm X Weekend, Harvard University, February 1982. https://www.blackpast.org/african-american-history/1982-audre-lorde-learning-60s/.

Malkki, Liisa. "National Geographic: The Rooting of Peoples and the Territorialization of National Identity among Scholars and Refugees." *Cultural Anthropology*, vol. 7, no. 1 (February 1992): 24–44.

Malkki, Liisa. *Purity and Exile*. Chicago: University of Chicago Press, 1995.

Malkki, Liisa. "Refugees and Exile: From 'Refugee Studies' to the National Order of Things." *Annual Review of Anthropology*, vol. 24 (1995): 495–523.

Mannaert, Celia. "Irregular Migration and Asylum in Turkey." UNHCR Evaluation and Policy Analysis Unit, New Issues in Refugee Research. Working Paper no. 89 (May 2003). http://www.unhcr.org/publ/RESEARCH/3ebf5c054.pdf.

Mercer, Kobena. *Welcome to the Jungle: New Positions in Black Cultural Studies*. New York: Routledge, 1994.

Moghissi, Haideh. *Populism and Feminism in Iran: Women's Struggle in a Male-Defined Revolutionary Movement*. Basingstoke: MacMillan Press, 1996.

Naficy, Hamid. *An Accented Cinema*. New Jersey: Princeton University Press, 2001.

Narlı, Nilüfer. "Transit Migration and Human Smuggling in Turkey: Preliminary Findings from the Field Work." *Turkish Review of Middle East Studies*, no. 3 (2002): 157–86.

Nassehy-Behnam, Vida. "Iranian Immigrants in France." In *Iranian Refugees and Exiles since Khomeini*, edited by Asghar Fathi, 102–18. Costa Mesa: Mazda Publishers, 1991.

Nemati, Edman. "1979 Sonrası İstanbul'da Bulunan İranlı Göçmenler Üzerine Saha Çalışması." Master's thesis, University of İstanbul, 1989.

O'Brien, M. E. *Family Abolition, Capitalism and the Communizing of Care*. London: Pluto Press, 2023.

Özbek, Nadir. "Alternatif Tarih Tahayyülleri: Siyaset, İdeoloji ve Osmanlı-Türkiye Tarihi." *Toplum ve Bilim*, no. 98 (Fall 2003): 234–57.

Özgür Baklacıoğlu, Nurcan. "'Open' Borders, Shifting Walls, at the Southeastern Borders of the EU." In *Turkey: Beyond the Fortress Paradigm at the Southeastern Borders of the EU*, edited by Nurcan Özgür Baklacıoğlu and Yeşim Özer, 383–418. Lewiston: Edwin Edgar Melen Press, 2013.

Papadopoulou, Aspasia. "Exploring the Asylum-Migration Nexus: A Case Study of Transit Migrants in Europe." *Global Migration Perspectives*, no. 23 (January 2005). https://www.refworld.org/docid/42ce4fa24.html.

Papadopoulou, Aspasia. "Smuggling into Europe: Transit Migrants in Greece." *Journal of Refugee Studies*, vol. 17, no. 2 (2004): 167–84.

Parla, Ayşe. Precarious Hope: Migration and Limits of Belonging in Turkey. Stanford: Stanford University Press, 2019.

Pinedo Caro, Luis. *Syrian Refugees in the Turkish Labour Market*. International Labour Organization, February 9, 2020. https://www.ilo.org/wcmsp5/groups/public/---europe/---ro-geneva/---ilo-ankara/documents/publication/wcms_738602.pdf.

Portelli, Alessandro. *The Battle of Vale Giulia: Oral History and the Art of Dialogue*. Wisconsin: The University of Wisconsin Press, 1997.

Portelli, Alessandro. *The Death of Luigi Trastulli and Other Stories*. New York: State University of New York State, 1991.

Portelli, Alessandro. "Oral History as Genre." In *Narrative and Genre*, edited by M. Chamberlain and P. R. Thompson, 23–45. London: Routledge, 1998.

Principe, Catarina. "From Mobilisation to Resistance: Portugal's Struggle against Austerity." *International Socialism*, issue 138 (2013). http://isj.org.uk/from-mobilisation-to-resistance-portugals-struggle-against-austerity/#138principe_1 (accessed May 3, 2023).

Qajar, Nahid. "My Beloved Organization." In *Fada'i Guerilla Praxis in Iran, 1970–1979: Narratives and Reflections on Everyday Life*, edited by Touraj Atabaki, Nasser Mohajer, and Siavush Randjbar-Daemi, 121–49. London: I.B. Tauris, 2023.

Rahnema, Ali. *Call to Arms: Iran's Marxist Revolutionaries: Formation and Evolution of the Fada'is, 1964–1976*. London: Oneworld, 2021.

Riceour, Paul. *Memory, History, Forgetting*. Chicago: University of Chicago Press, 2004.

Rose, Gillian. *Visual Methodologies*. London: Sage, 2001.

Safaii-Farahani, Ali Akbar (or Bijan Jazani). *Anche yek Enghelabi Bayad Bedanad*, Summer 1970. https://iran-archive.com/sites/default/files/2021-08/safaii-farahani-anche-yek-enghelabi-bayad-bedanad.pdf?fbclid=IwAR0y1FSmrtRHSV0jKE1ydSDpn8NZEKfjl7xxDJIodYaLaO314vsH9pM4VmU (accessed April 15, 2023).

Said, Edward. *Reflections on Exile and Other Essays*. London: Granta Books, 2001.

Saktanber, Ayşe. "Türkiye'de Medyada Kadın: Serbest Müsait Kadın veya İyi Eş, Fedakar Anne." In *Kadın Bakış Açısından 1980'ler Türkiye'sinde Kadın*, edited by Şirin Tekeli, 211–33. Istanbul: İletişim Yayınları, 1990.

Sancar, Mithat. *Geçmişle Hesaplaşma*. İstanbul: İletişim Yayınları, 2007.

Sazman-i Chirikha-yi Fada'i-yi Khalq-i Iran. *Iran's People's Struggle: Theory and Practice*, 1977. IISG archives Bro 5594/8. Reference link: https://hdl.handle.net/10622/096F758A-94E3-4850-9B92-FAD018765775 (accessed February 22, 2024)

Scott, James C. "Everyday Forms of Resistance." *Copenhagen Journal of Asian Studies*, vol. 4 (1989). https://rauli.cbs.dk/index.php/cjas/article/view/1765 (accessed May 3, 2023).

Scott, James C. *Weapons of the Weak: Everyday Forms of Peasant Resistance*. New Haven: Yale University Press, 1985.

Sert, Deniz. "Elements of Uncertainty in Turkey's Refugee System." *Turkish Policy Quarterly*, vol. 13, no. 1 (2014): 159–64.

Shahidian, Hammed. "Iranian Exiles and Sexual Politics: Issues of Gender Relations and Identity." *Journal of Refugee Studies*, vol. 9, no. 1 (1996): 43–72.

Shahidian, Hammed. "The Iranian Left and the 'Woman Question' in the Revolution of 1978–79." *International Journal of Middle East Studies*, vol. 26, no. 2 (May 1994): 223–47.

Shahidian, Hammed. "Women and Clandestine Politics in Iran, 1970–1985." *Feminist Studies*, vol. 23, no. 1 (Spring 1997): 7–42.

Shamlu, Ahmad. "'Eshq-e Umumi." In *Majmu'e Asare Ahmad Shamlu*, volume one, edited by Niyaz Yaghubshahi, 233–5. Tehran: Zamaneh, 1999.

Shayegan, Daryush. *Yaralı Bilinç*. İstanbul: Metis Yayınları, 2007.

Şimşek Ademi, Asiye. *"Afgan Suriyeli" Göçmen Kadınlar: Kaynanalardan Terör Örgütlerine Uluslararası Zorunlu Göçün Nedenleri-Sonuçları*. Ankara: Nobel Bilimsel Eserler, 2021.

Sirkeci, Ibrahim, and Neli Esipova. "Turkish Migration in Europe and Desire to Migrate to and from Turkey." *Border Crossing*, vol. 3, no. 1301 (2013). https://bordercrossing.uk/bc/article/view/522/515 (accessed February 22, 2024).

Skeggs, Beverly. *Formations of Class and Gender/Becoming Respectable*. London: Sage Smith Dorothy, 1998.

SODEV. *Suriye Göçünün 10. Yılında Türkiye'de Suriyeli Göçmenler*. Istanbul, 2021. https://sodev.org.tr/sodev-suriye-gocunun-10-yilinda-turkiyede-suriyeli-gocmenler/.

Spellman, Kathryn. *Religion and Nation: Iranian Local and Transnational Networks in Britain*. New York: Berghahn Books, 2004.

Sreberny-Mohammadi, Annabelle, and Ali Mohammadi. "Iranian Exiles as Opposition: Some Theses on the Dilemmas of Political Communication Inside and Outside Iran." In *Iranian Refugees and Exiles since Khomeini*, edited by Asghar Fathi, 205–27. Costa Mesa: Mazda Publishers, 1991.

Standing, Guy. "The Precariat and Class Struggle." *RCCS Annual Review, A Selection from the Portuguese journal Revista Crítica de Ciências Sociais*, issue 7 (2015): 3–16. https://journals.openedition.org/rccsar/pdf/585.

Standing, Guy. *The Precariat: The New Dangerous Class*. London: Bloomsbury, 2011.

Terry, Kyilah. *The EU-Turkey Deal, Five Years On: A Frayed and Controversial but Enduring Blueprint*. Migration Policy Institute, April 8, 2021. https://www.migrationpolicy.org/article/eu-turkey-deal-five-years-on.

The Economist. "The Effects on Turkey of Syria's Civil War." *Erdogan's Empire-Special Report*, January 21, 2023. https://www.economist.com/special-report/2023/01/16/the-effects-on-turkey-of-syrias-civil-war (accessed May 3, 2023).

Thompson, E. P. *The Making of the English Working Class*. New York: Vintage Books, 1966.

Tugal, Cihan. *The Fall of the Turkish Model: How the Arab Uprisings Brought Down Islamic Liberalism*. London: Verso, 2016.

UN. *The World's Women 2020, Trends and Statistics*. https://unstats.un.org/unsd/demographic-social/products/worldswomen/documents/WW2020_Executive Summary.pdf (accessed April 15, 2023).

UNHCR. *Age, Gender and Diversity Accountability Report 2018–2019*. https://www.unhcr.org/5f04946d4/unhcr-age-gender-diversity-accountability-report-2018-2019 (accessed April 15, 2023).

UNHCR. *Gender-Based Violence Information Management System (GBVIMS) Annual Report 2016.* https://data.unhcr.org/en/documents/download/62067 (accessed May 4, 2023).

UNHCR. *Gender-Based Violence Information Management System 2017 Report Jordan.* https://data.unhcr.org/ar/documents/download/66315 (accessed May 4, 2023).

UNHCR. *Global Trends Report 2021.* https://www.unhcr.org/62a9d1494/global-trends-report-2021 (accessed April 15, 2023).

Vahabzadeh, Peyman. *A Guerrilla Odyssey: Modernization, Secularism, Democracy, and the Fadai Period of National Liberation in Iran, 1971–1979.* Syracuse: Syracuse University Press, 2010.

Van der Linden, Marcel. "San Precario: A New Inspiration for Labor Historians," *Labor*, vol. 11, issue 1 (2014): 9–21.

Yaghmaian, Behzad. *Embracing the Infidel: Stories of Muslim Migrants on the Journey West.* New York: Bantam Dell, 2006.

Yalfani, Mehri. *Afsaneh's Moon.* Ontario: McGilligan Books, 2002.

Index

Afghan 2, 4, 14, 39, 63, 107, 123, 132, 135–6, 139, 141, 146
    men 134–6
    panic 134–6
    scare 139
    women 87–8, 136
Afghanistan 30, 63, 87–8, 126, 131, 134–6
Afsaneh's Moon 6, 104–5, 115
AKP (Justice and Development Party) 91–3, 139, 141–2, 144
Aksaray 32, 46–7, 52, 56, 89, 106–11, 116–17, 119. *See also* Laleli
Alan Kurdi 136
Alessandro Portelli 7–8, 10
Alexandra Kollontai 100
Amnesty International 26, 29, 131–2, 136, 138, 143
Anti-terror
    Counterterrorism and Security, Netherlands 138
    laws 63, 137–8, 146
    Unit (JITEM) 30
Aquarium 108
Arab 137–9
    Arabic 25, 140
    Spring 33–4
Armenian 3, 30, 64, 133
Assad 142
    regime 133, 142, 144
authoritarian 3, 13, 18, 62–3, 124, 131, 139, 141–2, 144, 146
    Islamist 141
    modernism 139–40
autonomy 5, 14, 17, 33, 35, 37, 120–1, 124

Baha'i 19, 40–1, 43, 64, 120
Baskale, Van 30, 45
Başörtüsü 92. *See also* headscarf
Bijan Jazani 81
Bolsheviks 100
Bulgaria 19, 20–1, 35–6, 47, 71, 114, 125

Bulgarian 20–1, 123, 128, 146
burden of representation 6–7
burqa 87

campism 42, 141, 144
capitalism 99–100, 110
    racial 33, 35
capitalist 2–3, 17, 34, 42, 99, 100, 110
chador 99
class 1, 29–32, 52, 57, 70, 80, 90, 92–3, 96, 100–1, 106, 122, 128, 139, 141
Cold War 42, 63
collective memory 14, 30, 103–5, 113, 115–16
conversion 66, 120
converts 120
Covid-19 87
Cultural Revolution 65

displaced (people) 20, 63, 69, 86, 88, 107
draft evaders 12, 20, 27, 74, 77–8
Dublin
    Brothers 66
    Regulation 66, 145

Erdoğan (Recep Tayyip) 92–3, 133, 141–4
Ethos 93
everyday resistance 71–3
Evin prison 46–9

femonationalism 138
France 30, 42, 63, 68, 91, 112, 114, 116, 138
    French 46, 68, 112
Frontex 125, 137, 145

gender 15, 32, 53, 85–7, 89, 94, 97–9, 134, 138
    based oppression 2, 5, 12, 14, 85–6, 89, 99, 101, 128, 136, 140. *See also* patriarchy
    dynamics 85–6, 88, 136

normative 85, 98–9
performativity 75
Geographical limitation/reservation (to 1951 Geneva Convention) 4, 18, 134
Geneva Convention (1951) 4, 18, 125, 134
Germany 5–6, 29, 39, 40, 56, 59, 63, 65, 67, 75, 95, 117, 137
　East 110–11
　West 31–2
Gezi (Park) protests 3, 143, 146
　trials 143
giriş-çıkış 70–1, 114

Halabja massacre 4, 20
headscarf 89–93
Helsinki Citizens' Assembly 26, 61
hijab 97
Human Rights Association (IHD) 24, 26
hunger strike 24, 131

internal exile 13, 40, 42, 53–7, 60, 126
International Catholic Migration Commission (ICMC) 109–10
International Labor Organization (ILO) 35, 134
International Organization for Migration (IOM) 125
intersectionality 4, 10, 35, 62, 86–7, 119
Iranian Refugees' Alliance 22–3
Iran-Iraq War 20, 45, 65, 67, 74, 114
Iraq 18–21, 29, 52, 63, 116, 131, 136, 138
　Iraqi 4, 22, 40, 61, 63, 104, 132
　northern 20, 22, 29
Islamophobia 63, 140

Judith Butler 35–6, 75

Kemalism 140
Khoy 49, 59
Kurdish 25, 30, 51, 122–3, 131, 136, 143. *See also* Kurds
　armed resistance 44, 143 (*see also* PKK)
　Peace Process 3, 143, 146
　question 141
Kurdistan 44, 57, 76
Kurdistan Democratic Party 23, 68
Kurds 4, 20–2, 29, 107, 128, 133, 142, 146. *See also* Kurdish

Laleli 106–8. *See also* Aksaray
LGBTQI 7, 12, 63, 128

Marxism 80, 99
　Marxist 31, 41, 68, 90, 99
military coup
　1980 3, 13, 17, 100, 131
　2016 3, 143, 145–6
migration-asylum nexus 63–4, 125
Mohamed Bouazizi 33
monarchists 12, 19, 31, 68
morality 94–5, 97
　political 77, 79, 85, 90, 116
moral panic 94, 96, 99, 135
Muslim scare 137, 139–40

Nassim Khaksar 113
Netherlands 3, 6, 55, 66, 73, 111–14, 138, 147
nine-eleven (9/11) 15, 63, 136
1994 Asylum regulation 13, 19–27, 146
non-Convention refugees 19, 22, 24–5, 27, 134
North African 63, 114, 137, 139

oral history 8, 10

Pahlavi regime 19, 110, 113
Paris 42, 46, 68, 80, 137
patriarchy 86–8, 91, 94, 98, 135. *See also* gender-based oppression
People's Fadaiyan 6, 12, 31, 47, 68, 74, 76, 80–2, 90–91, 97–8, 101
　Majority 41–2, 46, 52–3
　Minority 41–2
People's Mojahedin 68, 12, 23, 29, 31, 42, 68
PKK 3, 22–3, 30, 51, 143. *See also* Kurdish armed resistance
Political Islam 92, 140–1
politics of survival 5, 66, 69, 72–3, 85, 101, 119
precarity 4, 8, 13, 17–18, 32–7, 57–60, 86, 88, 96, 102, 121, 134, 139
prostitution 78, 94–6. *See also* sex-work

racial profiling 137–8
refugee crisis (2015) 3, 122–3, 136, 138

revolutionary guards 49, 50, 55
Reza Allamezadeh 6, 14, 30, 44, 113–14
Rojava 142–3

Salmas 43, 58
Second World War 63
   post 18, 34
sexuality 85, 90, 92–7, 98, 100
sex work 95–6. *See also* prostitution
smugglers 31–2, 40, 42–5, 47, 52, 56, 58,
     60, 63, 74, 107–9, 111–12
   smuggling 44, 50
Soviet Union 18, 19, 72, 100. *See also* USSR
Stockholm 5, 51, 74, 104, 110, 113, 115
sur place (refugees) 24, 74
Sweden 5–6, 40, 47, 49, 50, 75, 79, 95, 104,
     110–13, 117, 138
Syria 3, 34, 69, 125, 131, 136, 138, 142–4
   northern 142–3
Syrians 3–4, 14, 57, 69, 87–8, 123, 131–4,
     139, 144–6

Taliban 87, 134–6

temporary protection (of Syrians) 4, 132–4
The Guests of Hotel Astoria 6, 14, 30, 79,
     96, 111–14, 116
The Little Man 6, 106–7
Tehran 31, 40–2, 46–8, 57, 68
thick dialogue 10–11
torture 29, 131–2
Turkey-EU Deal (2016) 145–6
Turkish model 142–3

Ukraine 123, 125, 141
Ukrainian 123, 132
United Socialist Party (USP) 23–4, 74
United States (of America) 8, 19, 31, 63–4,
     72, 108–11, 115, 134, 138, 141
USSR 29, 52, 100, 115. *See also*
   Soviet Union

Van 30, 43, 45, 58, 78

whore stigma 96

Yassin Al Haj Saleh 57, 69

www.ingramcontent.com/pod-product-compliance
Lightning Source LLC
Chambersburg PA
CBHW052118300426
44116CB00010B/1710